Beginning Power BI
with Excel 2013

Self-Service Business Intelligence Using
Power Pivot, Power View, Power Query,
and Power Map

Dan Clark

Apress®

Beginning Power BI with Excel 2013: Self-Service Business Intelligence Using Power Pivot, Power View, Power Query, and Power Map

ISBN-13 (pbk): 978-1-4302-6445-3

ISBN-13 (electronic): 978-1-4302-6446-0

Publisher: Heinz Weinheimer
Lead Editor: Gwenan Spearing
Technical Reviewers: Melissa Demsak and Jen Underwood
Editorial Board: Steve Anglin, Mark Beckner, Ewan Buckingham, Gary Cornell, Louise Corrigan, Jim DeWolf, Jonathan Gennick, Jonathan Hassell, Robert Hutchinson, Michelle Lowman, James Markham, Matthew Moodie, Jeff Olson, Jeffrey Pepper, Douglas Pundick, Ben Renow-Clarke, Dominic Shakeshaft, Gwenan Spearing, Matt Wade, Steve Weiss
Coordinating Editor: Christine Ricketts
Copy Editor: Rebecca Rider
Compositor: SPi Global
Indexer: SPi Global
Artist: SPi Global
Cover Designer: Anna Ishchenko

Distributed to the book trade worldwide by Springer Science+Business Media New York, 233 Spring Street, 6th Floor, New York, NY 10013. Phone 1-800-SPRINGER, fax (201) 348-4505, e-mail orders-ny@springer-sbm.com, or visit www.springeronline.com. Apress Media, LLC is a California LLC and the sole member (owner) is Springer Science + Business Media Finance Inc (SSBM Finance Inc). SSBM Finance Inc is a Delaware corporation.

For information on translations, please e-mail rights@apress.com, or visit www.apress.com.

Apress and friends of ED books may be purchased in bulk for academic, corporate, or promotional use. eBook versions and licenses are also available for most titles. For more information, reference our Special Bulk Sales–eBook Licensing web page at www.apress.com/bulk-sales.

Any source code or other supplementary material referenced by the author in this text is available to readers at www.apress.com. For detailed information about how to locate your book's source code, go to www.apress.com/source-code/.

This book is dedicated to Tilly and Bella who were beside me every step of the way!

Contents at a Glance

Contents

About the Author

Dan Clark is a senior business intelligence (BI)/programming consultant specializing in Microsoft technologies. He is focused on learning new BI/data technologies and on training others how to best implement the technology. Dan has published several books and numerous articles on .NET programming and BI development. He is a regular speaker at various developer/database conferences and user group meetings and enjoys interacting with the Microsoft developer and database communities. In a previous life, he was a physics teacher; he is still inspired by the wonder and awe of studying the universe and figuring out why things behave the way they do. Dan can be reached at Clark.drc@gmail.com.

About the Technical Reviewers

Melissa Demsak is a data professional with an extensive corporate data career leading data teams and working as the liaison between business and technical organizations. She is experienced with a broad range of verticals including pharmaceutical, real estate, finance, consumer products, credit/marketing services, and insurance organizations. Her interests include driving business goals with data, data strategies, leading data analytic teams, data insights, and data visualization. Her perfect work day includes analyzing raw data and working with business partners and IT professionals to provide data insights that impact business value. You can contact Melissa via LinkedIn at https://www.linkedin.com/in/sqldiva and via Twitter @SQLDiva.

Jen Underwood has almost 20 years of experience in data warehousing, business intelligence, and predictive analytics. She advises, develops, reviews technical solutions, and performs industry analysis. Prior to launching Impact Analytix, she was a Microsoft global business intelligence technical product manager for offerings spanning across Microsoft SQL Server, Excel, and SharePoint. She also held roles as an enterprise data platform specialist, a tableau technology evangelist, and a business intelligence consultant for Big 4 systems integration firms. Throughout most of her career, she has been researching, designing, and implementing analytic solutions across a variety of open source, niche, and enterprise vendor landscapes including Microsoft, Oracle, IBM, and SAP.

As an industry analyst, presenter, author, blogger, and trainer, Jen is quite active in the global technical community. Recently she was honored with a Boulder Business Intelligence Brain Trust (BBBT) membership, a 2013 Tableau Zen Master award, a PASS Worldwide Excel BI Chapter leadership role, and a Dun & Bradstreet MVP. She writes articles for *SQL Server Pro*, BeyeNETWORK, and other industry media channels.

Jen holds a bachelor of business administration degree from the University of Wisconsin, Milwaukee, and a post graduate certificate in computer science—data mining from the University of California, San Diego.

Acknowledgments

Once again, thanks to the team at Apress for making the writing of this book an enjoyable experience. A special thanks goes out to Gwenan and Christine for helping to guide me through this process. And last but not least, to my technical reviewers, Melissa and Jen—thank you for your attention to detail and excellent suggestions while reviewing this book.

—Dan Clark

Introduction

Self-service business intelligence (BI) is all the rage. You have heard the hype, seen the sales demos, and are ready to give it a try. Now what? If you are like me, you have probably already checked out a few web sites for examples, given them a try, and learned a thing or two. But you are still left wondering how all these tools fit together and how you go about creating a complete solution, right? If so, this book is for you. It takes you step by step through the process of analyzing data using the various tools that are at the core of Microsoft's self-service BI offering.

At the center of Microsoft's self-service BI offering is Power Pivot. I will show you how to create robust, scalable data models using Power Pivot; these will serve as the foundation of your data analysis. Since Power Pivot is the core tool you will use to create self-service BI solutions, it is covered extensively in this book. Next up is Power View. I will show you how to use Power View to easily build interactive visualizations that allow you to explore your data to discover trends and gain insight. In addition, I will show you how Power Pivot allows you to create a data model that will take full advantage of the features available in Power View.

Two other tools that are becoming increasingly important to have in your BI arsenal are Power Query and Power Map. Quite often, you will need to take your raw data and transform it in some way before you load it into the data model. You may need to filter, aggregate, or clean the raw data. I will show you how Power Query allows you to easily transform and refine data before incorporating it into your data model. While analyzing data, you may also be required to incorporate locational awareness with visualizations into a map. Power Map uses Microsoft's Bing mapping engine to easily incorporate data on an interactive map. I will show you how to use Power Map to create interesting visualizations of your data.

One additional topic that I have included is Excel's table analysis tools. These tools allow you to run some interesting data analysis including analyzing key influencers, identifying data groupings, and forecasting future trends. Although these tools are not part of Microsoft's self-service BI tool set, I think they are worth covering. They will get you thinking about the value of predictive analytics when you are analyzing your data.

I strongly believe one of the most important aspects of learning is doing. You can't learn how to ride a bike without jumping on a bike, and you can't learn to use the BI tools without actually interacting with them. Any successful training program includes both theory and hands-on activities. For this reason, I have included a hands-on activity at the end of every chapter designed to solidify the concepts covered in the chapter. I encourage you to work through these activities diligently. It is well worth the effort.

PART 1

Building Models in Power Pivot

CHAPTER 1

■ ■ ■

Introducing Power Pivot

The core of Microsoft's self-service business intelligence (BI) toolset is Power Pivot. The rest of the tools, Power View, Power Query, and Power Map, build on top of a Power Pivot tabular model. In the case of Power View this is obvious because you are explicitly connecting to the model. In the case of Power Query and Power Map it may not be as obvious because the Power Pivot tabular model is created for you behind the scenes. Regardless of how it is created, to get the most out of the tool set and gain insight into the data you need to know how Power Pivot works.

This chapter provides you with some background information on why Power Pivot is such an important tool and what makes Power Pivot perform so well. It instructs you on the requirements for running Power Pivot and how to enable it. The chapter also provides you with an overview of the Power Pivot interface and provides you with some experience using the different areas of the interface.

After reading this chapter you will be familiar with the following:

- Why use Power Pivot?

- The xVelocity in-memory analytics engine

- Enabling Power Pivot for Excel

- Exploring the Data Model Management interface

Why Use Power Pivot?

You may have been involved in a traditional BI project consisting of a centralized data warehouse where the various data stores of the organization are loaded, scrubbed, and then moved to an OLAP (online analytical processing) database for reporting and analysis. Some goals of this approach are to create a data repository for historical data, create one version of the truth, reduce silos of data, clean the company data and make sure it conforms to standards, and provide insight into data trends through dashboards. Although these are admirable goals and are great reasons to provide a centralized data warehouse, there are some downsides to this approach. The most notable is the complexity of building the system and implementing change. Ask anyone who has tried to get new fields or measures added to an enterprise-wide warehouse. Typically this is a long, drawn-out process requiring IT involvement along with data steward committee reviews, development, and testing cycles. What is needed is a solution that allows for agile data analysis without so much reliance on IT and formalized processes. To solve these problems many business analysts have used Excel to create pivot tables and perform ad hoc analysis on sets of data gleaned from various data sources. Some problems with using isolated Excel workbooks for analysis are conflicting versions of the truth, silos of data, and data security.

So how can you solve this dilemma of the centralized data warehouse being too rigid while the Excel solution is too loose? This is where Microsoft's self-service BI tool set comes in. These tools do not replace your centralized data warehouse solution but rather augment it to promote agile data analysis. Using Power Pivot you can pull data from the data warehouse, extend it with other sources of data such as text files or web data feeds, build custom measures, and analyze the data using pivot tables and pivot charts. You can create quick proofs of concepts that can be easily promoted to become part of the enterprise wide solution. Power Pivot also promotes one-off data analysis projects without the overhead of a drawn-out development cycle. When combined with SharePoint, Power Pivot, workbooks can be secured and managed by IT, including data refresh scheduling and resource usage. This goes a long way to satisfying IT's need for governance without impeding the business user's need for agility.

Here are some of the benefits of Power Pivot:

- Functions as a free add-in to Excel

- Easily integrates data from a variety of sources

- Handles large amounts of data upward of tens to hundreds of millions of rows

- Uses familiar Excel pivot tables and pivot charts for data analysis

- Includes a powerful new Data Analysis Expressions (DAX) language

- Has data in the model that is read only, which increases security and integrity

When Power Pivot is hosted in SharePoint, here are some of its added benefits:

- Enables the sharing and collaboration of Power Pivot BI Solutions

- Can schedule and automate data refresh

- Can audit changes through version management

- Can secure users for read-only and updateable access

Now that you know some of the benefits of Power Pivot, let's see what makes it tick.

The xVelocity In-memory Analytics Engine

The special sauce behind Power Pivot is the xVelocity in-memory analytics engine (yes, that is really the name!). This allows Power Pivot to provide fast performance on large amounts of data. One of the keys to this is it uses a columnar database to store the data. Traditional row-based data storage stores all the data in the row together and is efficient at retrieving and updating data based on the row key, for example, updating or retrieving an order based on an order ID. This is great for the order entry system but not so great when you want to perform analysis on historical orders (say you want to look at trends for the past year to determine how products are selling, for example). Row-based storage also takes up more space by repeating values for each row; if you have a large number of customers, common names like John or Smith are repeated many times. A columnar database stores only the distinct values for each column and then stores the row as a set of pointers back to the column values. This built-in indexing saves a lot of space and allows for significant optimization when coupled with data compression techniques that are built into the xVelocity engine. It also means that data aggregations (like those used in typical data analysis) of the column values are extremely fast.

Another benefit provided by the xVelocity engine is the in-memory analytics. Most processing bottlenecks associated with querying data occur when data is read off of or written to a disk. With in-memory analytics, the data is loaded into the RAM memory of the computer and then queried. This results in much faster processing times and limits the need to store pre-aggregated values on disk. This advantage is especially apparent when you move from 32-bit to 64-bit operating systems and applications, which are becoming the norm these days.

In addition to the benefits provided by the xVelocity engine, another benefit that is worth mentioning is the tabular structure of the Power Pivot model. The model consists of tables and table relationships. This tabular model is more familiar to most business analysts and database developers. Traditional OLAP databases such as SSAS (SQL Server Analysis Server) present the data model as a three dimensional cube structure that is more difficult to work with and requires a complex query language, MDX (Multidimensional Expressions). I find, in most cases (but not all), that it is easier to work with tabular models and DAX than OLAP cubes and MDX.

Enabling Power Pivot for Excel

Power Pivot is a free add-in to Excel available in the Office Professional Plus and Office 365 Professional Plus editions. If you are using Excel 2010, you need to download and install the add-in from the Microsoft Office web site. If you are using Excel 2013 (the version covered in this book), the add-in is already installed and you just have to enable it. To check what edition you have installed, select the File menu in Excel and select the Account tab as shown in Figure 1-1.

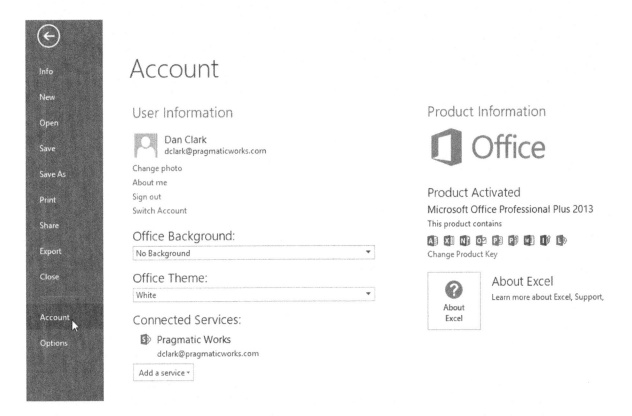

Figure 1-1. *Checking for the Excel version*

On the Excel Account tab click the About Excel button. You are presented with a screen showing version details as shown in Figure 1-2. Take note of the edition and the version. It should be the Professional Plus edition and ideally the 64-bit version. The 32-bit version will work fine for smaller data sets, but to get the optimal performance and experience from Power Pivot you should use the 64-bit version running on a 64-bit version of Windows with about 8 gigs of RAM.

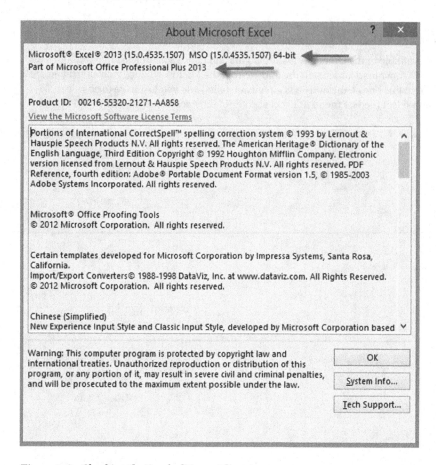

Figure 1-2. *Checking the Excel edition and version*

Once you have determined you are running the correct version, you can enable the Power Pivot add-in by going to the File menu and selecting the Options tab. In the Excel Options window select the Add-Ins tab. In the Manage drop-down select Com Add-Ins and click the Go button (see Figure 1-3).

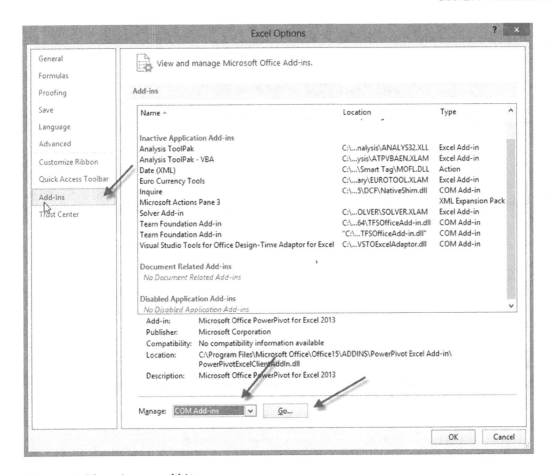

Figure 1-3. *Managing com add-ins*

You are presented with the Com Add-Ins window (see Figure 1-4). Select Microsoft Office PowerPivot for Excel 2013 and click OK.

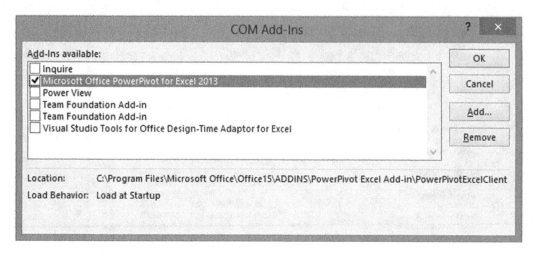

Figure 1-4. *Selecting the Power Pivot add-in*

Now that you have enabled the Power Pivot add-in for Excel, it is time to explore the Data Model Manager.

Exploring the Data Model Manager Interface

Once you enable Power Pivot, you should see a new Power Pivot tab in Excel (see Figure 1-5). If you click on the Manage button it launches the Data Model Management interface.

Figure 1-5. *Launching the Data Model Manager*

When the Data Model Manager launches you will have two separate but connected interfaces. You can switch back and forth between the normal Excel interface and the Data Model Management interface. This can be quite confusing for new Power Pivot users. Remember the Data Model Manager (Figure 1-6) is where you define the model including tables, table relationships, measures, calculated columns, and hierarchies. The Excel interface (Figure 1-7) is where you analyze the data using pivot tables and pivot charts.

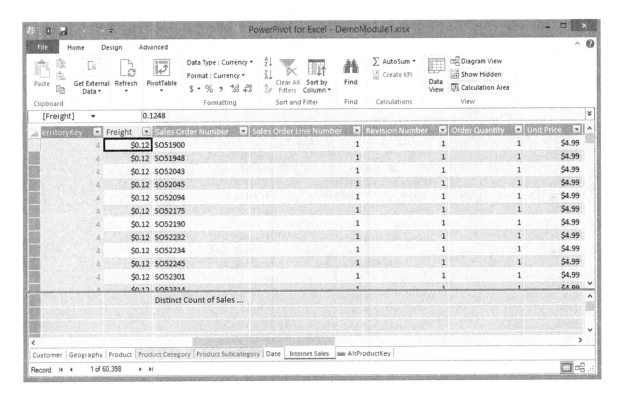

Figure 1-6. *The Data Model Manager interface*

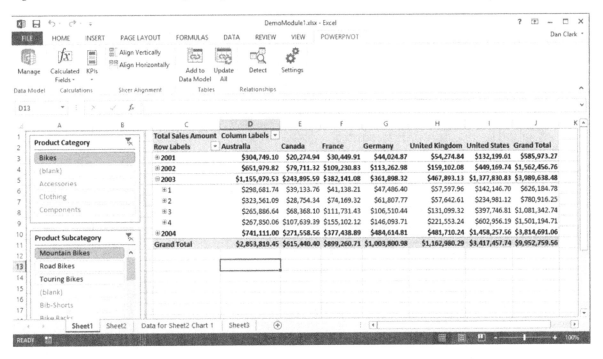

Figure 1-7. *The Excel Workbook interface*

There are two views of the data model in the Data Model Manager, the data view and the diagram view. When it first comes up, it is in the data view mode. In the data view mode you can see the data contained in the model. Each table in the model has its own tab in the view. Tables can include columns of data retrieved from a data source and also columns that are calculate using DAX. The calculated columns appear a little darker than the other columns. Figure 1-8 shows the Full Name column, which is derived by concatenating the First Name and Last Name columns.

[Full Name]	f_x =[First Name] & " " & [Last Name]				
First Name	Middle Name	Last Name	Full Name	Birth Date	
Latasha		Suarez	Latasha Suarez	9/25/1973 12:...	
Larry		Gill	Larry Gill	4/13/1977 12:...	
Edgar		Sanchez	Edgar Sanchez	6/3/1977 12:0...	
Shelby		Bailey	Shelby Bailey	6/3/1977 12:0...	
Alexa		Watson	Alexa Watson	8/25/1977 12:...	
Jacquelyn		Dominguez	Jacquelyn Dominguez	9/27/1977 12:...	
Kate		Shan	Kate Shan	1/24/1975 12:...	
Colleen		Lu	Colleen Lu	7/17/1973 12:...	
Dale		Shen	Dale Shen	3/16/1974 12:...	
Tammy		Sai	Tammy Sai	11/14/1974 1...	
Leah		Li	Leah Li	10/6/1976 12:...	
Andrea		Cox	Andrea Cox	8/3/1977 12:0...	
Alyssa		Lee	Alyssa Lee	8/13/1976 12:...	
Jill		Rubio	Jill Rubio	6/27/1976 12:...	
Dennis		Li	Dennis Li	7/17/1977 12:...	
Natasha		Sanz	Natasha Sanz	5/18/1977 12:...	
Autumn		Zhu	Autumn Zhu	10/23/1977 1...	

Figure 1-8. *A calculated column in the Data Model Manager*

Each tab also contains a grid area below the column data. The grid area is where you define measures in the model. The measures usually consist of some sort of aggregation function. For example, you may want to look at sales rolled up by month or by products. Figure 1-9 shows some measures associated with the Internet Sales table.

[Freight]	f_x Total Sales Amount:=SUM([Sales Amount])	
Freight	Sales Order Number	
$0.12	SO51900	
$0.12	SO51948	
$0.12	SO52043	
$0.12	SO52045	
$0.12	SO52094	
$0.12	SO52175	
Total Sales Amount: $29,358,677.22	Distinct Count of Sales Order:...	
Current Quarter Sales: 29358677.2207	Previous Quarter Sales: (blank)	
Current Quarter Sales Performance: (bla...	Previous Quarter Sales Propo...	

Figure 1-9. *The measures grid area in the Data Model Manager*

There are four menu tabs at the top of the designer: File, Home, Design, and Advanced. If you do not see the Advanced tab, you can show it by selecting the File menu tab and selecting Switch To Advanced Mode. You will become intimately familiar with the menus in the designer as you progress through this book. For now, suffice to say that this is where you initiate various actions such as connecting to data sources and creating data queries, formatting data, setting default properties, and creating KPIs (Key Performance Indicators). Figure 1-10 shows the Home menu in the Data Model Manager.

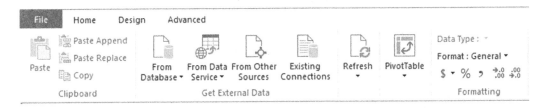

Figure 1-10. *The Home menu tab in the Data Model Manager*

On the right side of the Home menu you can switch from the data view mode to the diagram view mode. The diagram view shown in Figure 1-11 illustrates the tables and the relationships between the tables. This is where you generally go to establish relationships between tables and create hierarchies for drilling through the model. The menus are much the same in both the data view and the diagram view. You will find, however, that some things can only be done in the data view and some things can only be done in the diagram view.

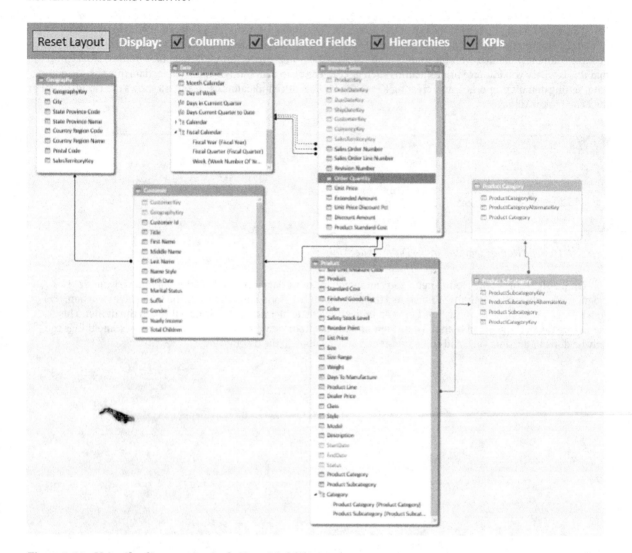

Figure 1-11. *Using the diagram view in the Data Model Manager*

Now that you are familiar with the various parts of the Data Model Manager, it is time to get your hands dirty and complete the following hands-on lab. This lab will help you become familiar with working in the Data Model Manager.

HANDS-ON LAB—EXPLORING POWER PIVOT

In the following lab you will

- Enable the Power Pivot add-in.

- Analyze data using pivot tables.

- Explore the Data Model Manager.

1. Open Excel 2013.

2. On the File menu select Account (see Figure 1-1).

3. Click About Excel so that you are using the Professional Plus edition and check the version (32-bit or 64-bit).

4. On the File menu select Options and then select the Add-Ins tab. In the Manage drop-down select Com Add-Ins and click the Go button.

5. In the Com Add-Ins window, check the Power Pivot add-in (see Figure 1-4).

6. After the installation, open the Chapter1Lab1.xlsx file located in the Lab Starters folder.

7. Click on Sheet1. You should see a basic pivot table showing sales by year and country as shown in Figure 1-12.

Total Sales Amount	Column Labels ▼						
Row Labels ▼	Australia	Canada	France	Germany	United Kingdom	United States	Grand Total
⊞ 2001	$1,309,047.20	$146,829.81	$180,571.69	$237,784.99	$291,590.52	$1,100,549.45	$3,266,373.66
⊞ 2002	$2,154,284.88	$621,602.38	$514,942.01	$521,230.85	$591,586.85	$2,126,696.55	$6,530,343.53
⊞ 2003	$3,033,784.21	$535,784.46	$1,026,324.97	$1,058,405.73	$1,298,248.57	$2,838,512.36	$9,791,060.30
⊞ 2004	$2,563,884.29	$673,628.21	$922,179.04	$1,076,890.77	$1,210,286.27	$3,324,031.16	$9,770,899.74
Grand Total	$9,061,000.58	$1,977,844.86	$2,644,017.71	$2,894,312.34	$3,391,712.21	$9,389,789.51	$29,358,677.22

Figure 1-12. *Using a pivot table*

8. Click anywhere on the pivot table. You should see the field list on the right side, as shown in Figure 1-13.

Figure 1-13. *The pivot table field list*

9. Below the field list are the drop areas for the filters, rows, columns, and values. You drag and drop the fields into these areas to create the pivot table.

10. Click on the All tab at the top of the PivotTable Fields window. Expand the Product table in the field list. Find the Product Category field and drag it to the Report Filter drop zone.

11. A filter drop-down appears above the pivot table. Click on the drop-down filter icon. You should see the Product Categories.

12. Change the filter to Bikes and notice the values changing in the pivot table.

13. When you select multiple items from a filter it is hard to tell what is being filtered on. Filter on Bikes and Clothing. Notice when the filter drop-down closes it just shows "(Multiple Items)."

14. Slicers act as filters but they give you a visual to easily determine what is selected. On the Insert menu click on the Slicer. In the pop-up window that appears, select the All tab and then select the Category hierarchy under the Product table as in Figure 1-14.

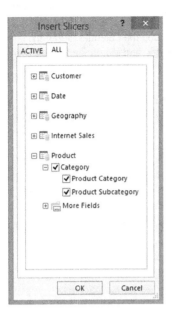

Figure 1-14. *Selecting slicer fields*

15. A Product Category and Product Subcategory slicer are inserted and are used to filter the pivot table. To filter by a value, click on the value button. To select multiple buttons, hold down the Ctrl key while clicking (see Figure 1-15). Notice that since these fields were set up as a hierarchy, selecting a product category automatically filters to the related subcategories in the Product Subcategory slicer.

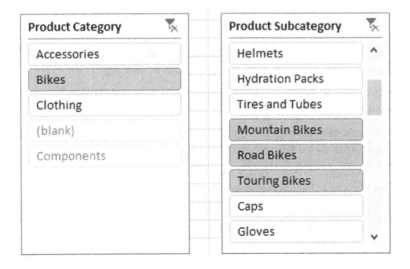

Figure 1-15. *Using slicers to filter a pivot table*

16. Hierarchies are groups of columns arranged in levels that make it easier to navigate the data. For example, if you expand the Date table in the field list you can see the Calendar hierarchy as shown in Figure 1-16. This hierarchy consists of the Year, Quarter, and Month fields and represents a natural way to drill down into the data.

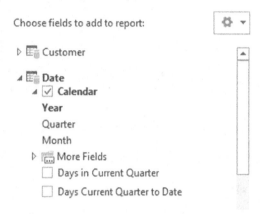

Figure 1-16. *Using hierarchies in a pivot table*

17. If you expand the Internet Sales table in the field list you will see a traffic light icon. This icon represents a KPI. KPIs are used to gauge the performance of a value. They are usually represented by a visual indicator to quickly determine performance.

18. Under the Power Pivot menu select the Manage Data Model button.

19. In the Data Model Manager select the different tabs at the bottom to switch between the different tables.

20. Go to the ProductAlternateKey column in the Products table. Notice that it is grayed out. This means it is hidden from any client tool. You can verify this by switching back to the Excel pivot table on sheet 1 and verifying that you cannot see the field in the field list.

21. In the Internet Sales table click on the Margin column. Notice this is a calculated column. It has also been formatted as currency.

22. Below the Sales Amount column in the Internet Sales table notice there is a measure called Total Sales Amount. Click on the measure and notice the DAX SUM function is used to calculate the measure.

23. Switch the Data Model Manager to the diagram view. Observe the relationships between the tables.

24. If you hover over the relationship with the mouse pointer you can see the fields involved in the relationship as shown in Figure 1-17.

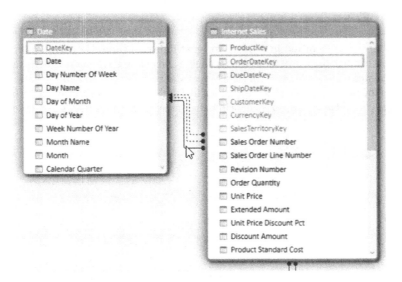

Figure 1-17. *Exploring relationships*

25. Click on the Date table in the diagram view. Notice the Create Hierarchy button in the upper right corner of the table (see Figure 1-18). This is how you define hierarchies for a table.

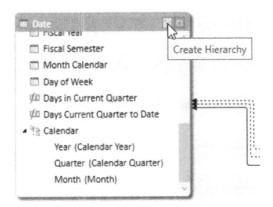

Figure 1-18. *Creating a hierarchy*

26. Take some time to explore the model and the pivot table. (Feel free to try to break things!) When you are done, close the file.

Summary

This chapter introduced you to the Power Pivot add-in to Excel. You got a little background into why Power Pivot can handle large amounts of data through the use of the xVelocity engine and columnar data storage. You also got to investigate and gain some experience with the Power Pivot Data Model Manager. Don't worry about the details of how you develop the various parts of the model just yet. This is explained in detail as you progress through the book. This begins in the next chapter where you will learn how to get data into the model from various kinds of data sources.

CHAPTER 2

■ ■ ■

Importing Data into Power Pivot

One of the first steps in creating the Power Pivot model is importing data. Traditionally when creating a BI solution based on an OLAP cube, you need to import the data into the data warehouse and then load it into the cube. It can take quite a while to get the data incorporated into the cube and available for your consumption. This is one of the greatest strengths of the Power Pivot model. You can easily and quickly combine data from a variety of sources into your model. The data sources can be from relational databases, text files, web services, and OLAP cubes, just to name a few. This chapter shows you how to incorporated data from a variety of these sources into a Power Pivot model.

After completing this chapter you will be able to

- Import data from relational databases.

- Import data from text files.

- Import data from a data feed.

- Import data from an OLAP cube.

- Reuse existing connections to update the model.

Importing Data from Relational Databases

One of the most common types of data sources you will run into is a relational database. Relational database management systems (RDMS), such as SQL Server, Oracle, DB2, and Access, consist of tables and relationships between the tables based on keys. For example Figure 2-1 shows a purchase order detail table and a product table. They are related by the ProductID column. This is an example of a one-to-many relationship. For every one row in the product table there are many rows in the purchase order detail table. The keys in a table are referred to as primary and foreign keys. Every table needs a primary key that uniquely identifies a row in the table. For example, the ProductID is the primary key in the product table. The ProductID is considered a foreign key in the purchase order detail table. Foreign keys point back to a primary key in a related table. Notice a primary key can consist of a combination of columns; for example, the primary key of the purchase order detail table is the combination of the PurchaseOrderID and the PurchaseOrderDetailID.

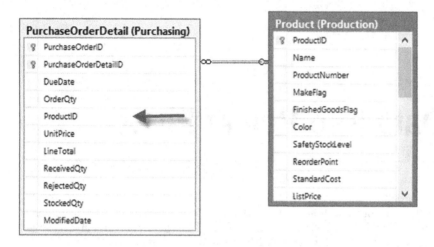

Figure 2-1. *A one-to-many relationship*

Although one-to-many relationships are the most common, you will run into another type of relationship that is fairly prevalent—the many-to-many. Figure 2-2 shows an example of a many-to-many relationship. A person can have multiple phone numbers of different types. For example they may have two fax numbers. You cannot relate these tables directly. Instead you need to use a junction table that contains the primary keys from the tables. The combination of the keys in the junction table must be unique.

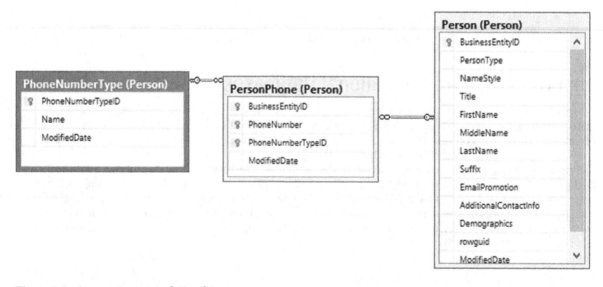

Figure 2-2. *A many-to-many relationship*

Notice that the junction table can contain information related to the association; for example, the PhoneNumber is associated with the customer and phone number type. A customer cannot have the same phone number listed as two different types.

One nice aspect of obtaining data from a relational database is that the model is very similar to a model you will create in Power Pivot. In fact, if the relationships are defined in the database, the Power Pivot import wizard can detect these and set them up in the model for you.

The first step to getting data from a relational database is to create a connection. On the Home tab of the Model Designer there is a Get External Data grouping (see Figure 2-3).

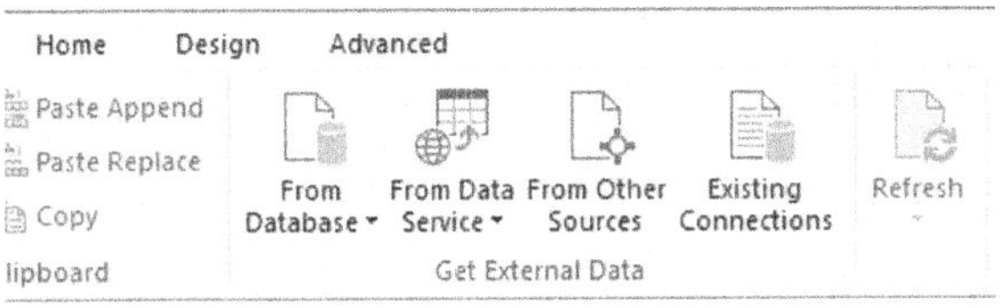

Figure 2-3. *Setting up a connection*

The From Database drop-down allows you to connect to SQL Server, Access, Analysis Services, or from another Power Pivot model. If you click on the From Other Sources button, you can see all the various data sources available to connect to (see Figure 2-4). As you can see, you can connect to quite a few relational databases. If one you need to connect to is not listed, you may be able to install a driver from the database provider to connect to it. Chances are, you may also be able to use the generic ODBC (Open Database Connectivity) driver to connect to it.

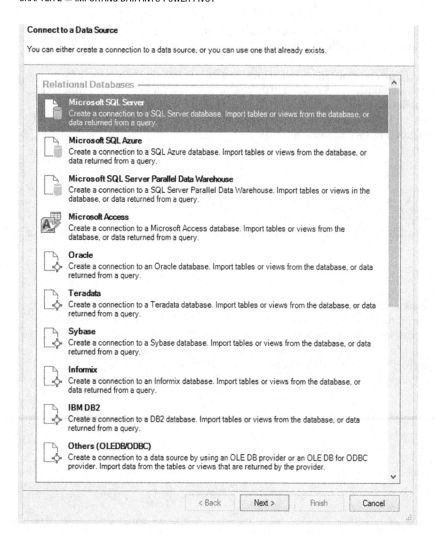

Figure 2-4. *Selecting a data source*

After selecting a data source, you are presented with a window to enter the connection information. The connection information depends on the data source you are connecting to. For most relational databases the information needed is very similar. Figure 2-5 shows the connection information for connecting to a SQL Server. Remember to click the Test Connection button to make sure everything is entered correctly.

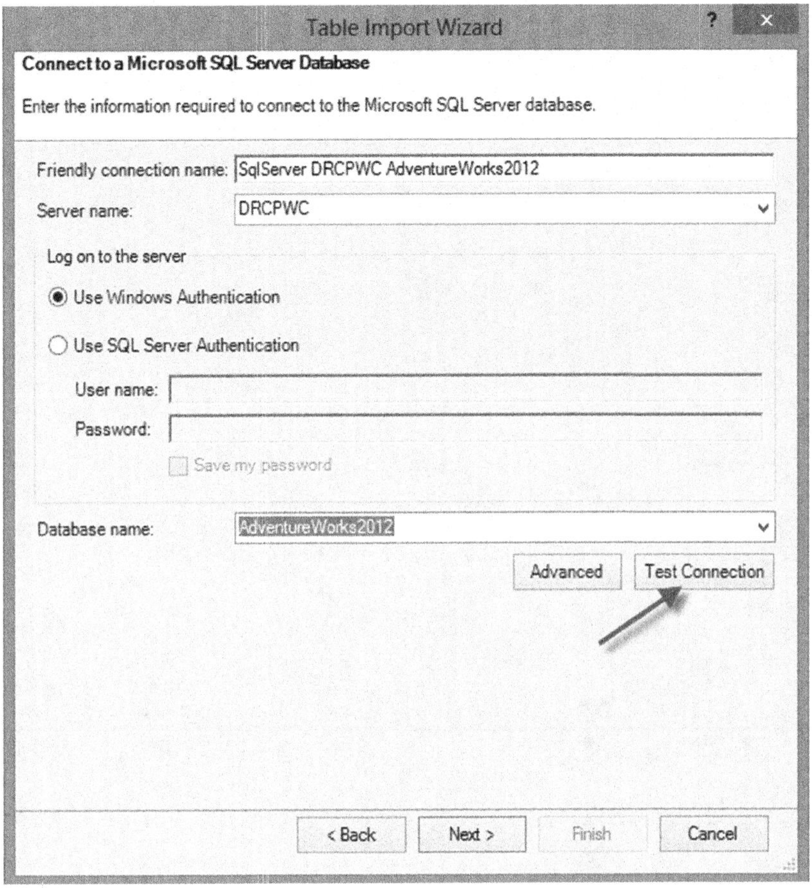

Figure 2-5. *Setting up a connection to a database*

After setting up the connection the next step is to query the database to retrieve the data. You have two choices at this point: You can choose to import the data from a list of tables and views or you can write a query to import the data (see Figure 2-6). Even if you select to import the data from a table or view under the covers, a query is created and sent to the database to retrieve the data.

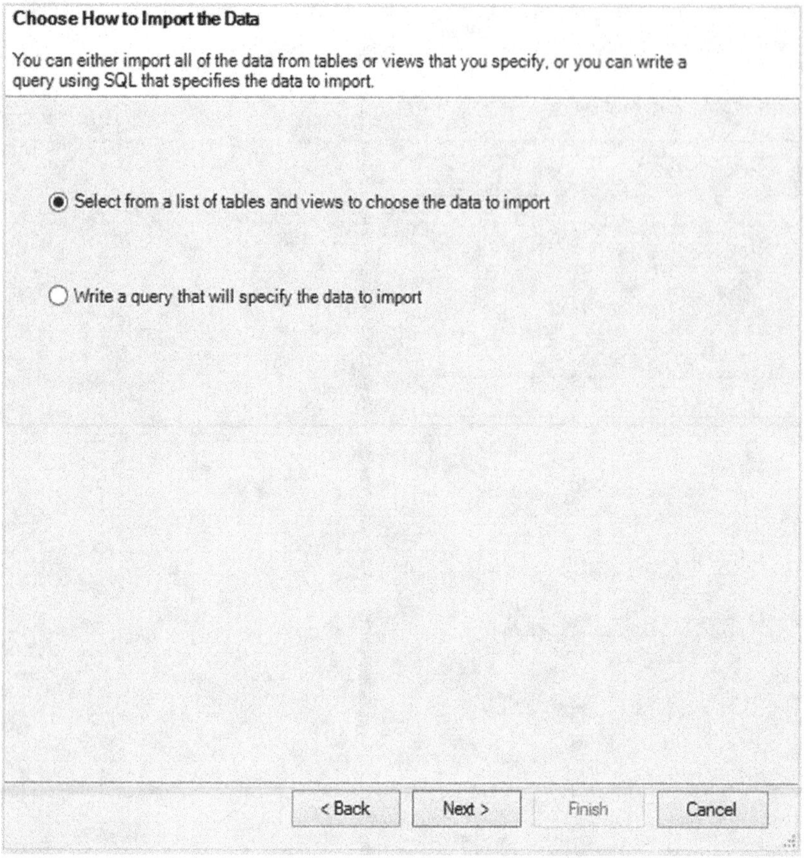

Choose How to Import the Data

You can either import all of the data from tables or views that you specify, or you can write a query using SQL that specifies the data to import.

◉ Select from a list of tables and views to choose the data to import

○ Write a query that will specify the data to import

| < Back | Next > | Finish | Cancel |

Figure 2-6. *Choosing how to retrieve the data*

If you choose to get the data from a list of tables and views, you are presented with the list in the next screen. From your perspective a view and a table look the same. In reality, a view is really a stored query in the database that masks the complexity of the query from you. Views are often used to show a simpler conceptual model of the database than the actual physical model. For example you may need a customer's address. Figure 2-7 shows the tables you need to include in a query to get the information. Instead of writing a complex query to retrieve the information, you can select from a view that combines the information in a virtual Customer Address table for you. Another common use of a view is to secure columns of the underlying table. Through the use of a view the database administrator can hide columns from various users.

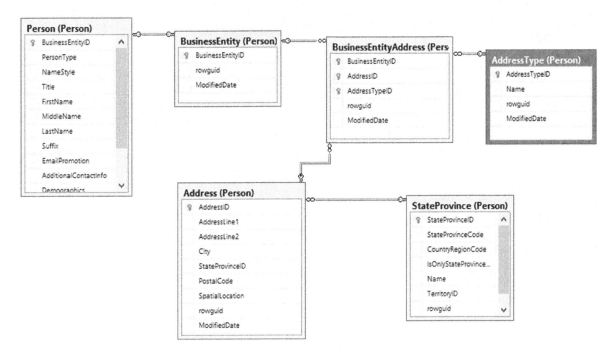

Figure 2-7. *Tables needed to get a customer address*

By selecting a table and clicking the Preview & Filter button (see Figure 2-8), you can preview the data in the table and filter the data selected.

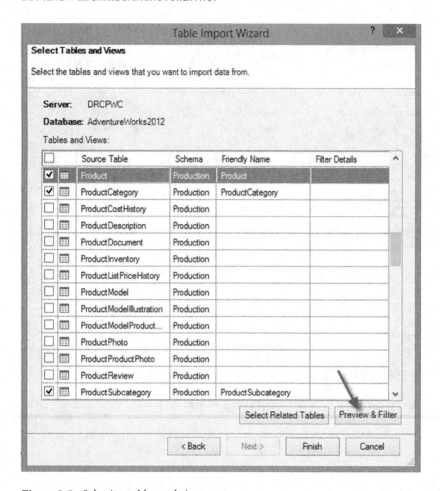

Figure 2-8. *Selecting tables and views*

In Figure 2-9 you can see the preview and filter screen.

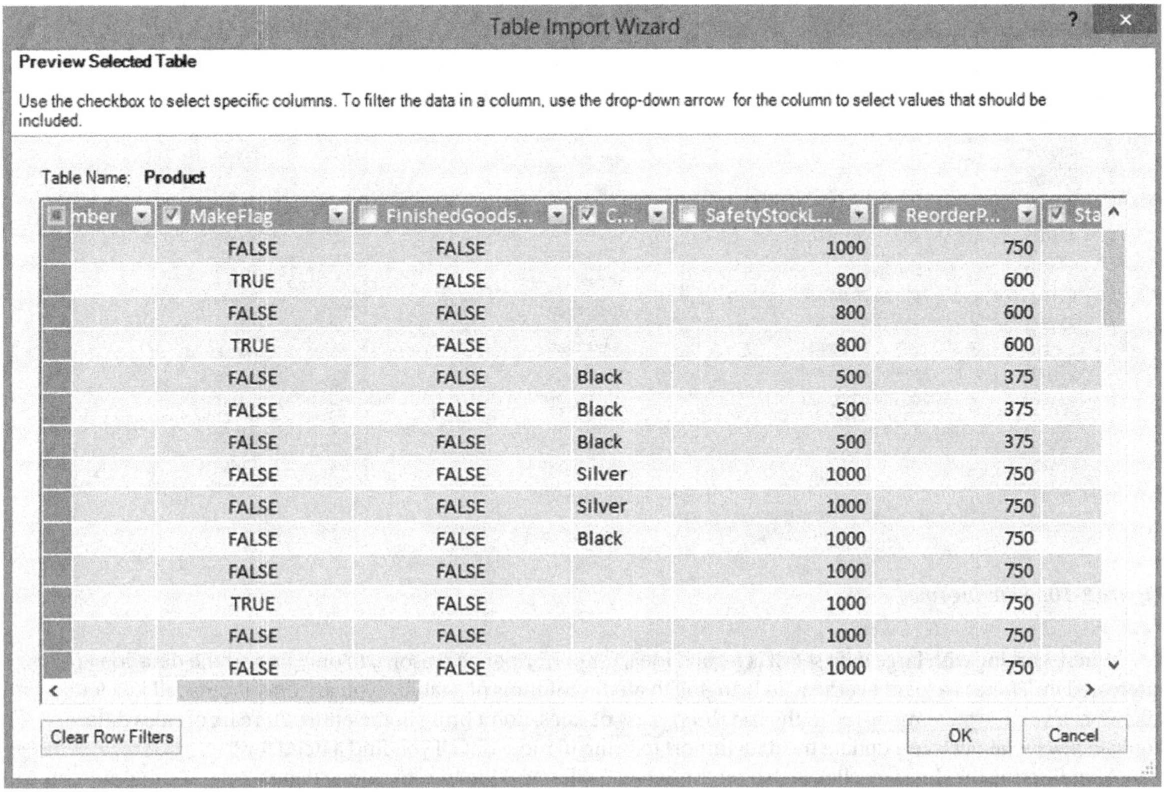

Figure 2-9. *Previewing and filtering the data*

One way you can filter a table is by selecting only the columns you are interested in. The other way is to limit the number of rows by placing a filter condition on the column. For example, you may only want sales after a certain year. Clicking on the drop-down next to a column allows you to enter a filter to limit the rows. Figure 2-10 shows the SalesOrderHeader table being filtered by order date.

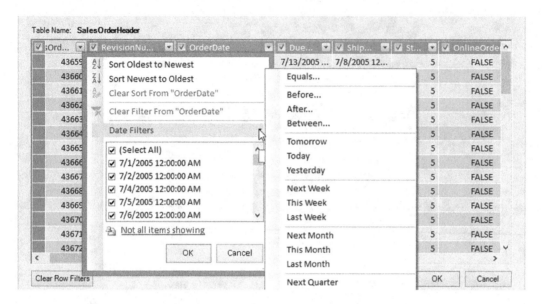

Figure 2-10. *Filtering rows*

When working with large data sets it is a good idea, for performance reasons, to only import the data you are interested in. There is a lot of overhead in bringing in all the columns of a table if you are only interested in a few. Likewise, if you are only interested in the last three years of sales, don't bring in the entire 20 years of sales data. You can always go back and update the data import to bring in more data if you find a need for it.

After filtering the data you click Finish on the Select Tables And Views screen (see Figure 2-8). At this point the data is brought into the model and you see a screen reporting the progress (see Figure 2-11). If there are no errors you can close the Table Import Wizard.

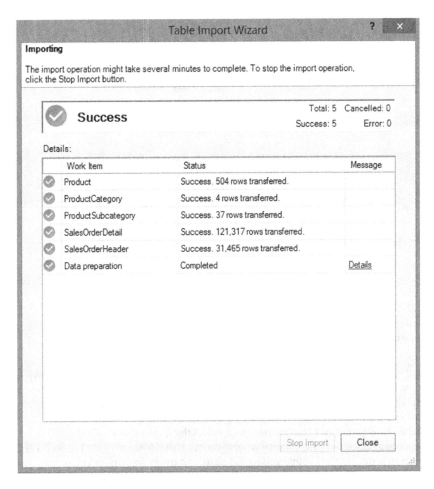

Figure 2-11. *Importing the data into the model*

When the wizard closes, you will see the data in the data view of the Model Designer.

■ **Note**   Remember that Power Pivot is only connected to the data source when it is retrieving the data. Once the data is retrieved the connection is closed and the data is part of the model.

If you switch to the diagram view of the Model Designer you will see the tables, and if the table relationships were defined in the database you will see the relationships between the tables. In Figure 2-12 you can see relationships defined between the product tables and one defined between the sales tables, but none defined between the SalesOrderDetail table and the Product table. You can create a relationship in the model even though one was not defined in the data source (more about this later).

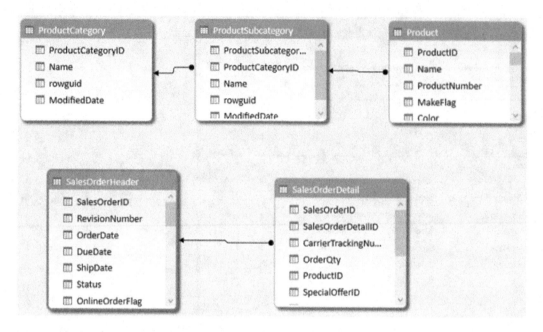

Figure 2-12. *Table relationships defined in the data source*

Although selecting from tables and views is an easy way to get data into the model without needing to explicitly write a query, it is not always possible. At times you may need to write your own queries; for example, you may want to combine data from several different tables and no view is available. Another factor is what is supported by the data source. Some data sources do not allow views and may require you to supply queries to extract the data. In these cases, when you get to the screen that asks how you want to retrieve the data, select the query option (Figure 2-6).

Once you select the query option you are presented with a screen where you can write in a query (see Figure 2-13). Although you may not write the query from scratch, this is where you would paste in a query written for you or one that you created in another tool such as Microsoft Management Studio or TOAD. Don't forget to name the query. It will become a table in the model with the name of the query.

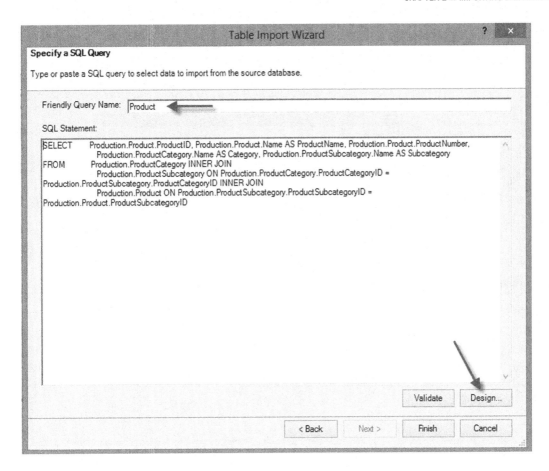

Figure 2-13. *Creating your own query*

If the data source supports it, you can launch a pretty nice query designer by clicking in the lower right corner of the query entry window (see Figure 2-13). This designer (see Figure 2-14) allows you to select the columns you want from the various tables and views. If the table relationships are defined in the database it will add the table joins for you. You can also apply filters and group and aggregate the data. One confusing aspect of the query designer is the parameter check box.

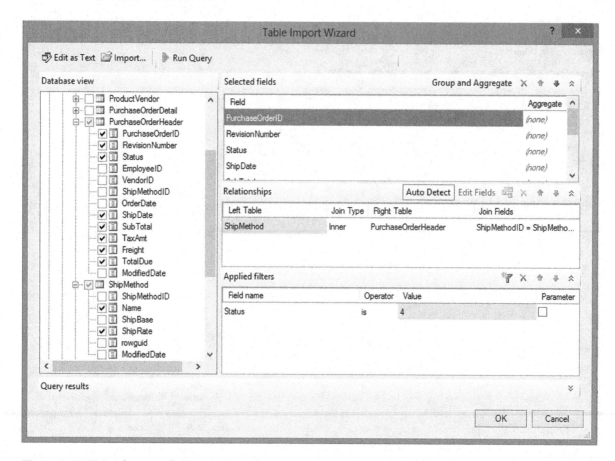

Figure 2-14. *Using the query designer*

___

■ **Note**   Parameters are not supported in the Power Pivot model and checking the box will give you an error message when you try to close the query designer.

___

After you are done designing the query, you should always run it to make sure it works the way you intended (see Figure 2-15).

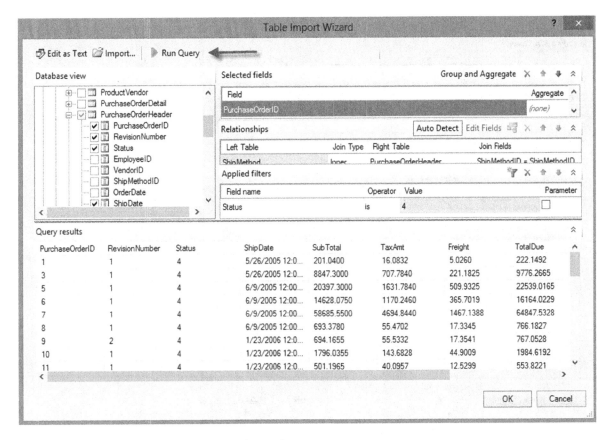

Figure 2-15. *Running the query and viewing the results*

Once you are satisfied with the query, selecting the OK button returns you to the previous screen with the query text entered. You can modify the query in this screen and use the Validate button to ensure it is still a valid query (see Figure 2-16). Clicking Finish will bring the data and table into the model.

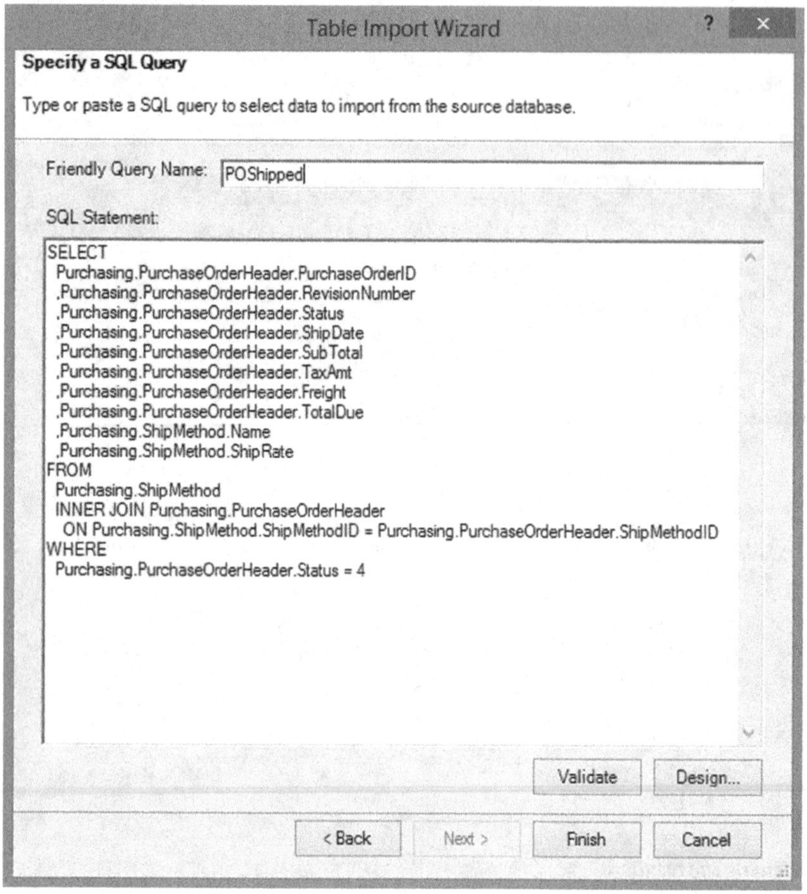

Figure 2-16. *Viewing and validating the query*

Now that you know how to import data from a database, let's see how you can add data to the model from a text file.

Importing Data from Text Files

There are many times when you need to combine data from several different sources. One of the most common sources of data is still the text file. This could be the result of receiving data as an output from another system; for example, you may need information from your company's ERP (enterprise resource planning) system, which is provided as a text file. You may also get data through third-party services that provide the data in a CSV (comma-separated value) format. For example, you may use a rating service to rate customers and the results can be returned in a CSV file.

Importing data into your model from a text file is similar to importing data from a relational database table. First you select the option to get external data from other sources on the Home menu, which brings up the option to connect to a data source. Scroll down to the bottom of the window and you can choose to import data from either an Excel file or a text file (see Figure 2-17).

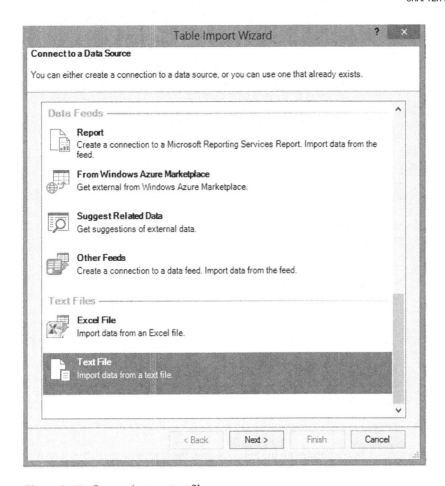

Figure 2-17. *Connecting to a text file*

Selecting the text file brings up a screen where you enter the path to the file and the file delimiter. Each text file is considered a table and the friendly connection name will be the name of the table in the model. Once you supply the connection information, the data is loaded for previewing and filtering (see Figure 2-18).

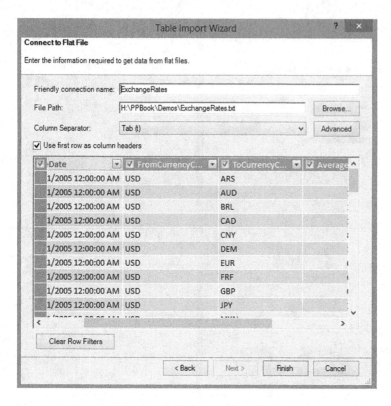

Figure 2-18. Previewing the data

Selecting the drop-down next to the column header brings up the ability to limit the rows brought in based on a filter criteria (see Figure 2-19).

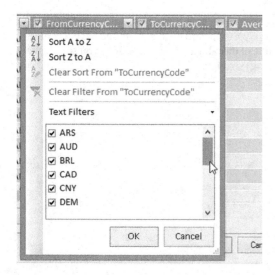

Figure 2-19. Filtering rows imported into the model

The main difference between importing data from a text file and importing data from an Excel file is that the Excel file can contain more than one table. By default each sheet is treated as a table (see Figure 2-20). Once you select the table you have the option to preview and filter the data just as you did for a text file.

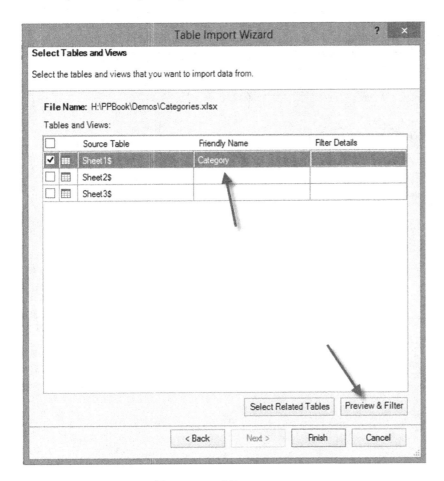

Figure 2-20. *Selecting a table in an Excel file*

In addition to importing data from a text file you may need to supplement your data model using data imported from a data feed. This is becoming a very common way to exchange data with business partners and you will see how to do this next.

Importing Data from a Data Feed

Although text files are one of the most popular ways of exchanging data, data feeds are becoming an increasingly prevalent way of exchanging data. Data feeds provide the data through web services, and to connect to the web service, you enter the web address of the web service. In Figure 2-17 you can see the data feed connections available to you. Most often you will know the address of the data service provided by a partner or data provider. In this case, you choose other feeds that then provide you with a connection information entry window, as shown in Figure 2-21.

Figure 2-21. *Connecting to a data feed*

Because the data feed contains not only the data but also the metadata (description of the data), once you make the connection, Power Pivot provides you with the ability to preview and filter the data, as shown in Figure 2-22.

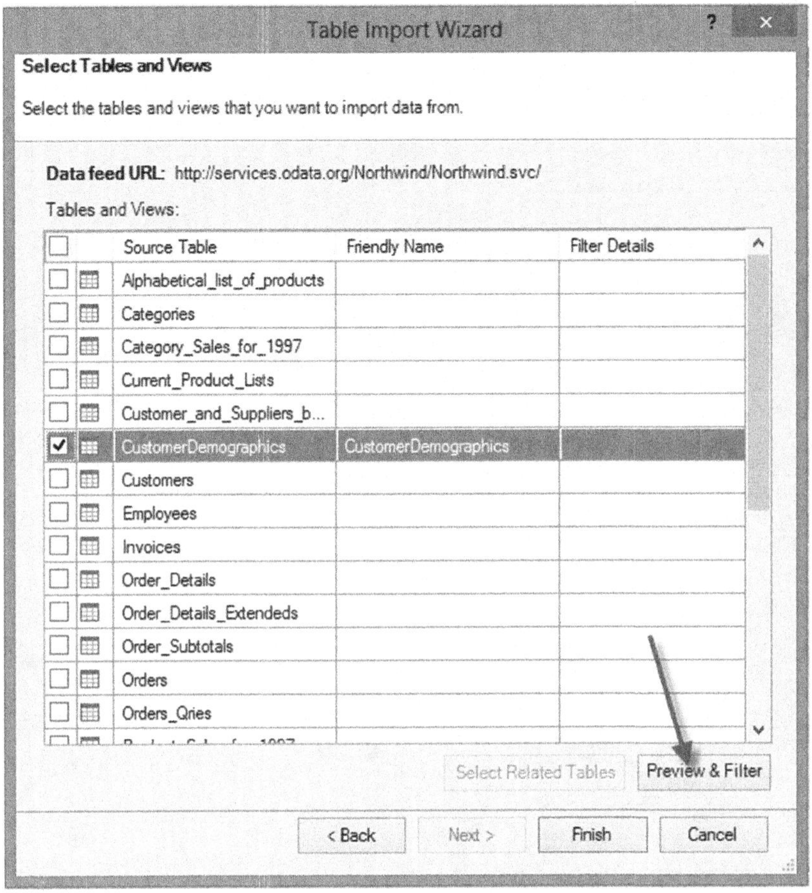

Figure 2-22. *Previewing and filtering data from a data feed*

A couple of interesting data feeds you can consume are data from Reporting Services reports and SharePoint lists. These applications can easily expose their data as data feeds that you can consume as a data source. In addition, many database vendors such as SAP support the ability to expose their data as data feeds.

Importing Data from an OLAP Cube

Many companies have invested a lot of money and effort into creating an enterprise reporting solution consisting of an enterprise-wide OLAP repository that feeds various dashboards and score cards. Using Power Pivot, you can easily integrate data from these repositories. From the connection choices in the connection window (Figure 2-17), choose the Microsoft SQL Server Analysis Services connection under Multidimensional Services. This launches the connection information window as shown in Figure 2-23. You can either connect to a multidimensional cube or a Power Pivot model published to SharePoint. To connect to a cube, enter the server name and the database name. To connect to a Power Pivot model, enter the URL to the Excel workbook (in a SharePoint library) and the model name.

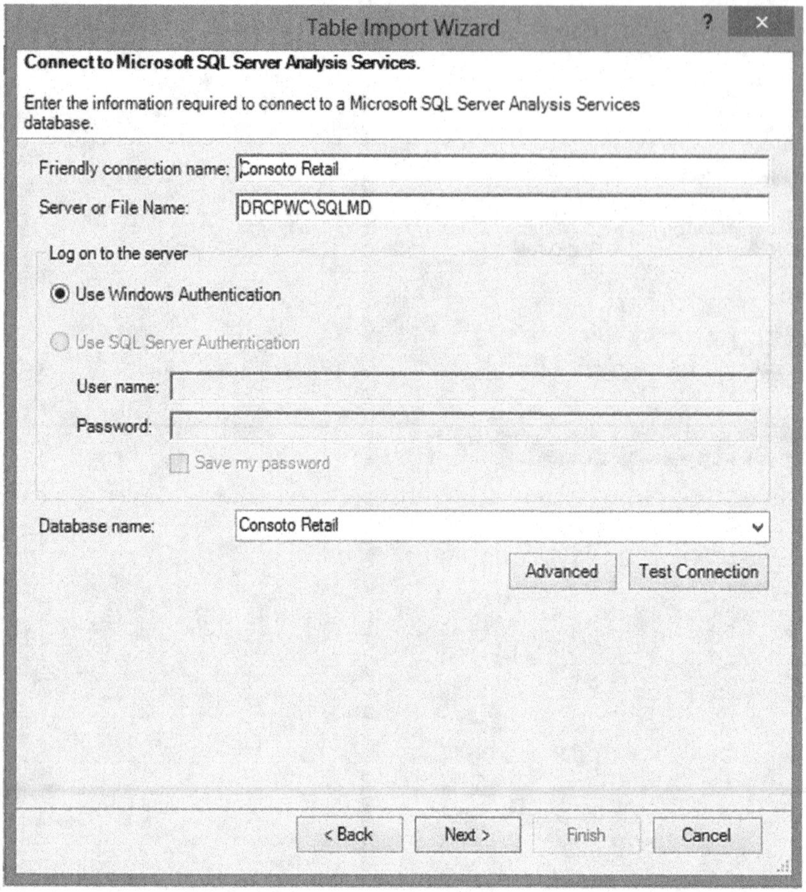

Figure 2-23. *Connecting to an Analysis Services cube*

Once you are connected to the cube you can enter an MDX query to retrieve the data (see Figure 2-24). Remember to validate the query to make sure it will run.

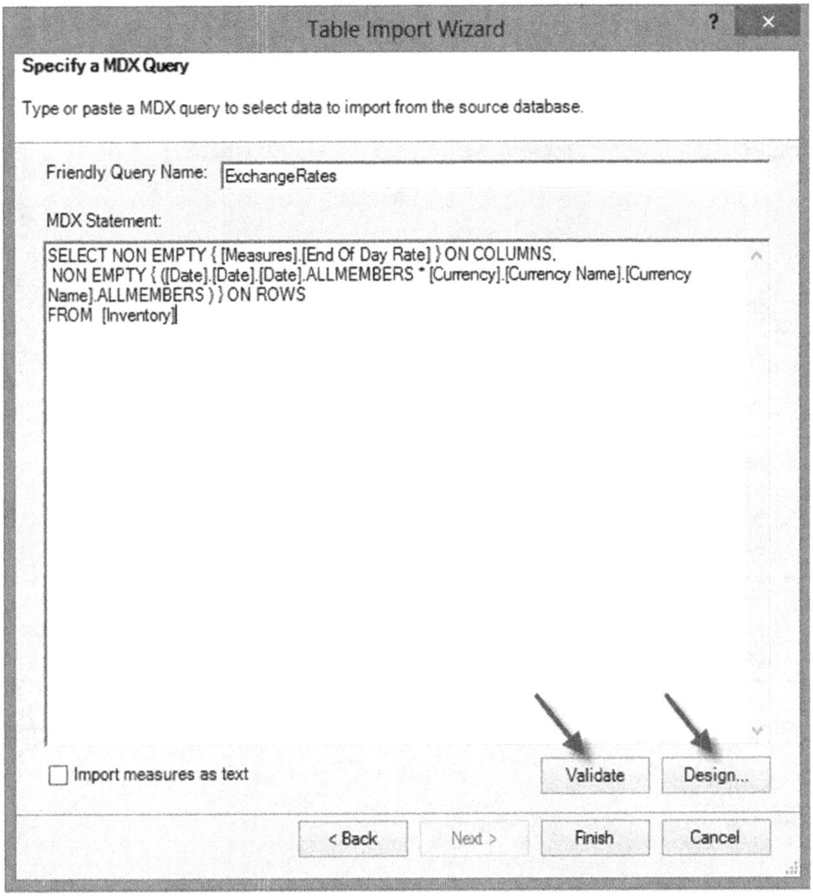

Figure 2-24. *Entering an MDX query*

If you do not know MDX, you can use a visual designer to create it, as shown in Figure 2-25. One of the nice features of the designer is the ability to preview the results.

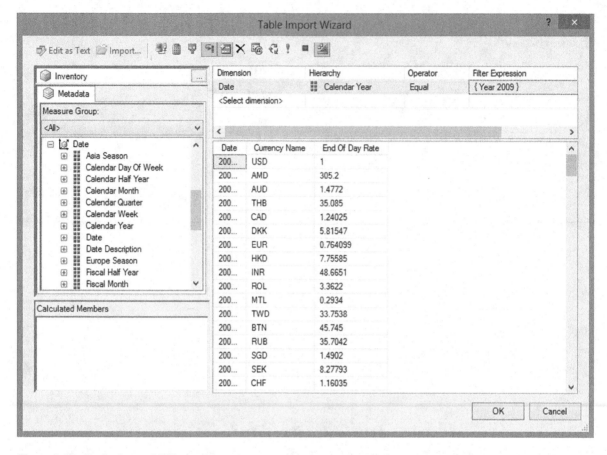

Figure 2-25. *Designing an MDX query*

When you are done designing the query, it is entered in to the MDX statement box, shown in Figure 2-24, where you can finish importing the data.

Reusing Existing Connections to Update the Model

There are two scenarios where you want to reuse an existing connection to a data source. You may need to retrieve additional data from a data source; for example, you need to get data from additional tables or views or issue a new query. In this case, you would choose the existing connections button located on the Home tab (see Figure 2-26).

Figure 2-26. *Selecting existing connections*

In the Existing Connections window, select the connection and click the Open button (see Figure 2-27). This will launch the screens (which depend on the connection type), covered previously, where you go through the process of selecting the data you want to import.

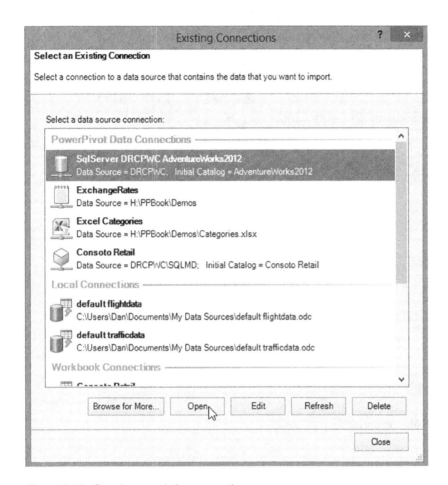

Figure 2-27. *Opening an existing connection*

The other scenario is when you want to change the filtering or add some columns to an existing table in the model. In this case, you need to select the table in the data view mode of the designer, and on the Design tab, select Table Properties (see Figure 2-28).

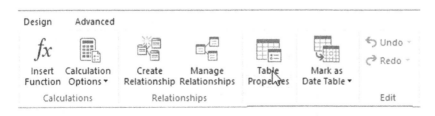

Figure 2-28. *Selecting table properties*

The Edit Table Properties window allows you to update the query used to populate the table with data. You can either update the table in the Table Preview mode (Figure 2-29) or Query mode (Figure 2-30). When in Query Editor mode you can also launch the query designer to update the query.

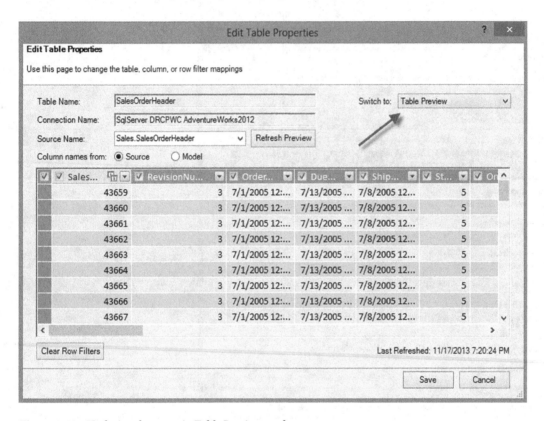

Figure 2-29. *Updating the query in Table Preview mode*

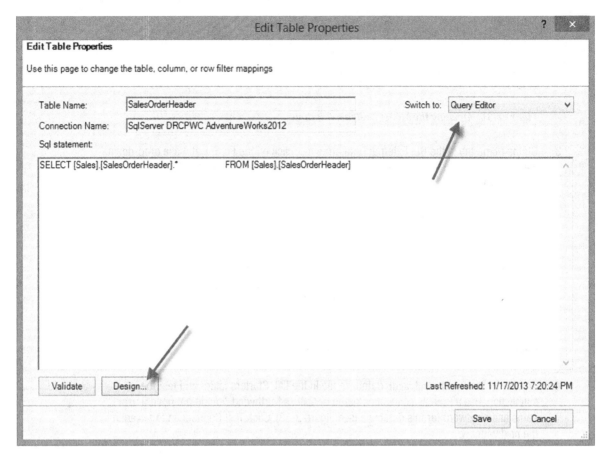

Figure 2-30. *Updating the query in Query Editor mode*

Now that you have seen how to import the data from various data sources into the Power Pivot data model, it is time to get some hands-on experience importing the data.

HANDS-ON LAB—LOADING DATA INTO POWER PIVOT

In the following lab you will

- Import data from an Access database.

- Import data from a text file.

1. Open Excel 2013 and create a new file called LabChapter2.xlsx

2. On the Power Pivot tab, click on the Manage Data Model button (see Figure 2-31).
   This launches the Power Pivot Model Designer window.

Figure 2-31. Opening the Model Designer window

3. On the Home tab in the Get External Data grouping, click on the From Database drop-down (see Figure 2-32). In the drop-down select From Access. This launches the Table Import Wizard.

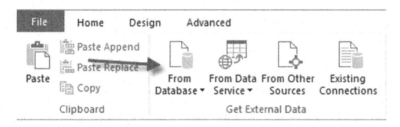

Figure 2-32. Launching the Table Import Wizard

4. Browse for the Northwind.acdb database file in the Lab Starters folder and test the connection. Use a friendly connection name of Access Northwind. You do not need a user name and password for this database (see Figure 2-33). Click Test Connection to advance to the next window.

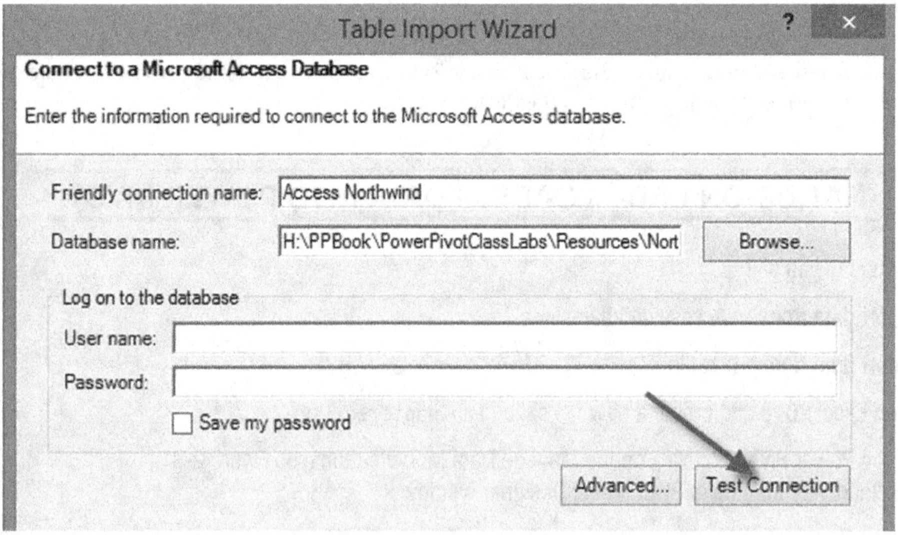

Figure 2-33. Connecting to an Access database

5. You have two options for importing the data: You can select from a list of tables and views or chose to write a query to select the data. Select from a list of tables and views.

6. In the Select Tables And Views window, select Customers and click on the row to highlight it. At the bottom of the window, select the Preview & Filter button to preview and filter the data (see Figure 2-34).

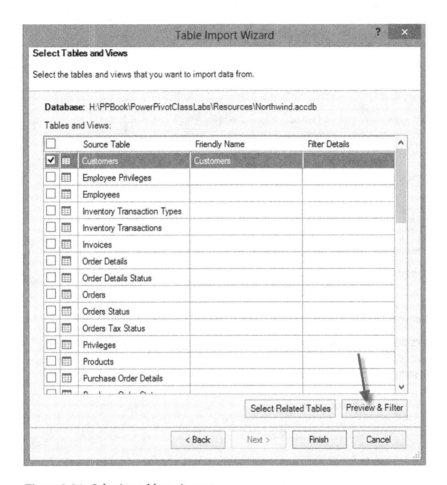

Figure 2-34. *Selecting tables to import*

7. In the Customers table, choose the following fields: ID, Company, Last Name, First Name, City, State/Province, and Country/Region. Uncheck the rest of the fields (see Figure 2-35). Checking the upper left check box will select or deselect all the columns.

Figure 2-35. *Filtering table columns*

8. From the Employees table select the following: ID, Last Name, First Name, and Job Title.

9. From the Orders table select these: Order ID, Employee ID, Customer ID, Order Date, Shipped Date, Shipper ID, Payment Type, and Paid Date. On the Status ID column, click the drop-down to filter the data. Uncheck status 0 and status 2. Status 3 represents a status of closed (see Figure 2-36).

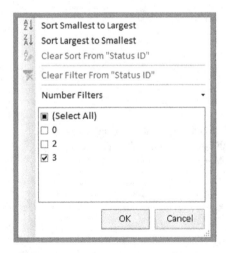

Figure 2-36. *Filtering table rows*

10. When you are done selecting the tables, click the Finish button to import the data. After importing, close the wizard. You should see each table as a tab in the Data View window (see Figure 2-37).

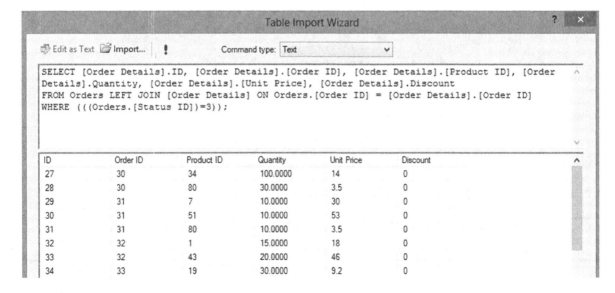

[ID] ▾					
Company	Last Name	First Name	City	StateProvince	CountryRegion
1 Company A	Bedecs	Anna	Seattle	WA	USA
2 Company B	Gratacos Sol...	Antonio	Boston	MA	USA
3 Company C	Axen	Thomas	Los A...	CA	USA
4 Company D	Lee	Christina	New Y...	NY	USA
5 Company E	O'Donnell	Martin	Minn...	MN	USA
6 Company F	Pérez-Olaeta	Francisco	Milwa...	WI	USA
7 Company G	Xie	Ming-Yang	Boise	ID	USA
8 Company H	Andersen	Elizabeth	Portla...	OR	USA

Customers | Employees | Orders

Figure 2-37. *Tables in the Data View window*

11. You are now going to select the order details using a query. In the Power Pivot Model Designer select the Home Tab. In the Home tab select the Existing Connections button. In the connections window select the Access Northwind connection and click Open.

12. This time, select Write A Query That Will Specify The Data To Import.

13. On the Specify A Query window, name the query **OrderDetails** and select the Design button to launch the Query Designer. (You could also write the query without the designer.) In the Query Designer, select Import and select the OrderDetailQuery.txt in the Lab Starters folder. Test the query by clicking the red exclamation (!) mark (see Figure 2-38). After testing the query, click the OK button.

Table Import Wizard

Edit as Text Import... ! Command type: Text

```
SELECT [Order Details].ID, [Order Details].[Order ID], [Order Details].[Product ID], [Order
Details].Quantity, [Order Details].[Unit Price], [Order Details].Discount
FROM Orders LEFT JOIN [Order Details] ON Orders.[Order ID] = [Order Details].[Order ID]
WHERE (((Orders.[Status ID])=3));
```

ID	Order ID	Product ID	Quantity	Unit Price	Discount
27	30	34	100.0000	14	0
28	30	80	30.0000	3.5	0
29	31	7	10.0000	30	0
30	31	51	10.0000	53	0
31	31	80	10.0000	3.5	0
32	32	1	15.0000	18	0
33	32	43	20.0000	46	0
34	33	19	30.0000	9.2	0

Figure 2-38. *Using a query to get data*

14. In the Table Import wizard, click the Finish button to import the data. After importing, close the wizard. You should see that an OrderDetail table tab has been added.

15. The final table you are going to import is contained in a tab-delimited text file. On the Home tab in the Get External Data section, click the From Other Sources button. In the data sources list select Text File and click Next.

16. In the connection information change the connection name to **Product**. In the File Path browse to the `ProductList.txt` file in the LabStarters folder. Select a tab column separator and check the Use First Row As Column Headers box. Click the Finish button to import the data (see Figure 2-39).

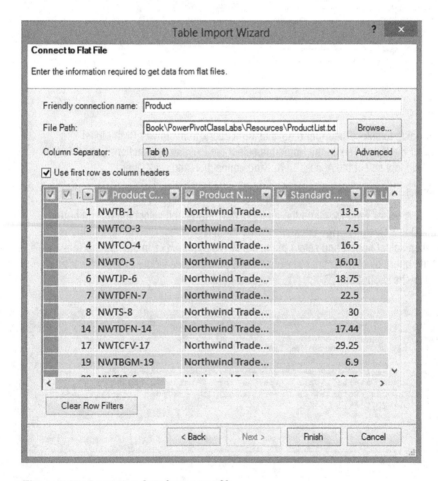

Figure 2-39. *Importing data from a text file*

17. After importing, close the wizard and you should see that a Product table tab has been added.

18. When you are finished save the file and close Excel.

Summary

One of the first steps in creating the Power Pivot model is importing data. In this chapter you learned how to import data from a variety of data sources. One of the nice features of importing data in Power Pivot is that the experience is similar when you import the data from the various data sources. You create a connection, supply a query or select tables, preview and filter the data, and then import it into the model. Now that you have imported the data into the various tables in your model, you need to set up relationships between these tables. In the next chapter you will learn the importance of setting up the relationships as well as how to augment the model with hierarchies to aid in data analysis.

CHAPTER 3

■ ■ ■

Creating the Data Model

Now that you know how to get data into the Power Pivot model, the next step is to understand what makes a good model. This is very important when dealing with data in Power Pivot. A good model will make Power Pivot perform amazingly fast and allow you to analyze the data in new and interesting ways. A bad model will cause Power Pivot to perform very slowly and at worst give misleading results when performing the data analysis. Traditional Excel pivot tables are based on a single table contained in an Excel sheet. Power Pivot pivot tables are based off of multiple tables contained in the data model. This chapter guides you through the process of creating a solid model that will become the foundation for your data analysis. In addition, you will look at how to present a user-friendly model to client tools. This includes renaming tables and fields, presenting appropriate data types, and hiding extraneous fields.

After completing this chapter you will be able to

- Explain what a data model is

- Create relationships between tables in the model

- Create and use a star schema

- Understand when and how to denormalize the data

- Create and use linked tables

- Create and use hierarchies

- Make a user-friendly model

What Is a Data Model?

Fundamentally a data model is made up of tables, columns, data types, and table relations. Typically data tables are constructed to hold data for a business entity; for example, customer data is contained in a customer table and employee data is contained in an employee table. Tables consist of columns that define the attributes of the entity. For example, you may want to hold information about customers such as name, address, birth date, household size, and so on. Each of these attributes has a data type that depends on what information the attribute holds—the name would be a string data type, the household size would be an integer, and the birth date would be a date. Each row in the table should be unique. Take a customer table, for example; if you had the same customer in multiple rows with different attributes, say birth date, you would not know which was correct.

In the previous example, you would know that one of the rows was incorrect because the same person could not have two different birthdays. There are many times, however, when you want to track changes in attribute values for an entity. For example, a product's list price will probably change over time. To track the change, you need to add a time stamp to make the row unique. Then each row can be identified by the product number and time stamp, as shown in Figure 3-1.

	Product Number	StandardCost	ListPrice	ProductLine	DealerPrice	ModelName	StartDate
1	FR-R38B-58	176.1997	297.6346	R	178.5808	LL Road Frame	2005-07-01 00:00:00.000
2	FR-R38B-58	170.1428	306.5636	R	183.9382	LL Road Frame	2006-07-01 00:00:00.000
3	FR-R38B-58	204.6251	337.22	R	202.332	LL Road Frame	2007-07-01 00:00:00.000

Figure 3-1. Using a time stamp to track changes

Once you have the tables of the model identified, it is important that you recognize whether the tables are set up to perform efficiently. This process is called *normalizing* the model. Normalization is the process of organizing the data to make data querying easier and more efficient. For example, you should not mix attributes of unrelated entities together in the same table—you would not want product data and employee data in the same table. Another example of proper normalization is not to hold more than one attribute in a column. For example, instead of having one customer address column, you would break it up into street, city, state, and zip. This would allow you to easily analyze the data by state or by city. The spread sheet shown in Figure 3-2 shows a typically non-normalized table. If you find that the data supplied to you is not sufficiently normalized, you may have to ask whoever is supplying the data to break the data up into multiple tables that you can then relate together in your model.

Customer Name	Address
Tom Smith	128 Elm St. Littleton, PA 12555
Jannet Jones	1399 Firestone Drive, San Francisco, CA 94109
Jon Yang	9539 Glenside Dr, Phoenix AZ 85004
Tom Smith	9707 Coldwater Drive, Orlando, FL 32804

Order Date	Item 1	Item 1 Description	Item 1 Price	Item 2	Item 2 Description	Item 2 Price
7/23/2013	FR-R38B-58	LL Road Frame	183	HB-R504	LL Road Handlebars	26.75
7/23/2013	FW-R623	Road Front Wheel	85.5			
8/1/2013	RB-9231	Rear Brakes	21.98			
8/1/2013	FW-R623	LL Road Front Wheel	85.5	RB-9231	Breaks	21.98

Figure 3-2. A non-normalized table

Once you are satisfied the tables in your model are adequately normalized, the next step is to determine how the tables are related. For example, you need to relate the customer table, sales table, and product table in order to analyze how various products are selling by age group. The way you relate the different tables is through the use of *keys*. Each row in a table needs a column or a combination of columns that uniquely identifies the row. This is called the *primary key*. The key may be easily identified, such as a sales order number or a customer number that has been assigned by the business when the data was entered. Sometimes you will need to do some analysis of a table to find the primary key, especially if you get the data from an outside source. For example, you may get data that contains potential customers. The fields are name, city, state, zip, birth date, and so on. You cannot just use the name as the key because it is very likely that you have more than one customer with the same name. If you use the combination of name and city, you have less of a chance of having more than one customer identified by the same key. As you use more columns, such as zip and birth date, your odds get even better.

When you go to relate tables in the model the primary key from one table becomes a foreign key in the related table. For example, to relate a customer to their sales, the customer key needs to be contained in the sales table where it is considered a foreign key. When extracting the data, the keys are used to get the related data. By far the best type of key to use for performance reasons is a single column integer. For this reason, a lot of database tables are designed with a surrogate key. This key is an integer that gets assigned to the record when it is loaded. Instead of using the natural key, the surrogate is used to connect the tables. Figure 3-3 shows a typical database table containing both the surrogate key (CustomerKey) and the natural key (CustomerAlternateKey).

CustomerKey	GeographyKey	CustomerAlternateKey	Title	FirstName	MiddleName	LastName	NameStyle	BirthDate
11000	26	AW00011000	NULL	Jon	V	Yang	0	1966-04-08
11001	37	AW00011001	NULL	Eugene	L	Huang	0	1965-05-14
11002	31	AW00011002	NULL	Ruben	NULL	Torres	0	1965-08-12
11003	11	AW00011003	NULL	Christy	NULL	Zhu	0	1968-02-15
11004	19	AW00011004	NULL	Elizabeth	NULL	Johnson	0	1968-08-08
11005	22	AW00011005	NULL	Julio	NULL	Ruiz	0	1965-08-05
11006	8	AW00011006	NULL	Janet	G	Alvarez	0	1965-12-06
11007	40	AW00011007	NULL	Marco	NULL	Mehta	0	1964-05-09
11008	32	AW00011008	NULL	Rob	NULL	Verhoff	0	1964-07-07
11009	25	AW00011009	NULL	Shannon	C	Carlson	0	1964-04-01

Figure 3-3. *A table containing both a surrogate key and a natural key*

It is important that you are aware of the keys used in your sources of data. If you can retrieve the keys from the source, you are much better off. This is usually not a problem when you are retrieving data from a relational database, but if you are combining data from different systems, make sure you have the appropriate keys.

Once you have the keys between the tables identified you are ready to create the relationships in the Power Pivot model.

Creating Table Relations

There are a few rules to remember when establishing table relationships in a Power Pivot model. First, you cannot use composite keys in the model. If your table uses a composite key, you will need to create a new column by concatenating the composite columns together and using this column as the key. Second, you can only have one active relationship path between two tables, but you can have multiple inactive relationships. Third, relationships are one to many; in other words, creating a relationship between the customer table (one side) and the sales table (many sides) is okay. Creating a direct relationship between the customers table and the products table is not allowed, however, because the customer can buy many products and the same product can be bought by many customers. In these cases you create a junction table to connect the tables together.

To create a relationship between two tables in the Power Pivot model you open up the Data Model Manager and switch to the diagram view. Right click on the table that represents the many side of the relationship and select Create Relationship. This launches the Create Relationship window. Select the related lookup table (the one side) and the key column. Figure 3-4 shows creating a relationship between the Sales table and the Store table. By default the first relationship created between the tables is marked as the active relationship.

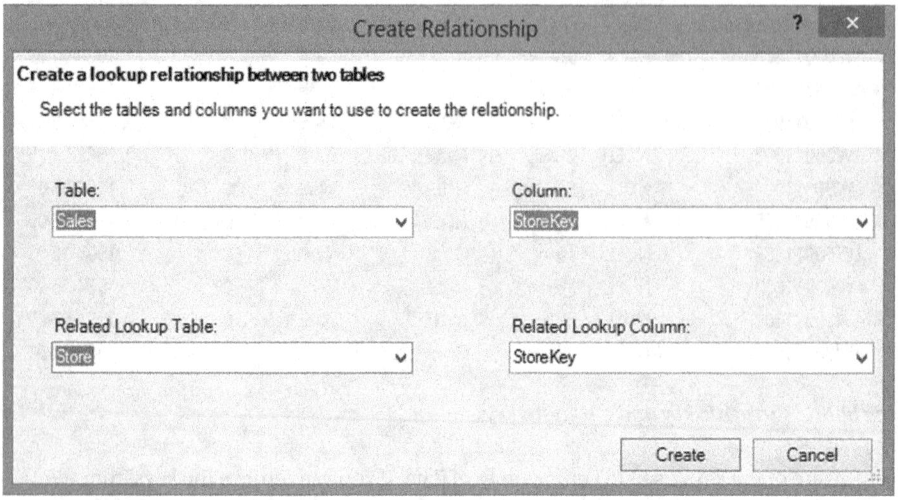

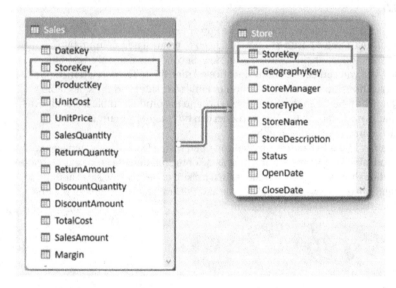

Figure 3-4. *Creating a table relationship*

Figure 3-5 shows the resulting relationship in the diagram view. If you click on the relationship arrow, the two key columns of the relationship are highlighted.

Figure 3-5. *Viewing a relationship in the diagram view*

You can create more than one relationship between two tables, but remember, only one can be the active relationship. If you try to make two active relationships, you get an error like the one shown in Figure 3-6.

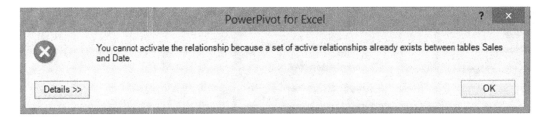

Figure 3-6. *Trying to create a second active relationship between two tables*

Sometimes the active relationship is not so obvious. Figure 3-7 shows an active relationship between the Sales table and the Date table and another one between the Sales table and the Store table. There is also an inactive relationship between the Store table and the Date table. If you try to make this one active, you get the same error message shown in Figure 3-6. This is because you can trace an active path from the Date table to the Sales table to the Store table.

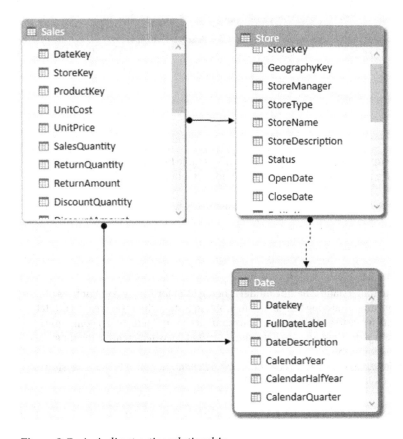

Figure 3-7. *An indirect active relationship*

Another common error you may run into is when you try to create a relationship between two tables and the key is not unique in at least one of the tables. Figure 3-8 shows a Product table and a Sales table that both contain duplicate ProductNumbers.

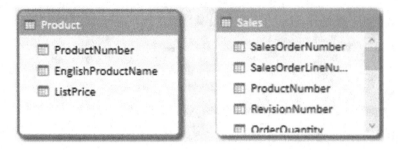

Figure 3-8. *The Product and Sales tables*

When you try to create a relationship between the tables you get the error shown in Figure 3-9.

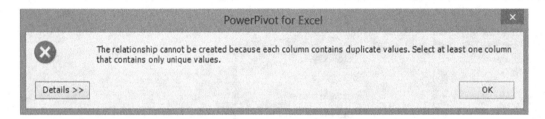

Figure 3-9. *Getting a duplicate value error*

In this example the ProductNumber is supposed to be unique in the Product table but it turns out there are duplicates. In order to fix this, you would have to change the query for the Product table data to ensure that you are not getting duplicates.

Now that you know how to create table relationships in the model, you are ready to look at the benefits of using a star schema.

Creating a Star Schema

When creating a data model it is important to understand what the model is being used for. The two major uses of databases are for capturing data and for reporting/analyzing the data. The problem is that when you create a model for efficient data capture, you decrease its efficiency to analyze the data. To combat this problem, many companies split off the data capturing database from their reporting/analysis database. Fortunately, when creating the data model in Power Pivot, we only need to tune it for reporting.

One of the best models to use when analyzing large sets of data is the *star schema*. The star schema consists of a central fact table surrounded by dimension tables, as shown in Figure 3-10.

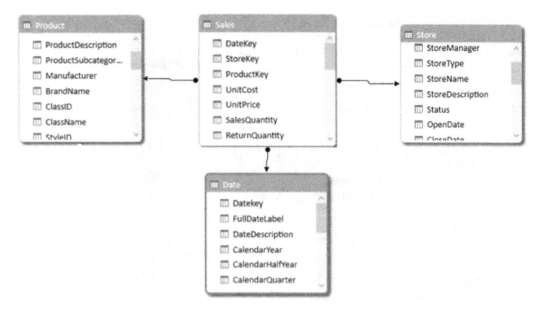

Figure 3-10. *A typical star schema*

The fact table contains quantitative data related to the business or process. For example, the Sales table in Figure 3-10 contains measurable aspects of a sale, such as total costs, sales amount, and quantity. Fact tables usually contain many rows and have a date or time component that records the time point at which the event occurred. The dimension tables contain attributes about the event. For example, the Date table can tell you when the sale occurred and allows you to roll up the data to the month, quarter, or year level. The Product table contains attributes about the product sold and you can look at sales by product line, color, and brand. The Store table contains attributes about the store involved in the sale. Dimension tables usually do not contain as many rows as the fact table but can contain quite a few columns. When you ask a question like "Which bikes are selling the best in the various age groups?" the measures (sales dollar values) come from the fact table whereas the categorizations (age and bike model) come from the dimension tables.

The main advantage of the star schema is that it provides fast query performance and aggregation processing. The disadvantage is that it usually requires a lot of preprocessing to move the data from a highly normalized transactional system to a more denormalized reporting system. The good news is that your business may have a reporting system feeding a traditional online analytical processing (OLAP) database such as Microsoft's Analysis Server or IBM's Cognos. If you can gain access to these systems, they are probably the best source for your core business data.

In order to create a star schema from your source data systems, you may have to perform some data denormalization, which is covered in the following section.

Understanding When to Denormalize the Data

Although transactional database systems tend to be highly normalized, reporting systems are denormalized into the star schema. If you do not have access to a reporting system where the denormalization is done for you, you will have to denormalize the data into a star schema to load your Power Pivot model. As an example, Figure 3-11 shows the tables that contain customer data in the Adventureworks transactional sales database.

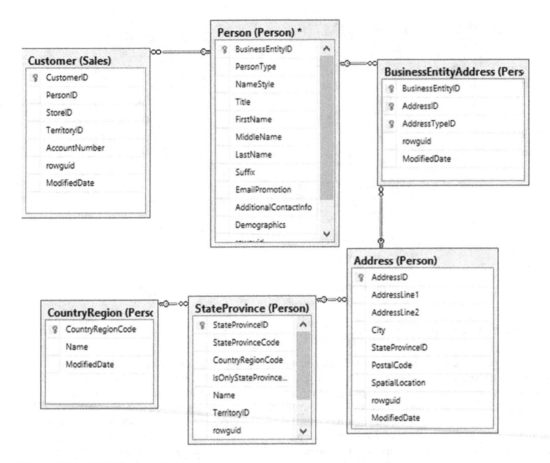

Figure 3-11. *A highly normalized schema*

In order to denormalize the customer data into your model, you need to create a query that combines the data into a single customer dimension table. If you are not familiar with creating complex queries, the easiest way to do this is to have the database developers create a view you can pull from that combines the tables for you. If the query is not too complex, you can probably create it yourself when you import the data. For example, Figure 3-12 shows a customer table and a geography table.

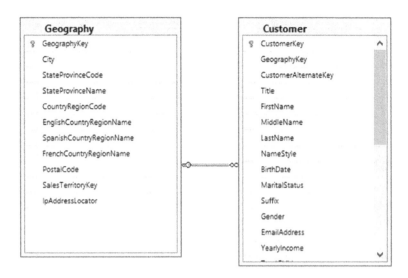

Figure 3-12. *Combining customer and customer location data*

You can combine these into one customer dimension table using the following query.

```
SELECT  c.CustomerKey, c.BirthDate, c.MaritalStatus, c.Gender,
        c.YearlyIncome, c.NumberChildrenAtHome, c.EnglishOccupation,
        c.HouseOwnerFlag,  c.NumberCarsOwned, c.CommuteDistance,
        g.City, g.StateProvinceName, g.EnglishCountryRegionName, g.PostalCode
FROM    Customer AS c INNER JOIN
        Geography AS g ON c.GeographyKey = g.GeographyKey
```

Although you do not have to be a query expert to get data into your Power Pivot model, it is very beneficial to know the basics of querying the data sources, even if it just helps to ask the right questions when you talk to the database developers.

Creating Linked Tables

One thing to remember about the data contained in the Power Pivot model is that it is read only. For the most part this is a good thing. You want to make sure that the data only gets changed in the source system. At times, however, as part of the data analysis, you will want to make adjustments on the fly and see how it affects the results. One example that happens fairly often is *bucket analysis*. For example, say you want to look a continuous measure such as age in discrete buckets (ranges) and you need to adjust the ranges during analysis. This is where linked tables shine.

To create the linked table you first set up the table on an Excel sheet. After entering the data, you highlight it and click on the quick analysis menu (see Figure 3-13). Under the Tables tab click on the Table button.

Age Group	Age Group	Age Group
Infant	0	2
Child	3	12
Teenager	13	18
Young Adult	19	25
Adult	25	59
Older Adult	60	120

FORMATTING	CHARTS	TOTALS	TABLES	SPARKLINES

Table   Blank
         PivotTable

Tables help you sort, filter, and summarize data.

Figure 3-13. *Creating an Excel table*

Once the table is created, it is a good idea to name it before importing it into the Power Pivot data model. You can do this by selecting the table and then entering the table name under the Tables tab in the Table Tools Design popup window (see Figure 3-14).

Table Name: Summarize with PivotTable
AgeGroups   Remove Duplicates
 Resize Table   Convert to Range
  Properties   Tools

Figure 3-14. *Renaming an Excel table*

Once you have the table named, select it, and on the Power Pivot tab, select Add To Data Model (see Figure 3-15).

FORMULAS	DATA	REVIEW	VIEW	POWERPIVOT

Add to   Update   Detect   Settings
Data Model All
    Tables   Relationships

Figure 3-15. *Adding the table to the model*

After the table is imported into the model, if you change some of the table values in the Excel sheet and select Update All on the PowerPivot tab (see Figure 3-15), the linked table in the model will update with the new values.

Creating Hierarchies

When analyzing data it is often helpful to use hierarchies to define various levels of aggregations. For example, it is common to have a calendar-based hierarchy based on year, quarter, and month levels. An aggregate like sales amount is then rolled up from month to quarter to year. Another common hierarchy might be from department to building to region. You could then roll cost up through the different levels. Creating hierarchies in a Power Pivot model is very easy. In the diagram view of the Model Designer select the table that has the attributes (columns) you want in the hierarchy. You will then see a Create Hierarchy button in the upper right corner of the table (see Figure 3-16). Click on the button to add the hierarchy and rename it. You can then drag and drop the fields onto the hierarchy to create the different levels. Make sure you arrange the fields so that they go from a higher level down to a lower level.

Figure 3-16. *Creating a hierarchy*

Creating hierarchies is one way to increase the usability of your model and help users instinctively gain more value in their data analysis. In the next section you will see some other things you can do to the model to increase its usability.

Making a User-Friendly Model

As you are creating your model one thing to keep in mind is making the model easy and intuitive to use. Chances are that the model may get used by others for analysis. The model may also be used for a wide variety of client reporting and analysis tools such as Power View, Power Map, and Reporting Services. There are properties and settings you can use that allow these client tools to gain more functionality from the model.

One of the most effective adjustments you can make is to rename the tables and columns. Use names that make sense for business users and not the cryptic naming convention that only makes sense to the database developers. Another good practice is to make sure the data types and formats of the columns are set correctly. A field from a text file may come in typed as a string when in reality it is numeric data. In addition you can hide fields that are of no use to the user, such as the surrogate keys used for linking the tables.

A common requirement is to change the sort order of a column from its natural sorting. The most common example is the months of the year. Since they are text by default, they are sorted alphabetically. In reality you want them sorted by month number. To fix this, you can sort one column by any other column in the table (see Figure 3-17). This is a nice feature and allows you to create your own business-related custom sorting.

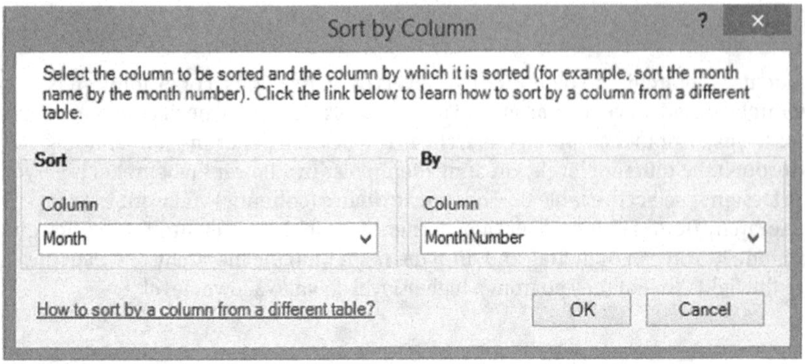

Figure 3-17. *Sorting one column by another column*

You can use some other settings to create good models for the various client tools. You will revisit this topic in more detail in Chapter 10, "Optimizing Tabular Models for Power View."

The following hands-on lab will help you solidify the topics covered in this chapter.

HANDS-ON LAB—CREATING A DATA MODEL IN POWER PIVOT

In the following lab you will

- Create table relations.

- Denormalize data.

- Create a linked table.

- Set up a hierarchy.

- Make a user-friendly model.

1. Open Excel 2013 and create a new file called LabChapter3.xlsx.

2. Using the Table Import Wizard in the Power Pivot data model, connect to the Adventureworks.accdb file in the LabStarters folder.

3. Select the tables and fields listed and import the data.

Source Table Name	Friendly Name	Fields
DimDate	Date	DateKey
		FullDateAlternateKey
		EnglishMonthName
		MonthNumberOfYear
		CalendarQuarter
		CalendarYear

(continued)

Source Table Name	Friendly Name	Fields
DimCustomer	Customer	CustomerKey BirthDate MaritalStatus Gender YearlyIncome TotalChildren HouseOwner NumberOfCars
FactInternetSales	Internet Sales	ProductKey OrderDateKey ShipDateKey CustomerKey SalesTerritoryKey SalesOrderNumber SalesOrderLineNumber OrderQuantity UnitPrice TotalProductCost SalesAmount

4. In the data view mode of the Power Pivot Model Designer, rename and hide the columns indicated in the table. To hide a column, right click on it and select Hide From Client Tools in the context menu.

Table	Column	Friendly Name	Hide
Date	DateKey		X
	FullDateAlternateKey	Date	
	EnglishMonthName	Month	
	MonthNumberOfYear	Month No	X
	CalendarQuarter	Quarter	
	CalendarYear	Year	X
Customer	CustomerKey		X
	BirthDate	Birth Date	
	MaritalStatus	Marital Status	
	Gender	Gender	
	YearlyIncome	Income	
	TotalChildren	Children	
	HouseOwner	Home Owner	
	NumberOfCars	Cars	

(continued)

Table	Column	Friendly Name	Hide
Internet Sales	ProductKey		X
	OrderDateKey		X
	ShipDateKey		X
	CustomerKey		X
	SalesTerritoryKey		X
	SalesOrderNumber	Order Number	
	SalesOrderLineNumber	Order Line Number	
	OrderQuantity	Quantity	
	UnitPrice	Unit Price	
	TotalProductCost	Product Cost	

5. Switch the Power Pivot window to diagram view. You should see the Date, Customer, and Internet Sales. The Customer table and the Internet Sales table have a relationship defined between them. This was discovered by the Table Import Wizard.

6. Drag the DateKey from the Date table and drop it on the OrderDateKey in the Internet Sales table. Similarly, create a relationship between the DateKey and the ShipDateKey. Double click on this relationship to launch the Edit Relationship window (see Figure 3-18). Try to make this an active relationship. You should get an error because you can only have one active relationship between two tables in the model.

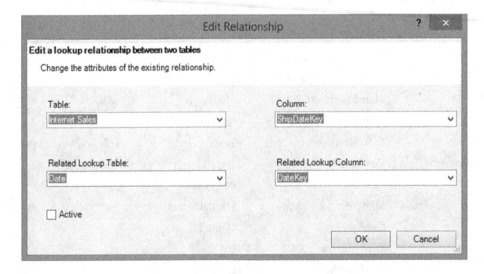

Figure 3-18. *Creating the table relationship*

7. On the Home tab of the Power Pivot Model Designer window, click the Existing Connections button. You should see the connection to the Adventureworks.acdb created earlier. Open this connection and select the query option for importing the data.

8. In the Specify A SQL Query window, change the query friendly name to Product and click the Design button.

9. In the designer click the Import button. Open the `ProductQuery.txt` file in the lab starter folder. Click the red exclamation mark (!) to run the query (see Figure 3-19). This query combines data (i.e., denormalizes) from the Product, ProductCategory, and ProductSubcategory tables.

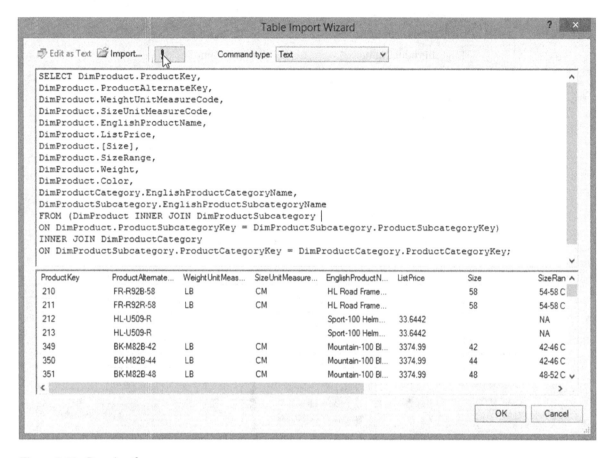

Figure 3-19. *Running the query*

10. After verifying that you are getting data, click the OK button and the Finish button on the next screen.

11. After importing the data, hide the ProductKey and update the column names as follows:

Table	Column	Friendly Name	Hide
Product	ProductKey		X
	ProductAlternateKey	Product Code	
	WeightUnitMeasureCode	Weight UofM Code	
	SizeUnitMeasureCode	Size UofM Code	
	EnglishProductName	Product Name	
	ListPrice	List Price	
	Size		
	SizeRange	Size Range	
	Weight		
	Color		
	EnglishProductCategoryName	Category	
	EnglishProductSubcategoryName	Subcategory	

12. Create a relationship between the Internet Sales and the Product tables using the ProductKey. Your final diagram should look like Figure 3-20.

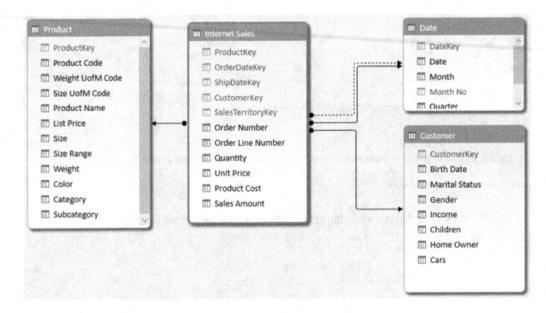

Figure 3-20. *Viewing the data model relationships*

13. To create a linked table, enter the data shown in Figure 3-21 into an empty spread sheet tab in Excel.

	A	B	C	D
1	SalesTerritoryKey	Region	Country	Group
2	1	Northwest	United States	North America
3	2	Northeast	United States	North America
4	3	Central	United States	North America
5	4	Southwest	United States	North America
6	5	Southeast	United States	North America
7	6	Canada	Canada	North America
8	7	France	France	Europe
9	8	Germany	Germany	Europe
10	9	Australia	Australia	Pacific
11	10	United Kingdom	United Kingdom	Europe
12	11	NA	NA	NA

Figure 3-21. *The linked table data*

14. Select the cells, right click, and in the Quick Analysis context menu, select the Table tab and click the Table button (see Figure 3-22). In the Table Tools Design tab, rename the table SalesTerritory.

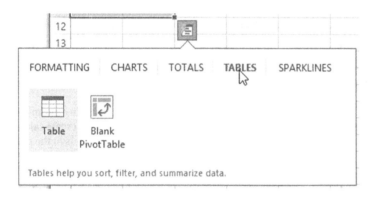

Figure 3-22. *The Quick Analysis Tables tab*

15. On the Power Pivot tab, click the Add To Data Model button. Once the table is in the model, change the name to Sales Territory, hide the SalesTerritoryKey, and create a relationship to the Internet Sales table.

16. To create a hierarchy, select the Sales Territory table in the Power Pivot window's diagram view and click the Create Hierarchy button. Drag and drop the Sales Territory Group, Country, and Region on the hierarchy. Rename the hierarchy **Sales Territory** (see Figure 3-23).

Figure 2-23. *The Sales Territory hierarchy*

17.   Create a Calendar hierarchy named **Calendar** in the Date table using Year, Quarter, and Month.

18.   Switch to the data view in the designer and select the Date Table tab. Select the Month column and set its Sort By Column to the Month No. column.

19.   When done save and close Excel.

Summary

When working in Power Pivot it is very important to understand what makes a good model. A good model will make Power Pivot perform incredibly fast and allow you to easily analyze large amounts of data. Unlike traditional Excel pivot tables, which are based on a single table contained in an Excel sheet, Power Pivot pivot tables are based off of multiple tables contained in the data model. This chapter guided you through the process of creating a solid model that will become the foundation for your data analysis. In addition, you saw how to present a user-friendly model to client tools.

Now that you have a solid foundation for your model, you are ready to extend the model with custom calculations. The next chapter introduces the Data Analysis Expressions (DAX) language and explains how to create calculated columns in the data model. It includes plenty of examples to help you create common calculations in the model.

■ ■ ■

CHAPTER 4

Creating Calculations with DAX

Now that you know how to create a robust data model to base your analysis on, the next step is to add to the model any calculations required to aid your exploration of the data. For example, you may have to translate code values into meaningful descriptions or parse out a string to obtain key information. This where Data Analysis Expressions (DAX) comes into play. This chapter introduces you to DAX and shows you how to use DAX to create calculated columns to add to the functionality of your model.

After completing this chapter you will be able to

- Use DAX to add calculated columns to a table.

- Implement DAX operators.

- Work with text functions in DAX.

- Use DAX date and time functions.

- Use conditional and logical functions.

- Get data from a related table.

- Use math, trig, and statistical functions.

What Is DAX?

DAX is a formula language used to create calculated columns and measures in the Power Pivot model. It is a new language developed specifically for the tabular data model Power Pivot is based on. If you are familiar with Excel's formula syntax, you will find that the DAX syntax is very familiar. In fact some of the DAX formulas have the same syntax and functionality as their Excel counterparts. The major difference, and one that you need to wrap your head around, is that Excel formulas are cell based whereas DAX is column based. For example, if you want to concatenate two values in Excel, you would use a formula like the following:

```
=A1 & " " & B1
```

where A1 is the cell in the first row and first column and B1 is the cell in the second column of the first row (see Figure 4-1).

Figure 4-1. *Entering a formula in Excel*

This is very similar to the DAX formula:

```
=[First Name] & " " & [Last Name]
```

where the First Name and Last Name are columns in a table in the model (see Figure 4-2).

[Full Name] ▾		fx =[First Name] & " " & [Last Name]	
First Name ▾	Last Name ▾	MiddleName ▾	Full Name ▾
Guy	Gilbert	R	Guy Gilbert
JoLynn	Dobney	M	JoLynn Dobney
Ruth	Ellerbrock	Ann	Ruth Ellerbrock
Barry	Johnson	K	Barry Johnson
Sidney	Higa	M	Sidney Higa
Taylor	Maxwell	R	Taylor Maxwell

Figure 4-2. *Entering a formula in Power Pivot*

The difference is that the DAX formula is applied to all rows in the table whereas the Excel formula only works on the specific cells. In Excel you need to re-create the formula in each row.

What this means is although you can do something like this in Excel:

```
=A1 & " " & B2
```

where you are taking a cell from the first row and concatenating a cell from the second row (see Figure 4-3), this can't be done in DAX.

C2	▾	⋮	✕	✓	fx	=A1 & " " & B2	
	A	B	C	D	E		
1	Dan	Clark	Dan Clark				
2	Al	Smith	Dan Smith				
3	Jane	Doe					

Figure 4-3. *Using cells in different rows*

When creating DAX formulas it is important to consider the data types and any conversions that may take place during the calculations. If you do not take these into account you may experience errors in the formula or unexpected results. The supported data types in the model are whole number, decimal number, currency, Boolean, text, and date. DAX also has a table data type that is used in many functions that take a table as an input value and return a table.

When you try to add a numeric data type with a text data type you get an implicit conversion. If DAX can convert the text to a numeric value it will add them as numbers, if it can't you will get an error. On the other hand, if you try to concatenate a numeric data type with a text data type, DAX will implicitly convert the numeric data type to text. Although most of the time implicit conversions give you the results you are looking for, they come at a performance cost and should be avoided if possible. For example, if you import data from a text file and the column is set to a text data type but you know it is in fact numeric, you should change the data type in the model.

When creating calculations in DAX you will need to reference tables and columns. If the table name does not contain spaces, you can just refer to it by name. If the table name contains spaces, you need to enclose it in single quotes. Columns and measures are enclosed in brackets. If you just list the column name in the formula, it is assumed that the column exists in the same table. If you are referring to a column in another table, you need to use the fully qualified name, which is the table name followed by the column name. The following code demonstrates the syntax:

```
=[SalesAmount] - [TotalCost]
=Sales[SalesAmount] - Sales[TotalCost]
='Internet Sales'[SalesAmount] - 'Internet Sales'[TotalCost]
```

Here are some other points to keep in mind when you are working with DAX:

- DAX formulas and expressions cannot modify or insert individual values in tables.

- You cannot create calculated rows by using DAX. You can create only calculated columns and measures.

- When defining calculated columns, you can nest functions to any level.

The first thing to understand when creating a calculation is what operators are supported and what the syntax to use them is. In the next section you will investigate the various DAX operators.

Implementing DAX Operators

DAX contains a robust set of operators that includes arithmetic, comparison, logic, and text concatenation. Most of these should be familiar to you and are listed in Table 4-1.

Table 4-1. *DAX Operators*

Category	Symbol	Use
Arithmetic operators		
	+	Addition
	-	Subtraction
	*	Multiplication
	/	Division
	^	Exponentiation

(continued)

Table 4-1. (*continued*)

Category	Symbol	Use
Comparison operators		
	=	Equal to
	>	Greater than
	<	Less than
	>=	Greater than or equal to
	<=	Less than or equal to
	<>	Not equal to
Text concatenation operator		
	&	Concatenation
		Logic operators
	&&	And
	||	Or

As an example of the arithmetic operator, the following code is used to divide the Margin column by the Total Cost column to create a new column, the Margin Percentage.

```
=[Margin]/[TotalCost]
```

It is very common to have several arithmetic operations in the same calculation. In this case you have to be aware of the order of operations. Exponents are evaluated first followed by multiplication/division and then addition/subtraction. You can control order of operations by using parentheses to group calculations; for example, the following formula will perform the subtraction before the division.

```
=([Sales Amount]-[Total Cost])/[Total Cost]
```

The comparison operators are primarily for if statements. For example, the following calculation checks to see if a store's selling area size is greater than 1000. If it is, it is classified as a large store, if not, it is classified as small.

```
=IF([Selling Area Size]>1000,"Large","Small")
```

The logical operators are used to create multiple comparison logic. The following code checks to see if the store size area is greater than 1000 or if it has more than 35 employees to classify it as large.

```
=IF([Selling Area Size]> 1000 || [Employee Count] > 35,"Large","Small")
```

When you start stringing together a series of logical conditions it is a good idea to use parentheses to control the order of operations. The following code checks to see if the store size area is greater than 1000 and if it has more than 35 employees to classify it as large. It will also classify it as large if it has annual sales of more than $1,000,000 regardless of its size area or number of employees.

```
=IF((([Selling Area Size]> 1000 && [Employee Count] > 35) || [Annual Sales] > 1000000,"Large","Small")
```

When working with DAX calculations you may need to nest one formula inside another. For example, the following code nests an IF statement inside the false part of another IF statement. If the employee count is not greater than 35 it jumps to the next if statement to check if it is greater than 20.

```
=IF(Store[EmployeeCount]>35,"Large",IF(Store[EmployeeCount]>20,"Medium","Small"))
```

DAX contains many useful functions for creating calculations and measures. These functions include text functions, date and time functions, statistical functions, math functions, and informational functions. In the next few sections you will look at using the various function types in your calculations.

Working with Text Functions

A lot of calculations involve some kind of text manipulation. You may need to truncate, parse, search, or format the text values that you load from the source systems. DAX contains many useful functions for working with text. The functions are listed in Table 4-2 along with a description of what they are used for.

Table 4-2. *DAX Text Functions*

Function	Description
BLANK	Returns a blank.
CONCATENATE	Joins two text strings into one text string.
EXACT	Compares two text strings and returns TRUE if they are exactly the same, FALSE otherwise.
FIND	Returns the starting position of one text string within another text string.
FIXED	Rounds a number to the specified number of decimals and returns the result as text.
FORMAT	Converts a value to text according to the specified format.
LEFT	Returns the specified number of characters from the start of a text string.
LEN	Returns the number of characters in a text string.
LOWER	Converts all letters in a text string to lowercase.
MID	Returns a string of characters from a text string, given a starting position and length.
REPLACE	Replaces part of a text string with a different text string.
REPT	Repeats text a given number of times. Use REPT to fill a cell with a number of instances of a text string.
RIGHT	Returns the last character or characters in a text string, based on the number of characters you specify.
SEARCH	Returns the number of the character at which a specific character or text string is first found, reading left to right.
SUBSTITUTE	Replaces existing text with new text in a text string.
TRIM	Removes all spaces from text except for single spaces between words.
UPPER	Converts a text string to all uppercase letters.
VALUE	Converts a text string that represents a number to a number.

As an example of using a text function in a calculation, let's say you have a product code column in a products table where the first two characters represent the product family. To create the product family column, you would use the Left function as follows:

```
=Left([Product Code],2)
```

You can use the FIND function to search a text for a subtext. You can use a (?) to match any single character and a (*) to match any sequence of characters. You have the option of indicating the starting position for the search. The FIND function returns the starting position of the substring found. If it doesn't find the substring, it can return a 0, -1, or a blank value. The following code searches the product description column for the word mountain.

```
=FIND("mountain",[Description],1,-1)
```

The FORMAT function converts a value to text based on the format provided. For example, you may need to convert a date to a specific format. The following code converts a date data type to a string with a format like "Mon - Dec 02, 2013".

```
=FORMAT([StartDate],"ddd - MMM dd, yyyy")
```

Along with the ability to create your own format there are also predefined formats you can use. The following code demonstrates using the Long Date format "Monday, December 2, 2013".

```
=FORMAT([StartDate],"Long Date")
```

Now that you have seen how to use some of the text functions, the next type of function to look at are the built-in date and time functions.

Using DAX Date and Time Functions

Most likely you will find that your data analysis has a date component associated with it. You may need to look at sales or energy consumption and need to know the day of the week the event occurred. You may have to calculate age or maturity dates. DAX has quite a few date and time functions to help create these types of calculations. Table 4-3 summarizes the various date and time functions available.

Table 4-3. *DAX Date and Time Functions*

Function	Description
DATE	Returns the specified date in datetime format
DATEVALUE	Converts a date in the form of text to a date in datetime format
DAY	Returns the day of the month
EDATE	Returns the date that is the indicated number of months before or after the start date
EOMONTH	Returns the date in datetime format of the last day of the month, before or after a specified number of months
HOUR	Returns the hour as a number from 0 (12:00 A.M.) to 23 (11:00 P.M.)
MINUTE	Returns the minute as a number from 0 to 59

(*continued*)

Table 4-3. (*continued*)

Function	Description
MONTH	Returns the month as a number from 1 (January) to 12 (December)
NOW	Returns the current date and time in datetime format
SECOND	Returns the seconds of a time value, as a number from 0 to 59
TIME	Converts hours, minutes, and seconds given as numbers to a time in datetime format
TIMEVALUE	Converts a time in text format to a time in datetime format
TODAY	Returns the current date
WEEKDAY	Returns a number from 1 to 7 identifying the day of the week of a date
WEEKNUM	Returns the week number for the given date
YEAR	Returns the year of a date as a four digit integer
YEARFRAC	Calculates the fraction of the year represented by the number of whole days between two dates

As an example of using the date functions, you need to calculate years of service for employees. The first thing you need to do is find the difference between the current year and the year they were hired. The following code gets the year from today's date.

```
=YEAR(Today())
```

Now you can subtract the year of their hire date. Notice we are nesting one function inside of another. Nesting functions is a common requirement for many calculations.

```
=YEAR(TODAY()) - YEAR([HireDate])
```

Astute readers will realize that this calculation is only correct if the current month is greater than or equal to the month they were hired. You can adjust for this using a conditional if statement as follows:

```
= If (MONTH(TODAY())>=MONTH([HireDate]),YEAR(TODAY()) - YEAR([HireDate]),YEAR(TODAY()) -
YEAR([HireDate])-1)
```

As you can see, calculations can get quite complicated pretty quickly. The challenge is making sure the open and closing parentheses of each function line up correctly. One way to organize the code is to use multiple lines and indenting. To get a new line in the formula editor bar, you need to hold down the Shift key while you press Enter. I find the following easier to understand.

```
= If (MONTH(TODAY())>=MONTH([HireDate]),
      YEAR(TODAY()) - YEAR([HireDate]),
      YEAR(TODAY()) - YEAR([HireDate])-1
  )
```

Unfortunately you can't add comments to your code in Power Pivot.

There is often more than one way to create a calculation. You may find an easier way to make the calculation or one that performs better. The following calculates the years of service using the YEARFRAC function and the TRUNC function (one of the math functions) to drop the decimal part of the number.

```
=TRUNC(YEARFRAC([HireDate],TODAY()))
```

The next group of functions you are going to investigate are the informational and logical functions. These functions are important when you want to determine if a condition exists such as a blank value or an error is occurring due to a calculation. These functions allow you to trap for conditions and respond to them in an appropriate way.

Using Informational and Logical Functions

As you start building more complex calculations, you often need to use informational and logical functions to check for conditions and respond to various conditions. One common example is the need to check for blank values. The ISBLANK function returns TRUE if the value is blank and FALSE if it is not. The following code uses a different calculation depending on whether the middle name is blank.

```
=IF(ISBLANK([MiddleName]),
[FirstName] & " " & [LastName],
[FirstName] & " " & [MiddleName] & " " & [LastName]
)
```

The ISERROR function is used to check if a calculation or function returns an error. The following calculation checks to see if a divide by zero error occurs during a division.

```
=IF(ISERROR([TotalProductCost]/[SalesAmount]),
    BLANK(),
    [TotalProductCost]/[SalesAmount]
  )
```

Another way to create this calculation is to use the IFERROR function, which returns the value if no error occurs and an alternate value if an error occurs.

```
=IFERROR([TotalProductCost]/[SalesAmount],BLANK())
```

Tables 4-4 and 4-5 list the logical and informational functions available in DAX.

Table 4-4. *The DAX Logical Functions*

Function	Description
AND	Checks whether both arguments are TRUE.
FALSE	Returns the logical value FALSE.
IF	Checks if a condition provided as the first argument is met. Returns one value if the condition is TRUE, and returns another value if the condition is FALSE.
IFERROR	Evaluates an expression and returns a specified value if the expression returns an error; otherwise returns the value of the expression itself.
NOT	Changes FALSE to TRUE, or TRUE to FALSE.
OR	Checks whether one of the arguments is TRUE to return TRUE.
SWITCH	Evaluates an expression against a list of values and returns one of multiple possible result expressions.
TRUE	Returns the logical value TRUE.

Table 4-5. *The DAX Informational Functions*

Function	Description
CONTAINS	Returns true if values for all referred columns exist, or are contained, in those columns
ISBLANK	Checks whether a value is blank
ISERROR	Checks whether a value is an error
ISLOGICAL	Checks whether a value is a Boolean value
ISNONTEXT	Checks if a value is not text (blank cells are not text)
ISNUMBER	Checks whether a value is a number
ISTEXT	Checks if a value is text
LOOKUPVALUE	Returns the value in the column for the row that meets all criteria specified by a search

When you are analyzing data you often need to look up corresponding data from a related table. You may need to obtain descriptions from a related code or summarize data and import it into a table, such as lifetime sales. The following section looks at how you go about looking up related data using DAX.

Getting Data from Related Tables

There are times when you need to look up values in other tables to complete a calculation. If there is a relationship established between the tables you can use the RELATED function. This allows you to denormalize the tables and make it easier for users to navigate. For example, you may have a Customer table related to a Geography table (see Figure 4-4).

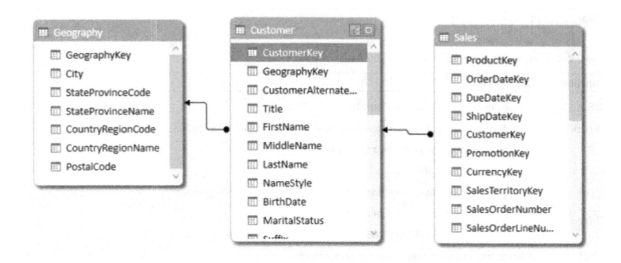

Figure 4-4. *Using the RELATED function*

If you need to look at sales by customer's country, you can use the related function to create a Country column in the Customers table.

```
=RELATED(Geography[CountryRegionName])
```

You can then hide the Geography table from client tools to keep the model cleaner and less confusing to users.

Although the related table returns a single value, there are times when you want to look at a set of related data and aggregate it before displaying the value in the column. For example, you may want to add a column to the Customers table that lists their lifetime sales amount. In this case, you would use the RELATEDTABLE function to get the related sales and then sum them up for each customer.

```
=SUMX(RELATEDTABLE(Sales),[SalesAmount])
```

■ **Note**   The previous code uses the SUMX function, which is used instead of the SUM function because you are applying a filter. Chapter 5 discusses this in more detail.

The final set of functions we look at are the math, trig, and statistical functions. These functions allow you to perform common analysis such as logs, standard deviation, rounding, and truncation.

Using Math, Trig, and Statistical Functions

Along with the functions discussed thus far, DAX also includes quite a few math, trig, and statistical functions. The math functions (see Table 4-6) are used for rounding, truncating, and summing up the data. They also contain functions you may use in scientific, engineering, and financial calculations; for example, you may need to calculate the volume of a sphere given the radius (see the following DAX calculation):

```
=4*PI()*POWER([Radius],3)/3
```

Table 4-6. *Some of the Math and Trig Functions Available in DAX*

Function	Description
ABS	Returns the absolute value of a number
CEILING	Rounds a number up to the nearest integer or to the nearest multiple of significance
EXP	Returns e raised to the power of a given number
FACT	Returns the factorial of a number
FLOOR	Rounds a number down, toward zero, to the nearest multiple of significance
LOG	Returns the logarithm of a number to the base you specify
PI	Returns the value of pi, 3.14159265358979, accurate to 15 digits
POWER	Returns the result of a number raised to a power
ROUND	Rounds a number to the specified number of digits
SQRT	Returns the square root of a number
SUM	Adds all the numbers in a column
TRUNC	Truncates a number to an integer by removing the decimal, or fractional, part of the number

As another example, say you want to calculate compounding interest on an investment. The following DAX calculation determines the compounding rate of return for an investment.

```
=[Principal]*POWER(1+([IntRate]/[CompoundRate]),[CompoundRate]*[Years])
```

When you are analyzing data, you often want to look at not only the relationship between the data but also the quality of the data and how well you can trust your predictions. This is where the statistical analysis of the data comes in to play. With statistics, you can do things like determine and account for outliers in the data, examine the volatility of the data, and detect fraud. As an example, you can use DAX to determine and filter out the outliers in your data using the standard deviation. The following DAX function calculates the standard deviation of the sales amount.

```
=STDEVX.P(RELATEDTABLE(Sales),Sales[SalesAmount])
```

Table 4-7 lists some of the statistical functions available in DAX.

Table 4-7. *Some of the Statistical Functions Available in DAX*

Function	Description
AVERAGE	Returns the average of all the numbers in a column
COUNT	Counts the number of cells in a column that contain numbers
COUNTA	Counts the number of cells in a column that are not empty
COUNTBLANK	Counts the number of blank cells in a column
COUNTROWS	Counts the number of rows in the specified table
DISTINCTCOUNT	Counts the number of different cells in a column of numbers
MAX	Returns the largest numeric value in a column
MIN	Returns the smallest numeric value in a column
RANK.EQ	Returns the ranking of a number in a list of numbers
RANKX	Returns the ranking of a number in a list of numbers for each row in the table argument
STDEV.S	Returns the standard deviation of a sample population
TOPN	Returns the top *N* rows of the specified table
VAR.S	Returns the variance of a sample population

Now that you have seen what functions you have available in Power Pivot and DAX. I want to review some tips on creating functions in general.

Tips for Creating Calculations in Power Pivot

Before turning you loose on a hands-on lab, I want to give you a few pointers on creating these calculations in Power Pivot. When entering a formula for a calculated column, right click on a column in the table in the Data View window of the model builder. In the context menu, select Insert Column (see Figure 4-5).

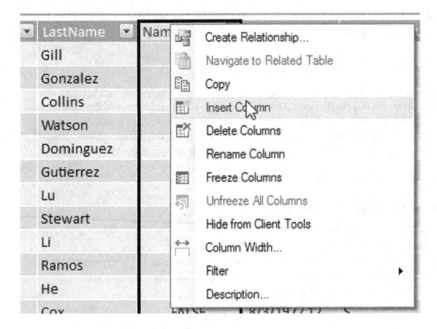

Figure 4-5. Adding a calculated column

Rename the column and then enter the formula in the formula editor bar. Formulas start with an equal sign (=) and table names are contained in single quotes (''), which is optional if the table name does not contain spaces. Table columns are contained in square brackets ([]). The formula editor bar supplies an autocomplete feature that you should take advantage of (see Figure 4-6). Select the function, table, or column from the drop-down list and press the Tab key to insert it into the formula. If you do not see the autofill drop-down, chances are there is an error in your formula.

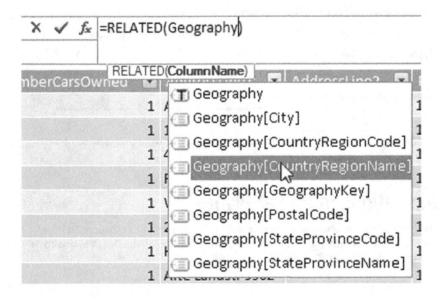

Figure 4-6. Using autocomplete when creating calculations

There are three buttons next to the formula editor bar: The X is used to cancel the changes you made; the check mark is used to commit the changes; and the function symbol is used to launch an Insert Function window (see Figure 4-7). You can peruse the various functions and gain information on the parameters expected by the functions.

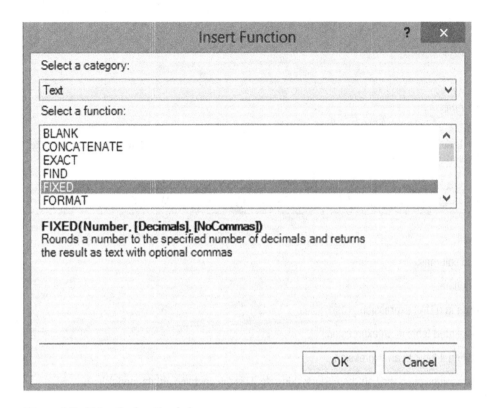

Figure 4-7. *Using the function helper*

When you create a calculation incorrectly, you may get an error indicator. You should click on the error dropdown and select Show Error (see Figure 4-8). This will display an error message (see Figure 4-9), which will give you useful information that can help you fix the error.

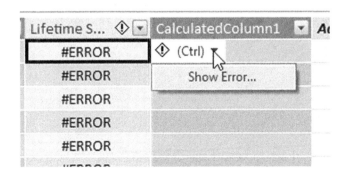

Figure 4-8. *Showing error information*

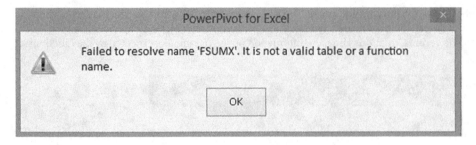

Figure 4-9. *Viewing the error message*

Now that you have seen how to create calculations with DAX and are familiar with the DAX functions available to you, it is time to gain some hands-on experience.

HANDS-ON LAB—CREATING CALCULATED COLUMNS IN POWER PIVOT

In the following lab you will

- Create calculated columns.

- Use DAX text functions.

- Use date functions in a DAX expression.

- Use data from a related table in an expression.

- Implement conditional logic in an expression.

1. In the Lab Starters folder, open the LabChap4Starter.xlsx file. This file contains a data model consisting of sales data, product data, and store data.

2. View the model in the Power Pivot window using the diagram view (see Figure 4-10).

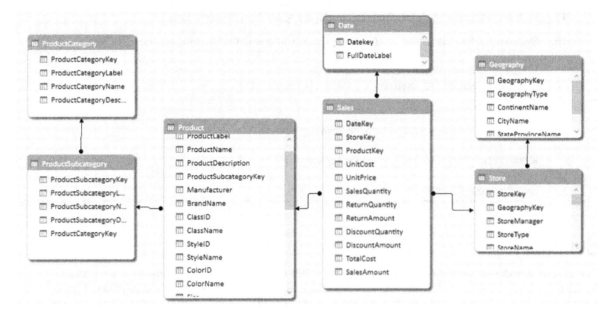

Figure 4-10. *The data model for store sales*

3. Switch to data view in the Power Pivot Window and select the Sales table.

4. After the SalesAmount column, click on the Add Column. In the formula bar above the table, enter the following to calculate margin:

```
=[SalesAmount] - [TotalCost]
```

5. Right click on the new column and rename it **Margin**.

6. Repeat this procedure to create a MarginPercent column with the following formula:

```
=[Margin]/[SalesAmount]
```

7. In the Data View window, select the Date table.

8. Use the Date functions to create a Year, Quarter, Month, Month Number, and Weekday column.

9. Using the Year, Quarter, and Month columns, create a Calendar hierarchy in the Date table.

10. In the Data View window, select the Product table.

11. Insert a Weight Label column with the following formula:

```
=if(ISBLANK([Weight]),BLANK(), [Weight] & " " & [WeightUnitMeasureID])
```

12. Next to ProductSubcategoryKey, create a ProductCategory column using the related function:

```
=RELATED('ProductCategory'[ProductCategoryName])
```

13. Using the related function, create a ProductSubcategory column.

14. Hide the ProductCategory and ProductSubcategory tables from the client tools.

15. Switch to the Store table and create a Years Open column with the following formula.

```
=TRUNC(YEARFRAC([OpenDate],
        If(ISBLANK([CloseDate]),TODAY(),[CloseDate]))
            ,0)
```

16. Create a LifetimeSales column using the following formula.

```
=SUMX(RELATEDTABLE(Sales),Sales[SalesAmount])
```

17. Save and close the Excel file.

Summary

This chapter introduced you to the DAX language and the built-in functions that you can use to create calculations. At this point, you should be comfortable with creating calculated columns and using the DAX functions. I strongly recommend that you become familiar with the various functions available and how to use them in your analysis. In the next chapter you will continue working with DAX to create measures. Measures are one of the most important parts of building your model in Power Pivot; the measures are the reason you are looking at your data. You want to answer questions such as how sales are doing or what influences energy consumption. Along with creating measures, you will also see how filter context effects measures. Filter context is one of the most important concepts you need to master in order to get the most out of Power Pivot.

■ ■ ■

CHAPTER 5

Creating Measures with DAX

Creating measures in DAX is the most important skill necessary to create solid data models. This chapter covers the common functions used to create measures in the data model. It also covers the important topic of data context and how to alter or override the context when creating measures.

After completing this chapter you will be able to

- Understand the difference between measures and attributes.

- Understand how context affects measurements.

- Create common aggregates.

- Know how and when to alter the filter context.

- Create KPIs.

Measures versus Attributes

If you look at a typical star model for a data warehouse, you have a fact table surrounded by dimension tables. For example, Figure 5-1 shows a financial fact table surrounded by several dimension tables.

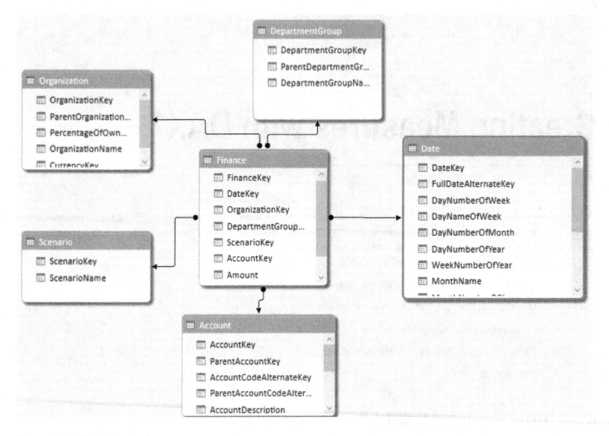

Figure 5-1. *Typical star schema*

Remember, the fact table contains numbers that you need to aggregate; for example, in the finance table, you have the amount, which is a monetary value that needs to be aggregated. In a sales fact table you may have a sales amount and item counts. In a human resources system you might have hours worked. The dimension tables contain the attributes that you are using to categorize and roll up the measures. For example, the financial measures are classified as profit, loss, and forecasted. You want to roll the values up to the department and organization level and you want to compare values between months and years.

When you start slicing and dicing the data in a pivot table, the attributes become the row and column headers whereas the measures are the values in the cells. Attributes are also commonly used as filters either in a filter drop-down or in a slicer. Figure 5-2 shows a pivot table containing research and development spending, actual and budgeted, for the months in the fiscal year 2006.

DepartmentGroupName	Research and Development ▼			
FiscalYear	2006 ▼			

SumAmount	Column Labels ▼			
Row Labels ▼	Actual	Budget	Grand Total	
⊟1	$1,993,567.08	$1,915,370.00	$3,908,937.08	
July	$392,972.36	$359,390.00	$752,362.36	
August	$961,235.94	$938,490.00	$1,899,725.94	
September	$639,358.78	$617,490.00	$1,256,848.78	
⊟2	$2,706,643.34	$2,794,280.00	$5,500,923.34	
October	$709,493.00	$732,960.00	$1,442,453.00	
November	$1,177,389.73	$1,248,960.00	$2,426,349.73	
December	$819,760.61	$812,360.00	$1,632,120.61	
⊟3	$2,424,910.23	$2,384,100.00	$4,809,010.23	
January	$518,208.94	$441,300.00	$959,508.94	
February	$916,732.01	$899,900.00	$1,816,632.01	
March	$989,969.28	$1,042,900.00	$2,032,869.28	
⊟4	$2,805,397.73	$2,766,330.00	$5,571,727.73	
April	$697,205.89	$640,910.00	$1,338,115.89	
May	$1,154,369.01	$1,157,810.00	$2,312,179.01	
June	$953,822.83	$967,610.00	$1,921,432.83	
Grand Total	$9,930,518.38	$9,860,080.00	$19,790,598.38	

OrganizationName ▾
Canadian Division
Central Division
Northeast Division
Northwest Division
Southeast Division
Southwest Division
AdventureWorks C...
Australia

Figure 5-2. *Analyzing data in a pivot table*

If you look at the filtering for each cell, you should realize they are all filtered a little differently. The two measures indicated by the green arrows differ by month, whereas the measures indicated by the red arrows differ by actual versus budgeted amount. As you change the fiscal year, department, or organization, the values for the measures must be recalculated because the query context has changed.

In the following section you will see how you can create some common aggregation measures in your Power Pivot model.

Creating Common Aggregates

It is very easy to create common aggregates such as sum, count, or average in Power Pivot. First you need to determine which table you want to associate the measure with. If you follow the star schema model, this will most likely be the fact table, but it does not have to be. In the data view mode of the Power Pivot model designer, select the tab of the table that is associated with the measure. The area below the data grid is where you place the measure formulas (see Figure 5-3). If you do not see a measures grid, you may need to unhide it by selecting the Calculation Area button on the Home tab (see Figure 5-4).

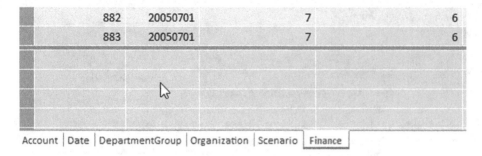

| | 882 | 20050701 | 7 | 6 |
| | 883 | 20050701 | 7 | 6 |

Account | Date | DepartmentGroup | Organization | Scenario | Finance

Figure 5-3. *The measure grid for the Finance table*

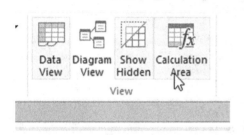

Figure 5-4. *Showing or hiding the measure grid*

The easiest way to create an aggregate is to select the column you want to aggregate and then select the AutoSum drop-down and choose the aggregate you need (see Figure 5-5).

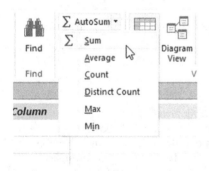

Figure 5-5. *Using the auto sum for common aggregates*

The aggregate is placed in the measure grid below the column (see Figure 5-6). If you select the cell you will see the formula in the formula bar (see Figure 5-7). The name of the measure is placed before the formula followed by a colon and equal sign (:=). Once you add the measure you can rename it by editing it in the formula editor.

1	73	$300.00	7/1/20...
1	74	$217.00	7/1/20...
1	76	$985.00	7/1/20...
	Sum of Amount: $1,358,640,412.70		

Figure 5-6. *The resulting measure below the column*

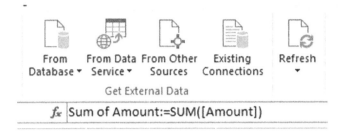

f_x | Sum of Amount:=SUM([Amount])

Figure 5-7. *Editing the measure formula*

The other way to create an aggregate measure is to select any cell in the measures grid and enter the formula in the formula bar. Although you can define a measure in any cell in the measures grid, it is a good idea to organize the measures in some fashion. I generally try to organize the measures along the left side of the grid so they are not spread out all over the grid (see Figure 5-8). You can easily move a definition from one cell to another using cut and paste.

	891	20050701
SumAmount: $1,358,640,412.70		
AveAmount: $34,475.38		
MaxAmount: $4,820,988.00		

Account | Date | DepartmentGroup | Organization | Scenario | Finance

Figure 5-8. *Organizing your measures*

You may have noticed that the aggregate functions such as SUM, AVE, MIN, and MAX have corresponding SUMX, AVEX, MINX, and MAXX functions. The X functions are used when you are evaluating an expression for each row in the table and not just a single column. As an example, the SUMX function is defined as follows:

SUMX(<table>, <expression>)

where the table is the table containing the rows to be evaluated and the expression is what will be evaluated for each row.

As an example, say you have a sales table that contains a Cost and a Gross column. To figure out the total net sales amount, you can take the gross amount minus the cost and sum the result for each row as in the following formula:

```
SumNet:=SUMX(Sales,[Gross]-[Cost])
```

Another way to get the same result is to create a net calculated column first and then use the SUM function on the net column. The difference is that calculated columns are pre-calculated and stored in the model. Measures are calculated when filters are applied to them in the pivot table and have to be recalculated every time the data context changes. So the more calculated columns you have the greater the size of your Power Pivot file. The more measures you have and the greater their complexity increases the more memory is necessary when you are working with the file.

Understanding how data context changes the measurement value is very important when creating measures and it is explored in the next section.

Mastering Data Context

Context plays an important role when creating measures in the Power Pivot model. Unlike static reports, Power Pivot models are designed for dynamic analysis by the client. When the user changes filters, drills down, and changes column and row headers in a pivot table, the context changes and the values are recalculated. Knowing how the context changes and how it affects the results is very essential to being able to build and troubleshoot formulas.

There are three types of context you need to consider: row, query, and filter. The row context comes into play when you are creating a calculated column. It includes the values from all the other columns of the current row as well as the values of any table related to the row. If you create a calculated column, say margin,

```
=[Gross] - [Cost]
```

DAX uses the row context to look up the values from the same row to complete the calculation. If you create a calculated column such as lifetime sales

```
=SUMX(RELATEDTABLE(Sales),[SalesAmount])
```

DAX automatically looks up the related values using the row context of the current row. The row context is set once the model is loaded and will not change until new data is loaded. This is why calculated columns are pre-calculated and only need to be recalculated when data is refreshed.

Query context is the filtering applied to a cell in the pivot table. When you drop a measure into a pivot table, the DAX query engine examines the row and column headers and any filters applied. Each cell has a different query context applied to it (see Figure 5-9) and returns the value associated with the context. Since you can change the query context on the fly by changing row or column headers and filter values, the cell values are calculated dynamically and the values are not held in the Power Pivot model.

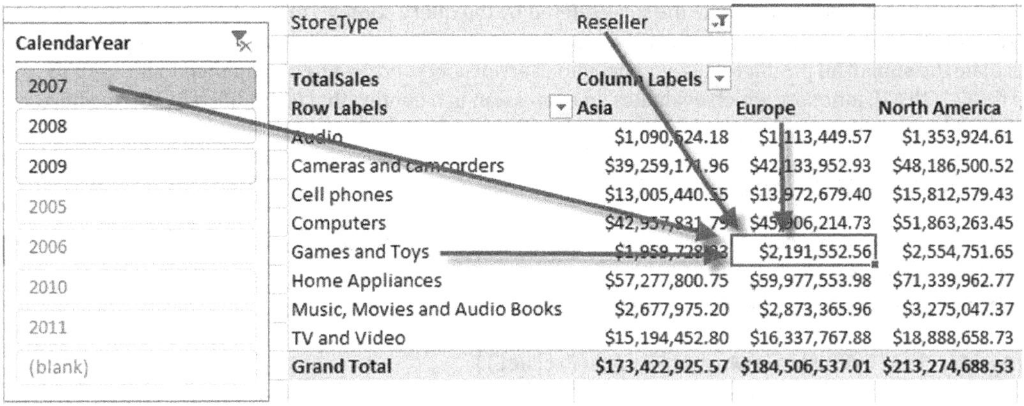

StoreType		Reseller	.T	
CalendarYear	🗙			
2007		**TotalSales**	Column Labels ▾	
2008		**Row Labels** ▾	Asia	Europe	North America
2009		Audio	$1,090,624.18	$1,113,449.57	$1,353,924.61
2005		Cameras and camcorders	$39,259,171.96	$42,133,952.93	$48,186,500.52
2006		Cell phones	$13,005,440.55	$13,972,679.40	$15,812,579.43
2010		Computers	$42,957,831.79	$45,906,214.73	$51,863,263.45
		Games and Toys	$1,959,728.32	$2,191,552.56	$2,554,751.65
2011		Home Appliances	$57,277,800.75	$59,977,553.98	$71,339,962.77
(blank)		Music, Movies and Audio Books	$2,677,975.20	$2,873,365.96	$3,275,047.37
		TV and Video	$15,194,452.80	$16,337,767.88	$18,888,658.73
		Grand Total	**$173,422,925.57**	**$184,506,537.01**	**$213,274,688.53**

Figure 5-9. *The query context of a measure*

Filter context is added to the measure using filter constraints as part of the formula. The filter context is applied in addition to the row and query contexts. You can alter the context by adding to it, replacing it, or selectively changing it using filter expressions. For example, if you used the following formula to calculate sales,

```
AllStoreSales:=CALCULATE(SUM(Sales[SalesAmount]),ALL(Store[StoreType]))
```

the filter context would clear any StoreType filter implemented by the query context.

In the next section you will see why knowing when and how to alter the query context is an important aspect of creating measures.

Altering the Query Context

When creating calculations you often need to alter the filter context being applied to the measure, for example, if you want to calculate the sales of a product category compared to the sales of all products (see Figure 5-10).

Row Labels ▾	ProductSales	ProductSalesRatio
Audio	$28,327,054.16	1.17 %
Cameras and camcorders	$497,254,487.87	20.50 %
Cell phones	$171,965,337.05	7.09 %
Computers	$635,370,758.16	26.19 %
Games and Toys	$31,323,167.21	1.29 %
Home Appliances	$771,257,471.64	31.79 %
Music, Movies and Audio Books	$32,047,454.50	1.32 %
TV and Video	$258,602,375.72	10.66 %
Grand Total	**$2,426,148,106.30**	**100.00 %**

Figure 5-10. *Viewing the product sales ratio*

To calculate the sales ratio, you need to take the sales filtered by the query context (in this case, categories) and divide it by the sales of all products regardless of the product query context. To calculate sales you just use the SUM function. To calculate the sum of all product sales, you need to override any product filtering applied to the cell. To do this, you use the CALCULATE function, which evaluates an expression in a context that is modified by the specified filters and has the following syntax:

```
CALCULATE(<expression>,<filter1>,<filter2>...)
```

where the expression is essentially a measure to be evaluated and the filters are Boolean expressions or a table expression that defines the filters.

So, to override any product filters, you use the following code:

```
AllProductSales:=CALCULATE(SUM([SalesAmount]), ALL(Product))
```

This uses the ALL function, which returns all the rows in a table or all the values in a column, ignoring any filters that might have been applied. So in this case, it clears all filters placed on the Product table. Figure 5-11 shows the measures in a pivot table.

Row Labels	ProductSales	AllProductSales	ProductSalesRatio
Audio	$28,327,054.16	$2,426,148,106.30	1.17 %
Cameras and camcorders	$497,254,487.87	$2,426,148,106.30	20.50 %
Cell phones	$171,965,337.05	$2,426,148,106.30	7.09 %
Computers	$635,370,758.16	$2,426,148,106.30	26.19 %
Games and Toys	$31,323,167.21	$2,426,148,106.30	1.29 %
Home Appliances	$771,257,471.64	$2,426,148,106.30	31.79 %
Music, Movies and Audio Books	$32,047,454.50	$2,426,148,106.30	1.32 %
TV and Video	$258,602,375.72	$2,426,148,106.30	10.66 %
Grand Total	$2,426,148,106.30	$2,426,148,106.30	100.00 %

Figure 5-11. Verifying the AllProductSales measure

Notice the ProductSales measure is affected by the product filter (category) whereas the AllProductSales is not. The final step to calculate the ProductSalesRatio measure is to divide the ProductSales by the AllProductSales. You can use a measure inside another measure as long as you do not have a circular reference. So the ProductSalesRatio is calculated as follows:

```
ProductSalesRatio:=[ProductSales]/[AllProductSales]
```

You can hide the AllProductSales measure from the client tools because, in this case, it is used as an intermediate measure and is not useful on its own.

In this section you saw how to use the CALCULATE function and a filter function to alter the filters applied to a measure. There are many filter functions available in DAX and it is important that you understand when to use them. In the next section you will look at several more important filter functions you can use.

Using Filter Functions

The filter functions in DAX allow you to create complex calculations that require you to interrogate and manipulate the data context of a row or cell in a pivot table. Table 5-1 lists and describes some of the filter functions available in DAX.

Table 5-1. *Some DAX Filter Functions*

Function	Description
ALL	Returns all the rows in a table, or all the values in a column, ignoring any filters that might have been applied.
ALLEXCEPT	Removes all context filters in the table except filters that have been applied to the specified columns.
ALLNONBLANKROW	Returns all rows but the blank row and disregards any context filters that might exist.
ALLSELECTED	Removes context filters from columns and rows, while retaining all other context filters or explicit filters.
CALCULATE	Evaluates an expression in a context that is modified by the specified filters.
CALCULATETABLE	Evaluates a table expression in a context modified by the given filters.
DISTINCT	Returns a one-column table that contains the distinct values from the specified column.
FILTER	Returns a table that represents a subset of another table or expression.
FILTERS	Returns the values that are directly applied as filters.
HASONEVALUE	Returns TRUE when the context has been filtered down to one distinct value.
ISFILTERED	Returns TRUE when a direct filter is being applied.
ISCROSSFILTERED	Returns TRUE when the column or another column in the same or related table is being filtered.
KEEPFILTERS	Modifies how filters are applied while evaluating a CALCULATE or CALCULATETABLE function. Keeps applied filters and adds additional filters.
RELATED	Returns a related value from another table.
USERELATIONSHIP	Specifies the relationship to be used in a specific calculation.
VALUES	Returns a one-column table that contains the distinct values from the specified column.

You have already seen how you can use the CALCULATE function in combination with the ALL function to calculate the total product sales ignoring any product filtering applied. Let's take a look at a few more examples.

Figure 5-12 shows a Power Pivot model for reseller sales. In the model there is an inactive relationship between the Employee and the SalesTerritory tables. You can use this relationship to calculate the number of salesman in each country.

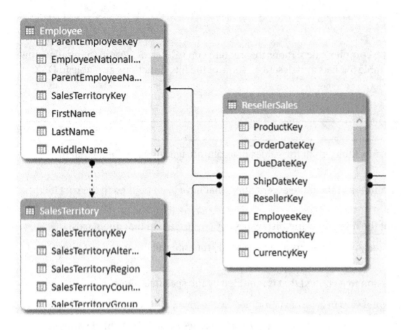

Figure 5-12. *An inactive relationship in the Power Pivot model*

You can use this to calculate the number of sales reps in each country using the following code:

```
Sales Rep Cnt:=CALCULATE(DISTINCTCOUNT(Employee[EmployeeNationalIDAlternateKey]),
USERELATIONSHIP(Employee[SalesTerritoryKey],SalesTerritory[SalesTerritoryKey]))
```

In this case you need to use the CALCULATE function so that you can apply the filter function USERELATIONSHIP to tell the DAX query engine which relationship to use. Figure 5-13 shows the resulting pivot table. It also shows the result you would get if you just used the DISTINCTCOUNT function without the USERELATIONSHIP filter.

Row Labels	Sales Rep Cnt	Sales Rep2 Cnt
Australia	1	20
Canada	2	20
France	1	20
Germany	1	20
NA	6	20
United Kingdom	1	20
United States	8	20
Grand Total	20	20

Figure 5-13. *Count of sales reps in each country*

In the next example you will look at the difference between the ALL and the ALLSELECTED filter functions. You can create three sales amount measures as follows:

```
Reseller Sales:=SUM([SalesAmount])
Reseller Grand Total:=calculate(sum([SalesAmount]), ALL('ResellerSales'))
Reseller Visual Total:=calculate(sum([SalesAmount]), ALLSELECTED())
```

Reseller Sales keeps all the data contexts applied to the measure. Reseller Grand Total removes all context associated with the ResellerSales table and any related table. Reseller Visual Total removes the column and row context from the measure. Figure 5-14 shows the resulting measures in a pivot table.

Row Labels	Reseller Sales	Reseller Grand Total	Reseller Visual Total
Value Added Reseller	$7,370,498.30	$80,450,596.98	$14,698,866.12
Warehouse	$7,328,367.81	$80,450,596.98	$14,698,866.12
Grand Total	$14,698,866.12	$80,450,596.98	$14,698,866.12

Figure 5-14. *Results of using different filters*

Now let's look at a more complex example. In this example you want to determine the best single order customers in a particular time period. The final pivot table is shown in Figure 5-15.

Row Labels	LargeSales	Top Sale
Brooks	$36,965.25	$3,028.02
Bryant	$43,876.23	$3,036.95
Butler	$36,828.66	$2,457.95
Coleman	$37,424.27	$2,492.32
Cox	$34,169.36	$2,428.05
Diaz	$38,220.87	$4,677.24
Flores	$31,637.93	$2,438.06
Gonzales	$40,326.89	$2,479.94
Griffin	$32,743.94	$2,443.55
Hernandez	$40,074.48	$3,086.31
Kelly	$32,683.80	$2,447.05
Powell	$33,407.10	$2,478.34
Reed	$31,468.15	$2,453.04
Rodriguez	$35,110.80	$2,543.44
Ross	$44,472.36	$3,182.00
Russell	$33,569.17	$2,554.20
Sanchez	$32,111.48	$4,950.93
Washington	$38,801.68	$3,316.26

CalendarYear

2005
2006
2007
2008
2009
2010

CountryRegionName

Australia
Canada
France
Germany
United Kingdom
United States

Figure 5-15. *Finding best single order customers*

The first step is to find the customers who spent a lot of money during the time period. To calculate customer sales, you use the following measure:

```
SumSales:=SUM([SalesAmount])
```

Next you want to only look at large spenders so you can filter out smaller values:

```
LargeSales:=IF([SumSales]>=30000,[SumSales],Blank())
```

The next step is to find the order amounts for the customer and take the maximum value:

```
Top Sale:=MAXX(VALUES(Date[DateKey]),[SumSales])
```

Since you only want to list the top sales for top customers, you can add an IF statement to make sure the customer has large sales:

```
Top Sale:=
IF(ISBLANK([LargeSales]),Blank(),MAXX(VALUES(Date[DateKey]),[SumSales]))
```

As a final example, say you are working with the HR department and you want to create a pivot table that will allow them to list employee counts for the departments at a particular date. There is an EmployeeDepartmentHistory table that lists employee, department, start date, and end date. There is also a Dates table that has a row for every date spanning the department histories. Figure 5-16 shows the pivot table containing employee counts for each department.

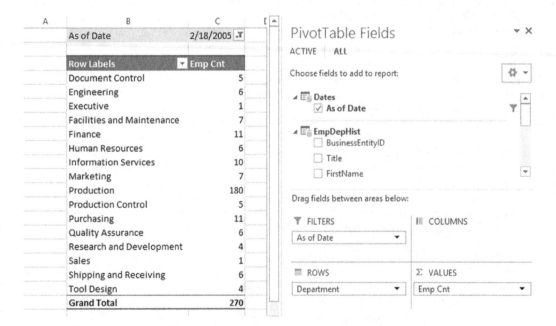

Figure 5-16. *Employee counts as of the selected date*

The As of Date is used as a filter and the Emp Cnt is the measure. When the As of Date is changed the Emp Cnt it is recalculated to show the employee counts on that date. Figure 5-17 shows new counts after the date is changed.

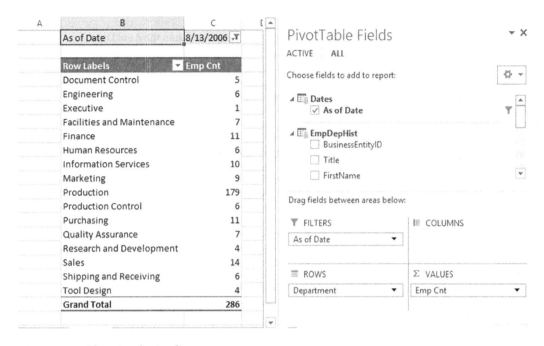

Figure 5-17. *Changing the As of Date*

The first step to creating the Emp Cnt is to use the COUNT function because you want to count the EmployeeID in the table:

```
Emp Cnt:=COUNT(EmpDepHist[BusinessEntityID])
```

Since you need to filter the table to only active employees at the date chosen, you need to change this to the COUNTX function:

```
Emp Cnt:=COUNTX(EmpDepHist, EmpDepHist[BusinessEntityID])
```

To filter the EmpDepHist table you use the FILTER function:

```
FILTER(<table>,<filter>)
```

The FILTER function is a Boolean expression that evaluates to TRUE. In this case you need to have the date that the employee started in the department less than or equal to the As of Date:

```
EmpDepHist[StartDate]<=Dates[As of Date]
```

Now, since the pivot table user can select more than one date and you want to make sure you only compare it to a single date, you can use the MAX function:

```
EmpDepHist[StartDate]<=MAX(Dates[As of Date])
```

You also want to make sure the date the employee left the department is greater than the As of Date:

```
EmpDepHist[EndDate] > Max(Dates[As of Date]
```

If the employee is currently in the department the EndDate will be blank:

```
ISBLANK(EmpDepHist[EndDate])
```

When you combine these filter conditions, you get the following filter condition:

```
EmpDepHist[StartDate]<=MAX(Dates[As of Date])
&& (ISBLANK(EmpDepHist[EndDate]) || EmpDepHist[EndDate] > Max(Dates[As of Date]))
```

The final FILTER function then becomes

```
FILTER(EmpDepHist,
EmpDepHist[StartDate]<=MAX(Dates[As of Date])
&& (ISBLANK(EmpDepHist[EndDate]) || EmpDepHist[EndDate] > Max(Dates[As of Date])))
```

and the final employee count measure becomes

```
Emp Cnt:=COUNTX(FILTER(EmpDepHist,
EmpDepHist[StartDate]<=MAX(Dates[As of Date])
&& (ISBLANK(EmpDepHist[EndDate]) || EmpDepHist[EndDate] > Max(Dates[As of Date]))),
EmpDepHist[BusinessEntityID])
```

As you can see, creating a measure can be quite complex, but if you break it up into steps, it becomes very manageable. Rest assured; the more you work with DAX and creating measures, the more intuitive and easier it becomes.

One type of measure commonly used in performance dashboards is the *Key Performance Indicator (KPI)*. A KPI is used to show performance and trends in a visual format. In the next section you will investigate creating KPIs in the Power Pivot model.

Creating KPIs

KPIs are a staple of many dashboards and provide a great way to quickly see trends and spot areas that need further analysis. The base value of a KPI is based on a measure; for example, you can create a KPI for current sales. The base value is then compared to a target value. The target value can be another measure; for example, last year's sales or an absolute numeric value like a target sales-to-expense ratio. The status thresholds establish what range is considered good, neutral, and bad. These thresholds are then used to determine the visual component of the KPI (i.e., green, yellow, red). Figure 5-18 shows KPIs for current sales compared to the previous sales.

Row Labels ▼	PrevQuarterSales	CurrentQuarterSales	SalesPerformance
⊟2005		$1,812,850.77	
3		$1,453,522.89	
4	$1,453,522.89	$1,812,850.77	⬤
⊟2006	$1,812,850.77	$1,327,799.32	⬤
1	$1,812,850.77	$1,791,698.45	◯
2	$1,791,698.45	$2,014,012.13	⬤
3	$2,014,012.13	$1,396,833.62	⬤
4	$1,396,833.62	$1,327,799.32	◯
⊟2007	$1,327,799.32	$4,009,218.46	⬤
1	$1,327,799.32	$1,413,530.30	⬤
2	$1,413,530.30	$1,623,971.06	⬤
3	$1,623,971.06	$2,744,340.48	⬤
4	$2,744,340.48	$4,009,218.46	⬤
⊟2008	$4,009,218.46	$50,840.63	⬤
1	$4,009,218.46	$4,283,629.96	⬤
2	$4,283,629.96	$5,436,429.15	⬤
3	$5,436,429.15	$50,840.63	⬤

Figure 5-18. *Sales KPI comparing current to previous sales*

To create a KPI, first create the base measure it will be based on. For example, production keeps track of scrapped parts, so you can base a KPI on the sum of the number of scrapped parts:

```
SumScrappedQty:=SUM([ScrappedQty])
```

You can compare this to the number of parts processed:

```
SumOrderQuantity:=SUM([OrderQty])
```

After creating the measures, right click on the base measure in the Power Pivot model designer. In the context menu, select Create KPI, which launches the KPI design window (see Figure 5-19).

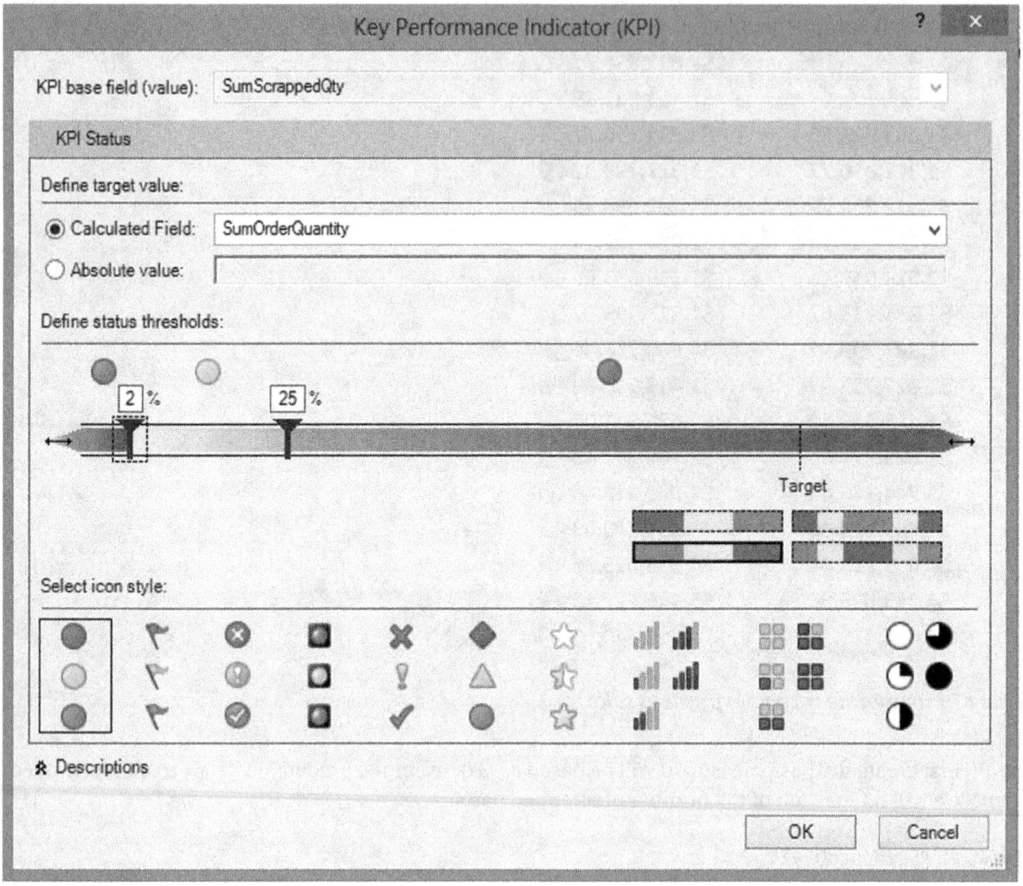

Figure 5-19. *The KPI design window*

You then set the target to the SumOrderQuantity measure and define the status thresholds. The style icons are used to show the status of the KPIs. When you are done creating the KPI you can use it in a pivot table in Excel (see Figure 5-20).

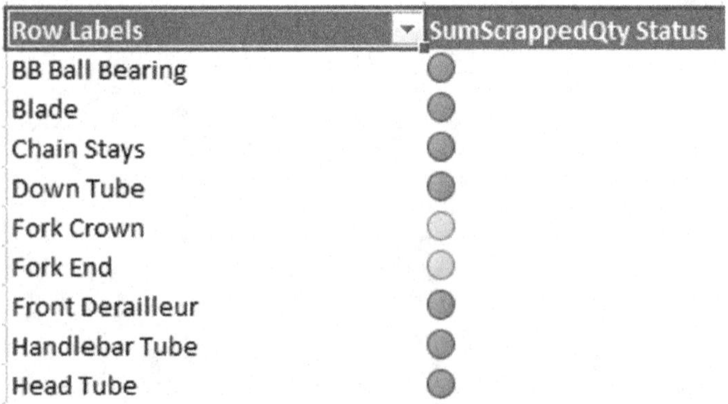

Figure 5-20. *Viewing a KPI in a pivot table*

Now that you have seen how to create measures and alter the data context using DAX, it is time to get your hands dirty and create some measures in the following lab.

HANDS-ON LAB—CREATING MEASURES IN POWER PIVOT

In the following lab you will

- Create aggregate measures.

- Alter the data context in a measure.

- Use a non-active relationship in a measure.

- Create a complex measure.

- Create a KPI.

1. In the Lab Starters folder, open the LabChapter5.xlsx file. This file contains a data model consisting of sales data, product data, and store data.

2. View the model in the Power Pivot window using the diagram view (Figure 5-21).

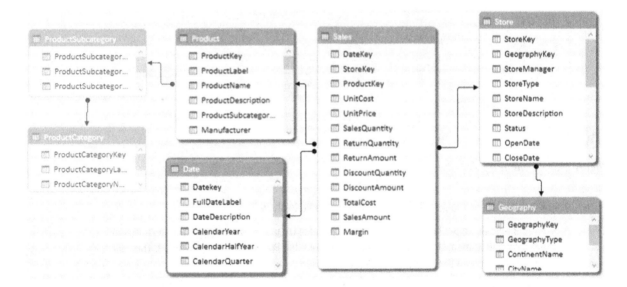

Figure 5-21. *The Power Pivot model*

3. Switch to data view in the Power Pivot window and select the Sales table.

4. Select the SalesAmount column. In the AutoSum drop-down select Sum (see Figure 5-22). You should see a measure added below the column. Rename the measure to Sum Sales.

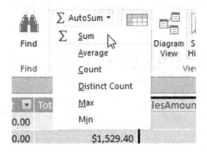

Figure 5-22. *Select the AutoSum drop-down*

5. Using the same technique as in step 4, create a Max Sales Quantity, a Min Sales Quantity, and an Ave Sales Quantity measure.

6. To test how the measures are recalculated as the filter context changes, click on the PivotTable in the Home tab and insert the PivotTable in Sheet1 cell B2 (see Figure 2-23).

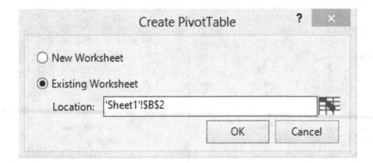

Figure 5-23. *Creating a pivot table*

7. If you do not see the field list click on the pivot table to show it.

8. From the Sales node check the Sales and Max Sales Quantity. This will add the measures to the Values drop area. Under the Product node check the ProductCategory attribute. This will add the attribute to the Row Labels drop area.

9. On the Insert tab click the Slicer button. In the Insert Slicers window select the All tab and select the ContinentName under the Geography node (see Figure 5-24).

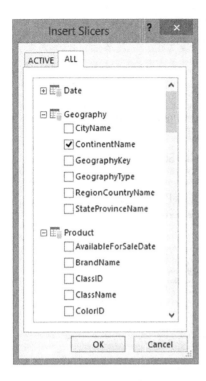

Figure 5-24. *Creating a slicer*

10. The pivot table should look like the one shown in Figure 5-25. Test the measures by clicking on the different continents. This changes the query context. Notice how the measure values are recalculated as the query context changes.

Row Labels	Max Sales Quantity
Audio	100
Cameras and camcorders	100
Cell phones	2880
Computers	180
Games and Toys	400
Home Appliances	96
Music, Movies and Audio Books	72
TV and Video	100
Grand Total	**2880**

ContinentName
Asia
Europe
North America

Figure 5-25. *Testing the query context*

11. Now suppose we want a sales ratio comparing the sales to the total sales for all products. Open the Power Pivot window in data view mode. Select the Sales table. Add the following measure to the Sales table:

```
All Product Sales:=CALCULATE([Sum Sales],ALL('Product'))
```

12. The All Product Sales measure uses the CALCULATE function to override any product filter applied to the query context. Format the measure as currency.

13. Switch to the pivot table. Replace the Max Sales Quantity measure with the Sum Sales and the All Product Sales measures.

14. Test the pivot table by clicking on different continents and notice that the All Product Sales measure is equal to the total product sales for each continent (see Figure 5-26).

Row Labels	Sum Sales	All Product Sales		ContinentName
Audio	$86,552,608.02	$7,287,305,516.43		Asia
Cameras and camcorders	$1,520,696,696.88	$7,287,305,516.43		
Cell phones	$525,926,798.18	$7,287,305,516.43		Europe
Computers	$1,904,003,431.02	$7,287,305,516.43		
Games and Toys	$76,256,100.91	$7,287,305,516.43		North America
Home Appliances	$2,278,755,400.00	$7,287,305,516.43		
Music, Movies and Audio Books	$99,362,624.96	$7,287,305,516.43		
TV and Video	$795,751,856.47	$7,287,305,516.43		
Grand Total	$7,287,305,516.43	$7,287,305,516.43		

Figure 5-26. *Testing the measure*

15. Switch back to the Power Pivot window and add the following measure to the Sales table. Format the measure as percentage.

```
Product Sales Ratio:=[Sum Sales]/[All Product Sales]
```

16. Open the Power Pivot window in diagram view mode. To create a relationship between the Date table and the Store table, drag the OpenDate field from the Store table and drop it on top of the DateKey in the Date table (see Figure 5-27). Notice that this is not the active relationship between the Store and the Date tables as indicated by the dashed line. This is because the active relationship goes from the Store table, through the Sales table, then to the Date table.

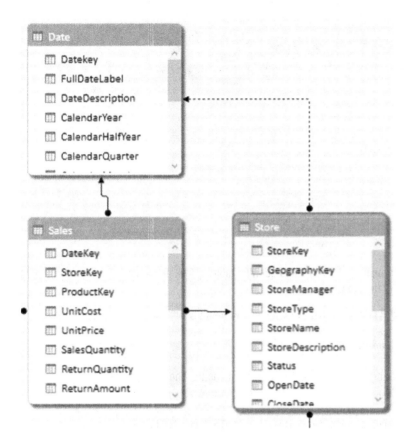

Figure 5-27. *Create an inactive relationship*

17. Switch to the data view mode and add the following measure to the Store table. Since you are using a non-active relationship, you need to use the USERELATIONSHIP function.

```
Store Count:=CALCULATE(DISTINCTCOUNT([StoreKey]),
USERELATIONSHIP(Store[OpenDate],'Date'[Datekey]))
```

18. To test the store count measure create a pivot table on Sheet2. Use the ContinentName as the column labels and the CalendarMonth as the row labels. Insert a slicer using CalendarYear. Your pivot table should look like Figure 5-28.

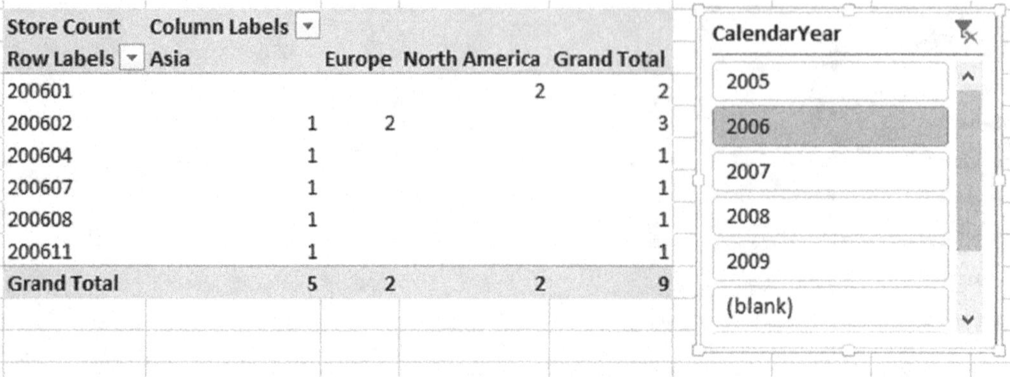

Store Count	Column Labels ▾			
Row Labels ▾	Asia	Europe	North America	Grand Total
200601			2	2
200602	1	2		3
200604	1			1
200607	1			1
200608	1			1
200611	1			1
Grand Total	5	2	2	9

CalendarYear

2005
2006
2007
2008
2009
(blank)

Figure 5-28. *Testing the store count measure*

19. The pivot table represents the number of stores opened during a month. Click the various years and observe the changes in the data.

20. To find out the best sales day for a product category create a Sale Quantity measure.

```
Sale Quantity:=SUM([SalesQuantity])
```

21. Use the Sale Quantity measure to create a Top Sale Day Quantity measure. The MAXX function is used to break any ties and returns the most recent DateKey.

```
Top Sale Day Quantity:=MAXX(values('Date'[Datekey]),[Sale Quantity])
```

22. To figure out the date of the top sales day, you first create a filter function that returns the dates when the Sale Quantity equals the Top Sale Day Quantity for the period.

```
Filter(VALUES('Date'[Datekey]),
[Sale Quantity]=CALCULATE([Top Sale Day Quantity],
VALUES('Date'[Datekey])))
```

23. This filter is then inserted into a CALCULATE function that returns the most recent date.

```
Top Sale Day:=CALCULATE(MAX('Date'[Datekey]),
Filter(VALUES('Date'[Datekey]),[Sale Quantity]=
CALCULATE([Top Sale Day Quantity],VALUES('Date'[Datekey]))))
```

24. Create a pivot table like the one in 5-29 to test your measures.

Row Labels	Top Sale Day Quantity	Top Sale Day
⊟ Audio	2477	11/26/2009
Bluetooth Headphones	1329	11/26/2009
MP4&MP3	1037	11/7/2009
Recording Pen	518	7/16/2009
⊞ Cameras and camcorders	9251	11/2/2007
⊞ Cell phones	27438	8/20/2009
⊞ Computers	12898	12/20/2009
⊞ Games and Toys	9674	7/15/2009
⊞ Home Appliances	12096	11/15/2009
⊞ Music, Movies and Audio Books	2344	2/15/2007
⊞ TV and Video	4334	12/18/2007
Grand Total	69757	12/27/2009

Figure 5-29. *Testing the Top Sale Day measure*

25. Create the following measures in the Sales table and format them as currency:

```
Ave Sales:=AVERAGE([SalesAmount])
Total Ave Sales:=If(ISBLANK([Ave Sales]),BLANK(),
                        CALCULATE([Ave Sales],ALLSELECTED()))
```

26. Select the Ave Sales measure in the measure grid. Right click it and select Create KPI in the context menu. In the KPI dialog, notice that the base measure is Ave Sales. Set the target value to Total Ave Sales. Set the low threshold to 90% and the high threshold to 110% (see Figure 5-30).

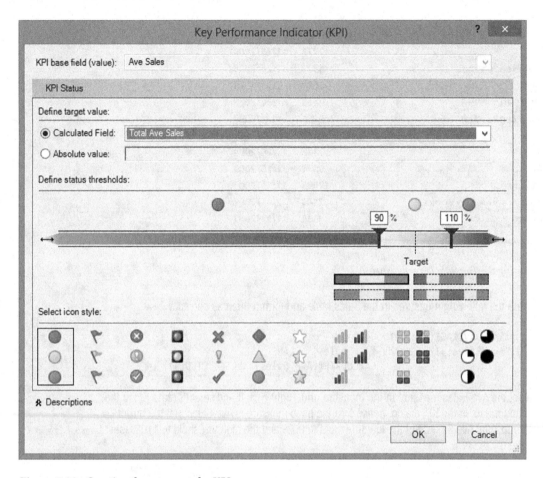

Figure 5-30. *Creating the average sales KPI*

27. Close the dialog and notice the Ave Sales measure has an icon indicating it has a KPI associated with it.

28. Create a pivot table like the one in 5-31 to test the KPI. You can compare the average sales of a store with the total average sales of all the stores showing.

Row Labels	Ave Sales	Total Ave Sales	Ave Sales Ratio	Ave Sales Status
Contoso Albany Store	$3,155.12	$3,159.62	99.86 %	○
Contoso Alexandria Store	$3,182.60	$3,159.62	100.73 %	○
Contoso Amsterdam Store	$2,842.46	$3,159.62	89.96 %	●
Contoso Annapolis Store	$3,273.27	$3,159.62	103.60 %	○
Contoso Knotty Ash Store	$2,838.54	$3,159.62	89.84 %	●
Contoso Kolkata Store	$3,422.66	$3,159.62	108.33 %	○
Contoso Kyoto Store	$3,988.35	$3,159.62	126.23 %	●
Grand Total	**$3,159.62**	**$3,159.62**	**100.00 %**	○

Figure 5-31. *Viewing the KPI*

Summary

This was a long and meaty chapter. You now have a firm grasp of how to create measures in your Power Pivot model. You should also understand data context and how it affects the measurements. This can be a very confusing concept when you start to develop more complex measures. Don't worry; the more you work with it the clearer it becomes.

The next chapter extends the concepts of this chapter. One of the most common types of data analysis is comparing values over time. Chapter 6 shows you how to correctly implement time-based analysis in Power Pivot. It includes setting up a date table and using the various built-in functions for analyzing values to date, comparing values from different periods, and performing semi-additive aggregations.

CHAPTER 6

■ ■ ■

Incorporating Time Intelligence

One of the most common types of data analysis is comparing values over time. This chapter shows the reader how to correctly implement time-based analysis in Power Pivot. It includes setting up a date table and using the various built-in functions for analyzing values to date, comparing values from different periods, and performing semi-additive aggregations.

After completing this chapter you will be able to

- Create a date table.

- Use DAX for time period–based evaluations.

- Shift the date context using filter functions.

- Create semi-additive measures.

Date-Based Analysis

A large percentage of data analysis involves some sort of date-time based aggregation and comparison. For example, you may need to look at usage or sales for the month-to-date (MTD) or year-to-date (YTD) as shown in Figure 6-1.

Row Labels	Sum of Sales	MTD Sales	YTD Sales
⊟2007	$571,204,151.10	$55,148,659.27	$571,204,151.10
Jan	$33,937,209.25	$33,937,209.25	$33,937,209.25
Feb	$39,627,318.77	$39,627,318.77	$73,564,528.02
Mar	$43,055,837.85	$43,055,837.85	$116,620,365.87
Apr	$45,152,238.05	$45,152,238.05	$161,772,603.92
May	$49,678,655.61	$49,678,655.61	$211,451,259.53
Jun	$49,431,542.53	$49,431,542.53	$260,882,802.06
Jul	$53,458,586.99	$53,458,586.99	$314,341,389.05
Aug	$50,771,841.27	$50,771,841.27	$365,113,230.32
Sep	$49,242,024.87	$49,242,024.87	$414,355,255.19
Oct	$47,437,924.07	$47,437,924.07	$461,793,179.26
Nov	$54,262,312.57	$54,262,312.57	$516,055,491.83
Dec	$55,148,659.27	$55,148,659.27	$571,204,151.10
⊞2008	$600,175,898.67	$56,659,783.37	$600,175,898.67
⊞2009	$543,817,781.67	$46,788,451.58	$543,817,781.67
Grand Total	$1,715,197,831.44	$46,788,451.58	$543,817,781.67

ChannelName

- Catalog
- Online
- Reseller
- Store

Figure 6-1. *Calculating year-to-date and month-to-date sales*

Another common example is looking at performance from one time period to the next. For example, you may want to compare previous month sales with current sales (see Figure 6-2) or sales for the current month to the same month a year before.

Row Labels ▾	Sum of Sales	Prev Month Sales	Monthly Sales Growth
⊟ 2007	$10,697,642.89	$9,510,697.85	12 %
Jan	$675,656.58		
Feb	$615,633.57	$675,656.58	-9 %
Mar	$614,046.66	$615,633.57	-0 %
Apr	$707,348.69	$614,046.66	15 %
May	$966,623.91	$707,348.69	37 %
Jun	$987,545.18	$966,623.91	2 %
Jul	$996,175.98	$987,545.18	1 %
Aug	$883,280.80	$996,175.98	-11 %
Sep	$983,234.05	$883,280.80	11 %
Oct	$908,519.60	$983,234.05	-8 %
Nov	$1,172,632.83	$908,519.60	29 %
Dec	$1,186,945.05	$1,172,632.83	1 %
⊞ 2008	$12,802,000.68	$12,699,939.76	1 %
⊞ 2009	$13,768,349.90	$13,810,604.03	-0 %
Grand Total	$37,267,993.47	$36,021,241.64	3 %

RegionCountryName

- Armenia
- Australia
- Bhutan
- Canada
- China
- Denmark
- France
- Germany

Figure 6-2. *Calculating sales growth*

In addition to these common data analytics, there are also times when you need to base your aggregations on measures that are non-additive, such as account balances or inventory. In these cases, you need to determine the last value entered and use that value to aggregate across the different time periods (see Figure 6-3).

ProductCategoryName	Computers
ContinentName	North America

InventoryLevel	Column Labels						
Row Labels ▾	Computers Accessories	Desktops	Laptops	Monitors	Printers, Scanners & Fax	Projectors & Screens	Grand Total
⊟ 2007	193503	50607	79254	66890	171471	135450	697175
⊞ 1	26594	7674	9703	8605	29331	17395	99302
⊞ 2	44557	13942	16425	14981	49660	34604	174169
⊞ 3	61478	19415	22563	19760	66319	49973	239508
⊞ 4	86206	27041	29382	26873	89536	70701	329739
⊞ 5	104439	32741	35188	34070	106874	86050	399362
⊞ 6	123307	37369	41335	43840	121873	97499	465223
⊞ 7	138290	40734	49853	50018	134701	107373	520969
⊞ 8	149119	42767	55503	54408	144543	115116	561456
⊞ 9	160183	44737	62361	57895	151789	120629	597594
⊞ 10	170744	46665	66411	61270	158035	125639	628764
⊞ 11	183597	48841	73882	65139	166232	131861	669552
⊞ 12	193503	50607	79254	66890	171471	135450	697175
⊞ 2008	395964	97223	177075	161823	243145	235876	1311106
⊞ 2009	607639	133436	286314	232460	304242	303520	1867611
Grand Total	607639	133436	286314	232460	304242	303520	1867611

Figure 6-3. *Aggregating inventory amounts*

DAX contains many functions that help you create the various date-time based analyses you may need. In the next section, you will see how to create a date table that is required to use many of the date-time based functions.

Creating a Date Table

In order to use the built-in time intelligence functions in DAX, you need to have a date table in your model for the functions to reference. The only requirement for the table is that it needs a distinct row for each day in the date range at which you are interested in looking. Each of these rows needs to contain the full date of the day. The date table can, and often does, have more columns, but it doesn't have to.

There are several ways to create the date table. If you are retrieving data from a data warehouse, you can import a date dimension into the model and use it. If you do not have access to a date table, you can create it in an Excel sheet and import it into the model. If you have access to a database, you can also write a SQL query to create a temporary table and load the dates into your model using the temporary table. The following code shows the SQL query you can use against a Microsoft SQL Server database. It uses a common table expression to populate a date table.

```
DECLARE
  @BeginDate DATE,
  @EndDate DATE

SET @BeginDate = '01/01/2010'
SET @EndDate = '12/31/2014'
;

WITH cteDate AS (
  SELECT @BeginDate AS CalendarDate
  UNION ALL
  SELECT DATEADD(DAY,1,CalendarDate)
    FROM cteDate
    WHERE CalendarDate < @EndDate)

SELECT
  (DATEPART(YEAR,CalendarDate) * 10000) + (DATEPART(MONTH,CalendarDate) * 100)  +
    DATEPART(DAY,CalendarDate) AS DateKey,
  CalendarDate,
  DATEPART(YEAR,CalendarDate) AS Year,
  DATEPART(MONTH,CalendarDate) AS MonthNumber,
  DATENAME(MONTH,CalendarDate) AS Month
  FROM cteDate
  OPTION (MAXRECURSION 0)
```

Once you have the table in the model, you need to mark it as the official date table (see Figure 6-4) and indicate which column is the unique key (see Figure 6-5). This tells the DAX query engine to use this table as a reference for constructing the set of dates needed for a calculation. For example, if you want to look at year-to-date sales, the query engine uses this table to get the set of dates it needs.

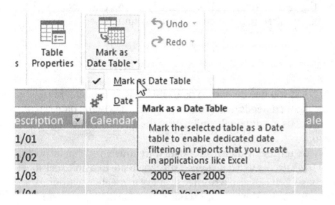

Figure 6-4. *Identifying the date table*

Figure 6-5. *Setting the date key*

Currently there are 35 built-in time intelligent functions in DAX. Some of these functions like FIRSTNONBLANK return a single date. Some return a set of dates such as PREVIOUSMONTH. And still others like TOTALQTD evaluate expressions over time. At this point, the DAX built-in time intelligence functions support the traditional calendar ending on December 31st. They also support a fiscal calendar that has a different year-end date and contains four quarters containing three months each. If you need to use a custom financial calendar, you need to create your own custom calculations.

Now that you understand how to create and designate the date table in your model, it is time to look at implementing some of the common time intelligent functions to analyze your data.

Time Period–Based Evaluations

A common analysis often employed in data analytics is looking at period-to-date values. For example, you may want to look at sales year-to-date or energy consumption month-to-date. DAX provides the TOTALMTD, TOTALQTD, and TOTALYTD functions that make this very easy. For instance, the total year-to-date is defined as follows:

```
TOTALYTD(<expression>,<dates>[,<filter>][,<year_end_date>])
```

where the expression is an expression that returns a scalar value. The dates is the date table's key column. The filter is an optional filter expression and the year_end_date is also optional—you can use it to indicate the year end of a fiscal calendar. The following expressions are used to calculate the sum of the sales and the sales year-to-date values.

```
Sum of Sales:=SUM(Sales[SalesAmount])
YTD Sales:=TOTALYTD([Sum of Sales],'Date'[Datekey])
```

If you want to calculate year-to-date sales for all products, use the following expression:

```
YTD Sales ALL Products:=TOTALYTD([Sum of Sales],'Date'[Datekey],ALL('Product'))
```

Figure 6-6 shows the measures in a pivot table. You can use these base measures to calculate further measures, such as percent of year-to-date sales and percent of all product sales.

ProductCategoryName	Row Labels	Sum of Sales	YTD Sales	YTD Sales ALL Products
Audio	2007	$1,146,469,996.57	$1,146,469,996.57	$4,561,940,955.02
Cameras and camcord...	January	$76,580,425.17	$76,580,425.17	$269,835,263.23
Cell phones	February	$88,914,528.27	$165,494,953.44	$568,051,231.58
Computers	March	$85,714,037.10	$251,208,990.54	$868,538,158.49
Games and Toys	April	$108,206,075.80	$359,415,066.34	$1,268,698,490.08
Home Appliances	May	$106,963,757.90	$466,378,824.24	$1,692,127,617.87
Music, Movies and Au...	June	$104,713,790.47	$571,092,614.71	$2,101,925,163.42
TV and Video	July	$97,226,447.91	$668,319,062.62	$2,491,542,535.70
	August	$92,298,097.12	$760,617,159.73	$2,879,972,362.81
	September	$88,743,351.91	$849,360,511.64	$3,259,116,962.37
	October	$95,184,597.09	$944,545,108.73	$3,682,330,203.21
	November	$104,034,888.68	$1,048,579,997.41	$4,136,080,412.45
	December	$97,889,999.17	$1,146,469,996.57	$4,561,940,955.02
	2008	$990,173,504.69	$990,173,504.69	$4,111,233,534.68
	January	$68,870,582.97	$68,870,582.97	$279,460,806.88
	February	$70,478,255.74	$139,348,838.71	$568,313,440.90
	March	$67,535,939.12	$206,884,777.83	$858,374,001.52
	April	$83,632,429.02	$290,517,206.85	$1,214,513,171.94

Figure 6-6. *Calculating year-to-date values*

You can also use another set of functions—DATESMTD, DATESQTD, and DATESYTD—to create the same measures. Just as with the previous to-date measures, you need to pass the date key from the date table to the functions. The following expression uses the CALCULATE function with the DATESYTD filter to get the sales year-to-date measure.

```
YTD Sales 2:=CALCULATE([Sum of Sales],DATESYTD('Date'[Datekey]))
```

Using the CALCULATE function and the DATES functions is more versatile than the total-to-date functions because you can use them for any type of aggregation, not just the sum. The following expressions are used to calculate the average sales year-to-date. The results are shown in Figure 6-7.

```
Ave Sales:=AVERAGE([SalesAmount])
YTD Ave Sales:=CALCULATE([Ave Sales],DATESYTD('Date'[Datekey]))
```

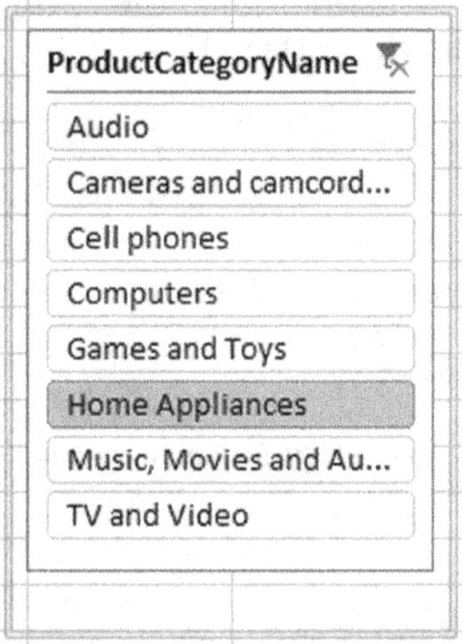 ProductCategoryName ⊽ₓ		Row Labels ▾	Ave Sales	YTD Ave Sales
Audio		⊟ 2007	$3,461.41	$3,461.41
Cameras and camcord...		January	$2,486.80	$2,486.80
Cell phones		February	$2,981.55	$2,731.41
Computers		March	$2,871.91	$2,781.89
Games and Toys		April	$3,005.07	$2,850.03
Home Appliances		May	$3,276.18	$2,949.96
Music, Movies and Au...		June	$3,268.40	$3,007.62
TV and Video		July	$3,745.67	$3,101.38
		August	$3,989.47	$3,202.06
		September	$4,032.18	$3,284.12
		October	$3,396.47	$3,296.99
		November	$4,672.36	$3,410.47
		December	$4,068.24	$3,461.41

Figure 6-7. *Calculating average year-to-date values*

Now that you know how to create time period–based calculations, you can use this to compare past performance with current performance. But first you need to know how to shift the date context to calculate past performance.

Shifting the Date Context

If you want to compare performance from one period to the same period in the past, say sales for the current month to sales for the same month a year ago, you need to shift the date context. DAX contains several functions that do this. One of the most versatile functions for shifting the date context is the PARALLELPERIOD function. As with the other time intelligence functions, you need to pass the key column of the date table to the function. You also need to indicate the number of intervals and the interval type of year, quarter, or month.

```
PARALLELPERIOD(<dates>,<number_of_intervals>,<interval>)
```

One thing to remember is that the PARALLELPERIOD function returns a set of dates that corresponds to the interval type. If you use the year, it returns a year of dates; the month interval returns a month's worth of dates. The following expression calculates the sales totals for the month of the previous year. Figure 6-8 shows the results of the calculation.

```
Month Sales Last Year:=Calculate([Sum of Sales],
PARALLELPERIOD('Date'[Datekey],-12,Month))
```

Row Labels	Sum of Sales	Month Sales Last Year
⊟ 2007	$571,204,151.10	
January	$33,937,209.25	
February	$39,627,318.77	
March	$43,055,837.85	
April	$45,152,238.05	
May	$49,678,655.61	
June	$49,431,542.53	
July	$53,458,586.99	
August	$50,771,841.27	
September	$49,242,024.87	
October	$47,437,924.07	
November	$54,262,312.57	
December	$55,148,659.27	
⊟ 2008	$600,175,898.67	$571,204,151.10
January	$41,172,371.61	$33,937,209.25
February	$44,356,169.32	$39,627,318.77
March	$44,067,571.51	$43,055,837.85
April	$53,070,715.43	$45,152,238.05
May	$53,183,905.20	$49,678,655.61
June	$51,653,752.92	$49,431,542.53
July	$56,149,796.74	$53,458,586.99
August	$49,966,766.60	$50,771,841.27

Figure 6-8. *Calculating sales for a parallel period*

Notice that if you drill down to the date level (see Figure 6-9), you still see the month totals for the month of the date for a year ago. As mentioned before, this is because the PARALLELPERIOD in this case always returns the set of dates for the same month as the row date for the previous year.

⊟2008	$600,175,898.67	$571,204,151.10
⊞January	$41,172,371.61	$33,937,209.25
⊟February	$44,356,169.32	$39,627,318.77
2/1/2008	$1,566,855.57	$39,627,318.77
2/2/2008	$1,463,784.54	$39,627,318.77
2/3/2008	$1,451,718.78	$39,627,318.77
2/4/2008	$1,373,878.11	$39,627,318.77
2/5/2008	$1,577,128.49	$39,627,318.77
2/6/2008	$1,401,943.35	$39,627,318.77
2/7/2008	$1,316,157.79	$39,627,318.77
2/8/2008	$1,640,352.74	$39,627,318.77
2/9/2008	$1,536,049.78	$39,627,318.77
2/10/2008	$1,544,487.02	$39,627,318.77
2/11/2008	$1,325,233.15	$39,627,318.77
2/12/2008	$1,621,591.76	$39,627,318.77
2/13/2008	$1,390,489.17	$39,627,318.77
2/14/2008	$1,484,512.08	$39,627,318.77

Figure 6-9. *Drilling to day level still shows month level aggregation*

Now that you can calculate the month sales of the previous year you can combine it with current sales to calculate the monthly sales growth from one year to the next. Figure 6-10 shows the results.

```
YOY Monthly Growth:=([Sum of Sales]-[Month Sales Last Year])/[Month Sales Last Year]
```

Row Labels ▼	Sum of Sales	Month Sales Last Year	YOY Monthly Growth
⊞2007	$571,204,151.10		#NUM!
⊟2008	$600,175,898.67	$571,204,151.10	5 %
January	$41,172,371.61	$33,937,209.25	21 %
February	$44,356,169.32	$39,627,318.77	12 %
March	$44,067,571.51	$43,055,837.85	2 %
April	$53,070,715.43	$45,152,238.05	18 %
May	$53,183,905.20	$49,678,655.61	7 %
June	$51,653,752.92	$49,431,542.53	4 %
July	$56,149,796.74	$53,458,586.99	5 %
August	$49,966,766.60	$50,771,841.27	-2 %
September	$49,627,897.65	$49,242,024.87	1 %
October	$46,947,843.65	$47,437,924.07	-1 %
November	$53,319,324.67	$54,262,312.57	-2 %
December	$56,659,783.37	$55,148,659.27	3 %

Figure 6-10. *Calculating year over year monthly growth*

Notice if there is no previous year sales you get an error in the pivot table. You can control this by checking if the month sales for last year is blank and inserting a blank value instead.

```
YOY Monthly Growth:=IF(
ISBLANK([Month Sales Last Year]),
BLANK(),
([Sum of Sales]-[Month Sales Last Year])/[Month Sales Last Year])
```

Another function commonly used to alter the date context is the DATEADD function. The DATEADD function is used to add a date interval to the current date context. You can add year, quarter, month, or day intervals.

```
DATEADD(<dates>,<number_of_intervals>,<interval>)
```

The following calculation is used to find the sum of the previous day sales using the DATEADD function as a filter.

```
Prev Day Sales:=Calculate([Sum of Sales],DATEADD('Date'[Datekey],-1,day))
```

Now that you know how to shift the date context, it is time to look at functions you can use in your filters that return a single date.

Using Single Date Functions

DAX contains a set of functions that return a single date. These are usually used when filtering the date context. For example the FIRSTDATE function returns the first date in the column of dates passed to it. As an example, you can use this in combination with the DATESBETWEEN function to get the range of dates from the first day to the 15th day of the current date context set of dates.

```
DATESBETWEEN('Date'[FullDateAlternateKey]
 ,FIRSTDATE('Date'[FullDateAlternateKey])
,DATEADD(FIRSTDATE('Date'[FullDateAlternateKey]), 14, DAY))
```

This can then be used as a filter in the CALCULATE function to get the sales during the first 15 days of the period. The resulting pivot table is shown in Figure 6-11.

Row Labels	TotalSales	First 15 Day Sales
⊟2005	$3,266,373.66	$198,963.36
⊞July	$473,388.16	$198,963.36
⊞August	$506,191.69	$245,773.41
⊞September	$473,943.03	$224,025.27
⊞October	$513,329.47	$274,285.55
⊟November	$543,993.41	$307,175.05
11/1/2005	$20,731.50	
11/2/2005	$10,734.81	
11/3/2005	$13,931.52	
11/4/2005	$18,412.17	
11/5/2005	$21,990.44	
11/6/2005	$17,509.79	
11/7/2005	$26,446.09	
11/8/2005	$28,626.16	
11/9/2005	$14,313.08	
11/10/2005	$21,762.16	
11/11/2005	$21,469.62	
11/12/2005	$19,289.55	
11/13/2005	$27,709.76	
11/14/2005	$28,740.42	
11/15/2005	$15,508.00	

Figure 6-11. *Calculating sales for the first 15 days of the month*

If you are just looking at the monthly periods, you can use the functions STARTOFMONTH and ENDOFMONTH (there are ones for year and quarter also.). The following expression is used to calculate the sum of the sales for the last 15 days of the month.

```
Last 15 Day Sales:=CALCULATE(SUM(InternetSales[SalesAmount]),
 DATESBETWEEN('Date'[FullDateAlternateKey]
 , DATEADD(ENDOFMONTH('Date'[FullDateAlternateKey]), -14, DAY)
,ENDOFMONTH('Date'[FullDateAlternateKey])))
```

Although the majority of measures you need to aggregate from a lower level to a higher level (for example, from days to months) are simple extensions of the base aggregate, at times you need to use special aggregations to roll up the measure. This type of measure is considered semi-additive and is covered in the next section.

Creating Semi-additive Measures

You often encounter semi-additive measures when analyzing data. Some common examples are inventory and account balances. For example, to determine the total amount of inventory at a current point in time, you add the inventory of all stores. However, to find the total inventory of a store at the end of the month, you do not add up the inventory for each day.

In order to deal with these situations DAX contains the FIRSTNONBLANK and LASTNONBLANK functions. These functions return the first or last date for a non-blank condition. For example, the following expression determines the last non-blank date for the product inventory entries.

```
LASTNONBLANK ('Date'[DateKey],CALCULATE (SUM(Inventory[UnitsInStock])))
```

This is then combined with the CALCULATE function to determine the total units in stock.

```
Product Units In Stock:=CALCULATE(SUM(Inventory[UnitsInStock]),
  LASTNONBLANK('Date'[DateKey],
  CALCULATE(SUM(Inventory[UnitsInStock])))))
```

Now if you want to add up the units in stock across products, you can use the following expression.

```
Total Units In Stock:=SUMX(VALUES('Inventory'[ProductKey]),[Product Units In Stock])
```

Figure 6-12 shows the resulting pivot table. Notice the Total Units In Stock measure is additive across the products but non-additive across the dates.

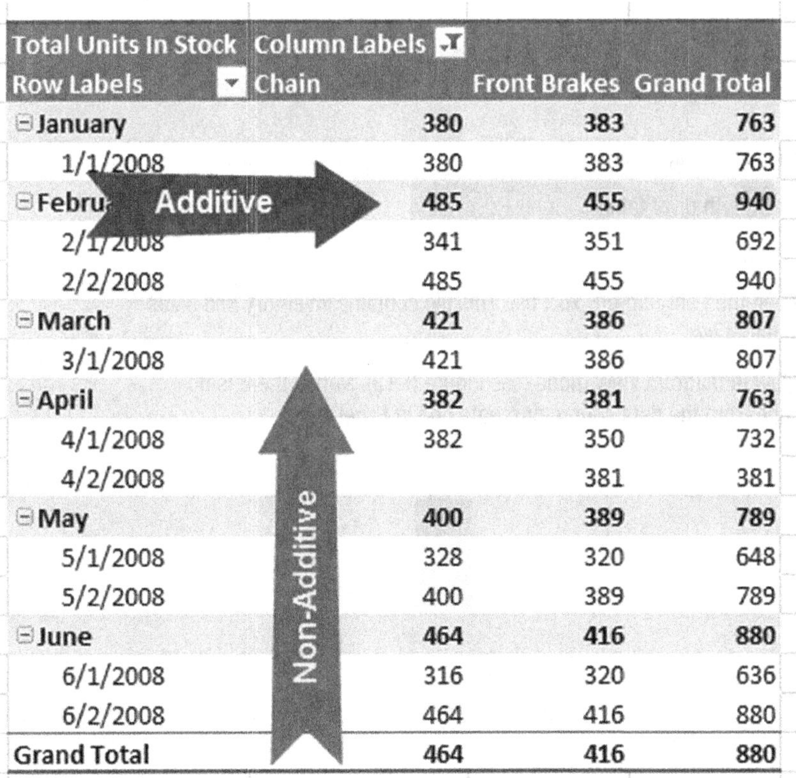

Total Units In Stock	Column Labels		
Row Labels	Chain	Front Brakes	Grand Total
⊟January	380	383	763
1/1/2008	380	383	763
⊟February	485	455	940
2/1/2008	341	351	692
2/2/2008	485	455	940
⊟March	421	386	807
3/1/2008	421	386	807
⊟April	382	381	763
4/1/2008	382	350	732
4/2/2008		381	381
⊟May	400	389	789
5/1/2008	328	320	648
5/2/2008	400	389	789
⊟June	464	416	880
6/1/2008	316	320	636
6/2/2008	464	416	880
Grand Total	464	416	880

Figure 6-12. Calculating units in stock

One of the advantages of DAX is that once you learn a pattern you can extend this to other scenarios. For example, you can employ the same techniques used in this inventory calculation when calculating measures in a cash flow analysis. The following calculation is used to calculate the ending balance.

```
Balance:=CALCULATE ( SUM ( Finance[Amount]),
  LASTNONBLANK ('Date'[DateKey],
  CALCULATE(SUM ( Finance[Amount]]))))
```

In the previous examples the inventory and balance were only entered as a row in the table when a change in inventory or balance occurred. Often the balance or inventory is entered every day and the same value is repeated until there is a change. In these cases, you can use the DAX functions CLOSINGBALANCEMONTH, CLOSINGBALANCEQUARTER, and CLOSINGBALANCYEAR. These functions look at the last date of the time period and use that as the value for the time period. In other words, whatever the value is on the last day of the month is returned by the CLOSINGBALANCEMONTH function.

At this point you should have a good grasp of how the various time functions work. In the following lab you will gain experience implementing some of these functions.

HANDS-ON LAB—IMPLEMENTING TIME INTELLIGENCE IN POWER PIVOT

In the following lab you will

- Create a date table.

- Use time intelligence functions to analyze data.

- Create a Month over Month Growth pivot table.

- Create an Inventory Level Report.

1. In the LabStarters folder, open the LabChapter6.xlsx file. This file contains inventory and sales data from the test Consoto database.

2. Open the Power Pivot window in diagram view mode (see Figure 6-13). Notice there is no Date table. We could load one from the data source or create one in Excel.

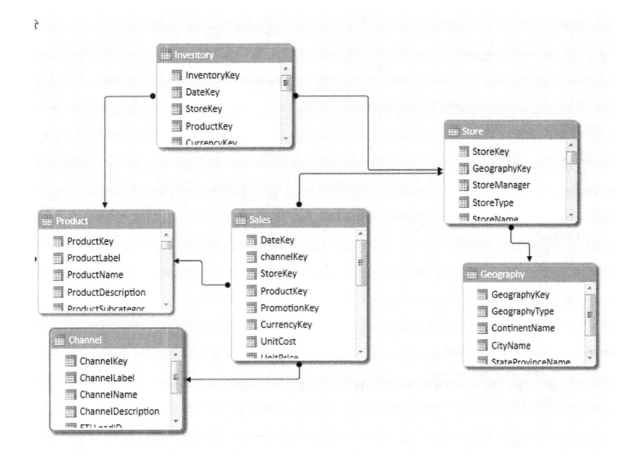

Figure 6-13. *The current Consoto data model*

3. To create the Date table in Excel, switch to sheet 3. Select the first cell and enter a column name of **DateKey**. In the second cell of the column enter a value of **1/1/2007**. Use the auto fill feature of Excel to add values through 12/31/2009.

4. To create a table from the values, select the values in column A. Under the Home tab select the Format As Table drop-down and select a format. Under the Table Tools Design tab change the table name to **Date** (see Figure 6-14).

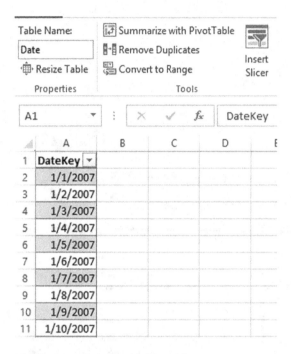

Figure 6-14. *Creating the date table*

5. To add the table to the model, select the table and under the PowerPivot tab click the Add To Data Model button (see Figure 6-15).

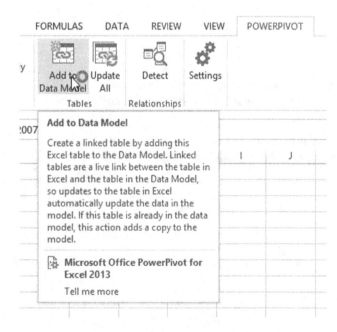

Figure 6-15. *Adding the Excel table to the data model*

6. You should see the table in the data view window of the Power Pivot design window. Click on the Design tab and select Mark As Date Table. Use the DateKey as the unique identifier.

7. Use the Date functions to create a Year, Month Number, and Month column (You have to use the FORMAT function to create the Month column). Sort the Month column by the Month Number column.

8. Switch to the diagram view of the model. Using the Year and Month, create a Calendar hierarchy in the Date table.

9. Create a relationship between the Sales table and Date table (see Figure 6-16).

Figure 6-16. *Creating the relationship between the Sales and Date table*

10. Select the Sales table in the Data View window. Add the following measures and format them as currency:

```
Sum of Sales:=SUM(Sales[SalesAmount])
YTD Sales:=TOTALYTD([Sum of Sales],'Date'[Datekey])
MTD Sales:=TOTALMTD([Sum of Sales],'Date'[Datekey])
```

11. To test the measures, go to Sheet1 in Excel and click on cell B2. On the Insert tab, select PivotTable. In the Create PivotTable window, select Use An External Data Source and click the Choose Connection button (see Figure 6-17).

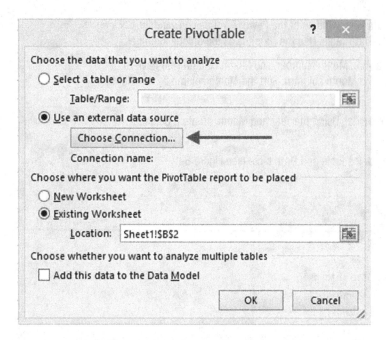

Figure 6-17. *Choosing an external data source*

12. In the Existing Connections window select the Tables tab. In the Tables tab select Tables In Workbook Data Model and click Open (see Figure 6-18). After selecting the connection, click OK in the Create PivotTable window.

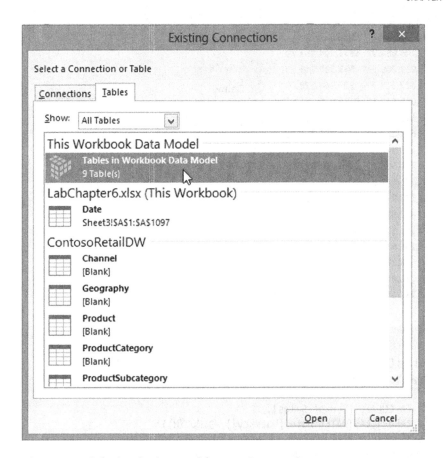

Figure 6-18. *Selecting the data model connection*

13. Add the measures Sum Of Sales, MTD Sales, and YTD Sales to the Values area and the Calendar hierarchy to the Rows area. In the Insert tab select Slicer and choose the ChannelName. Investigate the data and verify that is what you expected (see Figure 6-19).

Row Labels ▼	Sum of Sales	MTD Sales	YTD Sales
⊟ 2007	$571,204,151.10	$55,148,659.27	$571,204,151.10
Jan	$33,937,209.25	$33,937,209.25	$33,937,209.25
Feb	$39,627,318.77	$39,627,318.77	$73,564,528.02
Mar	$43,055,837.85	$43,055,837.85	$116,620,365.87
Apr	$45,152,238.05	$45,152,238.05	$161,772,603.92
May	$49,678,655.61	$49,678,655.61	$211,451,259.53
Jun	$49,431,542.53	$49,431,542.53	$260,882,802.06
Jul	$53,458,586.99	$53,458,586.99	$314,341,389.05
Aug	$50,771,841.27	$50,771,841.27	$365,113,230.32
Sep	$49,242,024.87	$49,242,024.87	$414,355,255.19
Oct	$47,437,924.07	$47,437,924.07	$461,793,179.26
Nov	$54,262,312.57	$54,262,312.57	$516,055,491.83
Dec	$55,148,659.27	$55,148,659.27	$571,204,151.10
⊞ 2008	$600,175,898.67	$56,659,783.37	$600,175,898.67
⊞ 2009	$543,817,781.67	$46,788,451.58	$543,817,781.67
Grand Total	$1,715,197,831.44	$46,788,451.58	$543,817,781.67

ChannelName	🏷
Catalog	
Online	
Reseller	
Store	

Figure 6-19. Verifying the year-to-date sales measure

14. Switch to the Sales table in the Data Model. Create a rolling 3 month sales measure with the following expression. Format the measure as currency.

```
Rolling 3 Month Sales:=CALCULATE([Sum of Sales],
DATESINPERIOD('Date'[Datekey],LASTDATE('Date'[Datekey]),-3,MONTH))
```

15. Add the measure to the pivot table on Sheet1 and verify it is working as expected.

16. Next you want to compare sales growth from one month to the next. First create a previous month's sales measure.

```
Prev Month Sales:=CALCULATE([Sum of Sales],
PARALLELPERIOD('Date'[DateKey],-1,MONTH))
```

17. Next use the previous sales and current sales to create a sales growth measure. Format the measure as percent. Notice you need to check to make sure the previous month sales exists. If it does not, you need to return a blank value.

```
Monthly Sales Growth:=if(NOT(ISBLANK([Prev Month Sales])),
([Sum of Sales] - [Prev Month Sales])/[Prev Month Sales],BLANK())
```

18. Create a pivot table like the one shown in Figure 6-20 on Sheet2 in Excel to test your results.

Row Labels ▾	Sum of Sales	Prev Month Sales	Monthly Sales Growth
⊟ 2007	$10,697,642.89	$9,510,697.85	12 %
Jan	$675,656.58		
Feb	$615,633.57	$675,656.58	-9 %
Mar	$614,046.66	$615,633.57	-0 %
Apr	$707,348.69	$614,046.66	15 %
May	$966,623.91	$707,348.69	37 %
Jun	$987,545.18	$966,623.91	2 %
Jul	$996,175.98	$987,545.18	1 %
Aug	$883,280.80	$996,175.98	-11 %
Sep	$983,234.05	$883,280.80	11 %
Oct	$908,519.60	$983,234.05	-8 %
Nov	$1,172,632.83	$908,519.60	29 %
Dec	$1,186,945.05	$1,172,632.83	1 %
⊞ 2008	$12,802,000.68	$12,699,939.76	1 %
⊞ 2009	$13,768,349.90	$13,810,604.03	-0 %
Grand Total	$37,267,993.47	$36,021,241.64	3 %

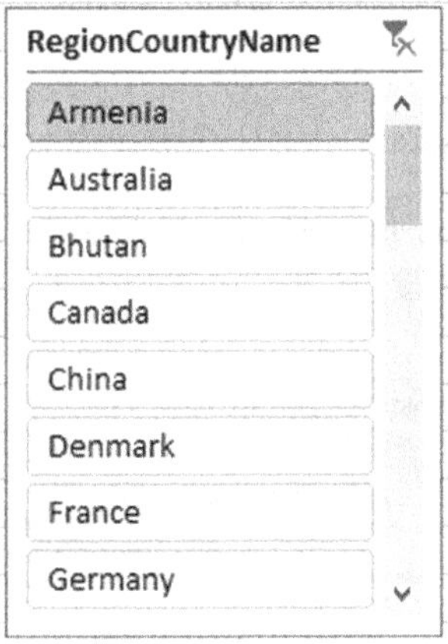

RegionCountryName

Armenia
Australia
Bhutan
Canada
China
Denmark
France
Germany

Figure 6-20. *Testing the Monthly Sales Growth measure*

19. To investigate semi-additive measures, you are going to create a pivot table that shows inventory counts. First create a relationship between the Inventory and Date tables.

20. Add the following inventory count measure to the Inventory table:

```
Inventory Count:=SUM([OnHandQuantity])
```

21. In order to calculate the inventory over time, you need to find the last non-blank entry for the time period. The following formula will give you the value. The date range initial value is blank (prior to the first date) and final date is the maximum date. You will use this formula as part of the formula in step 22.

```
LNB Date:=LASTNONBLANK(
DATESBETWEEN('Date'[Datekey],BLANK(),MAX('Date'[Datekey]))
,[Inventory Count])
```

22. Using the last non-blank filter and the CALCULATE function you can calculate the last non-blank quantity for a product. Add the following measure to the Inventory table.

```
LNB Quantity:=CALCULATE([Inventory Count],
LASTNONBLANK(DATESBETWEEN('Date'[Datekey],
BLANK(),MAX('Date'[Datekey])),[Inventory Count]))
```

23. You can now add up the product quantity for products chosen. Add the following measure to the Inventory table.

```
Product Quantity:=SUMX(
VALUES(Product[ProductKey]),[LNB Quantity])
```

24. The final step is to add up the inventory across all the stores selected using the following measure.

```
Inventory Level:=SUMX(Values(Store[StoreKey]),[Product Quantity])
```

25. To test the measure, add a new sheet in Excel and create a pivot table like the one in Figure 6-21.

ProductCategoryName	Audio			
Inventory Level	**Column Labels**			
Row Labels	**Bluetooth Headphones**	**MP4&MP3**	**Recording Pen**	**Grand Total**
⊟2007	1879	2002	965	4846
Jan	214	660	116	990
Feb	304	665	127	1096
Mar	474	702	350	1526
Apr	651	927	523	2101
May	858	1142	545	2545
Jun	1024	1351	588	2963
Jul	1295	1554	720	3569
Aug	1409	1522	690	3621
Sep	1658	1677	701	4036
Oct	1633	1684	816	4133
Nov	1984	2059	1054	5097
Dec	1879	2002	965	4846
⊞2008	6274	6175	2499	14948
⊞2009	11423	9639	4616	25678
Grand Total	**11423**	**9639**	**4616**	**25678**

Figure 6-21. *Testing the inventory measure*

Summary

This chapter provided you with the basics you need to successfully incorporate date-time based analysis using Power Pivot and DAX. You should now understand how to shift the date context to compare measures based on parallel periods. You should also feel comfortable aggregating measures using the period-to-date DAX formulas. Combine the concepts you learned in Chapter 5 and this chapter; when you do, you should start to recognize patterns in your analysis. Based on these patterns you can identify the DAX template you need to solve the problem. Because not all of you are familiar with creating pivot tables and pivot charts in Excel, the next chapter shows you the basics of how to create dashboards in Excel based on your model. If you are familiar with these concepts, you may want to skip Chapter 7.

■ ■ ■

Data Analysis with Pivot Tables and Charts

Once you have the data model created in Power Pivot, you need to create an interface for users to interact with the data model and perform data analysis using the model. You can use several programs to interface with the model depending on the type of analysis taking place; these include Power View, Power Map, Performance Point, and Reporting Services. Although all these tools are viable clients to use, one of the best client tools is Excel itself. Excel is a feature-rich environment for creating dashboards using pivot tables and pivot charts. Furthermore, it is very easy to share Excel files with colleagues or host the Excel workbook on SharePoint for increased performance and security. This chapter covers the basics of building an interface for analyzing the data contained in a Power Pivot model using pivot tables and pivot charts in Excel.

After completing this chapter you will be able to

- Use pivot tables to explore the data.

- Filter data using slicers.

- Add visualizations to a pivot table.

- Use pivot charts to explore trends.

- Use multiple charts and tables linked together.

- Use cube functions to query the data model

■ **Note**   This chapter contains references to color figures. If you are reading this book in print, or in a black-and-white eBook edition, you can find copies of color figures in the Source Code/Downloads package for the book at http://www.apress.com/9781430264453.

Pivot Table Fundamentals

One of the most widely used tools for analyzing data is the pivot table. The pivot table allows you to easily detect patterns and relationships from the data. For example, you can determine what products sell better during certain times during the year. Or you can see how marketing campaigns affect the sales of various products. Figure 7-1 shows the various areas of a pivot table.

The row and column fields contain the attributes that you are interested in using to summarize the data. For example, the pivot table in Figure 7-1 is aggregating the values by product categories and years. The filter is used to filter the values in the pivot table by some attribute. The filter in Figure 7-1 is limiting the results to the first quarter of each year. The slicer works the same as the filter in this case, limiting the values to large resellers. Slicers have the added advantage of filtering multiple pivot tables and pivot charts.

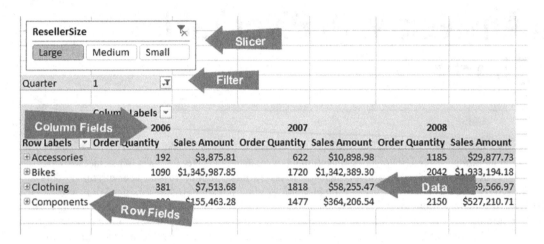

Figure 7-1. *The parts of a pivot table*

To construct the pivot table, drag and drop the fields from the Field List to the drop areas below the Field List, as shown in Figure 7-2. If you just click on the check box to select the fields, it will place text fields in the rows and any numeric values in the Values area. This can become quite annoying because it will place a field like Years in the Values area and treat it as a set of values to be summed. (In Chapter 8, I will show you how you can avoid this.)

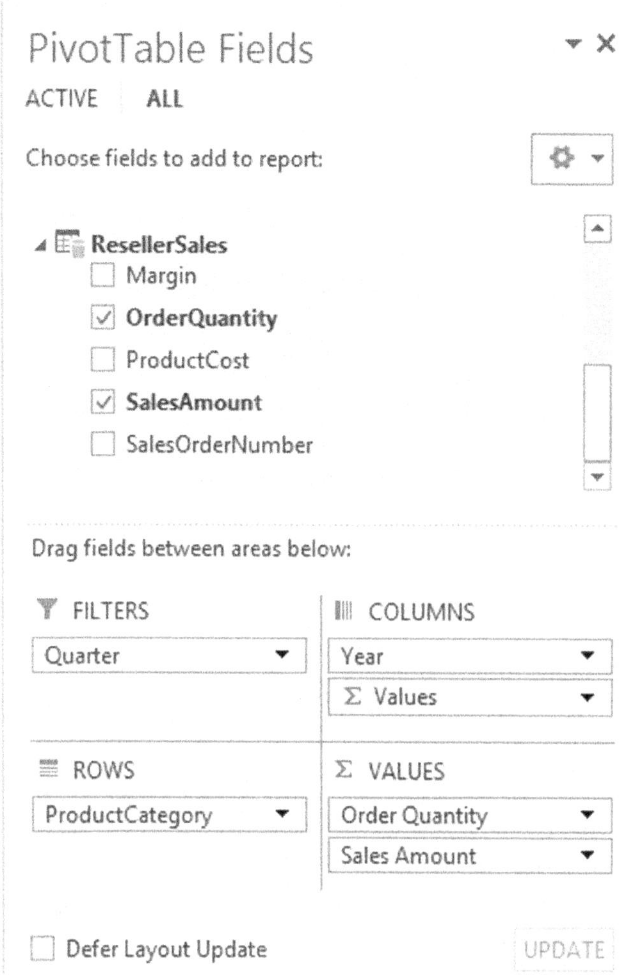

PivotTable Fields ▾ ✕

ACTIVE   **ALL**

Choose fields to add to report: ⚙ ▾

◢ 🎬 **ResellerSales**
  ☐ Margin
  ☑ **OrderQuantity**
  ☐ ProductCost
  ☑ **SalesAmount**
  ☐ SalesOrderNumber

Drag fields between areas below:

▼ FILTERS	▮▮▮ COLUMNS
Quarter ▼	Year ▼
	Σ Values ▼

☰ ROWS	Σ VALUES
ProductCategory ▼	Order Quantity ▼
	Sales Amount ▼

☐ Defer Layout Update   UPDATE

Figure 7-2. *Adding fields to the pivot table*

In order to add slicers to filter the pivot table, you need to go to the Insert tab in Excel and select the Slicer button. In the next section, you will look at adding slicers and controlling multiple pivot tables with the same slicer.

Slicing the Data

To add a slicer to filter a pivot table, click on the pivot table, and on the Insert tab, select the Slicer button. You should see a pick list containing the fields in the Power Pivot data model (see Figure 7-3).

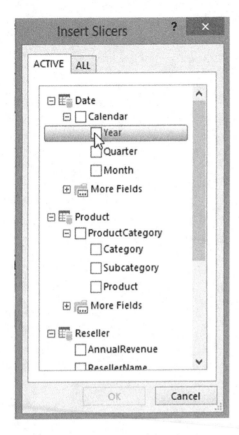

Figure 7-3. *Selecting the slicer field*

Since you had the pivot table selected when you inserted the slicer, it is automatically wired up to the pivot table. You can verify this by clicking on the slicer and selecting the Slicer Tools Options tab (see Figure 7-4). You can use this tab to format the slicer and choose the report connections for the slicer.

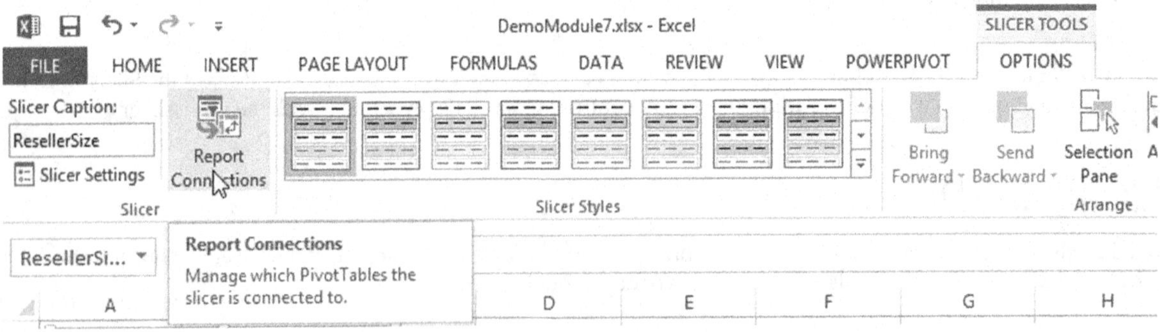

Figure 7-4. *Setting the slicer connections*

Figure 7-5 shows the Report Connections pick list for the slicer. Notice the pivot table does not have to be on the same sheet as the slicer. The names of the pivot tables are the generic names given to them by Excel when they were created. As you add more pivot tables, it is a good idea to give them more meaningful names. If you click on the pivot table and go to the PivotTable Tools Analyze tab, you will see a textbox where you can change the name of the pivot table.

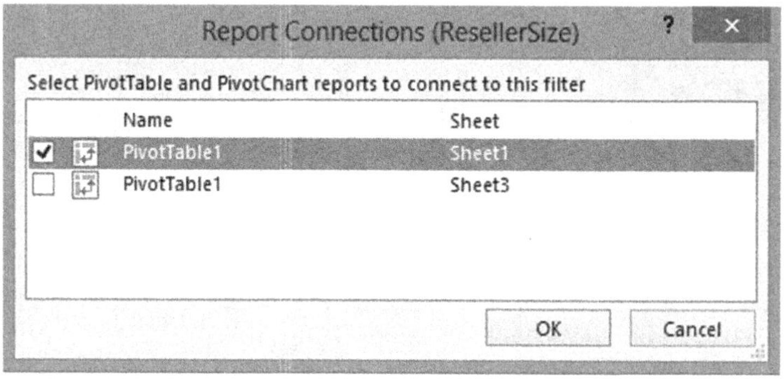

Figure 7-5. *Selecting connections for the slicer*

If you select the Slicer Settings button under the Slicer Tools Options tab, you launch the Slicer Settings window (see Figure 7-6) where you can change the name, caption, and sort order of the slicer. You can also choose how to show items with no data.

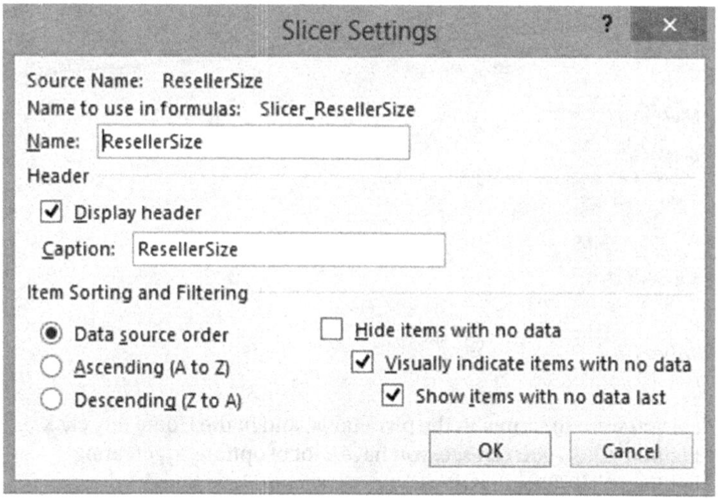

Figure 7-6. *Changing the slicer settings*

There are times when you need *cascading filters*—where one filter limits what can be chosen in the next filter. This is easy with slicers that are based on fields that are related in the model. When you select the related fields, the slicers are linked automatically for you. For example, Figure 7-7 shows a product category and product subcategory filter. If you select a product category, the corresponding product subcategories are highlighted.

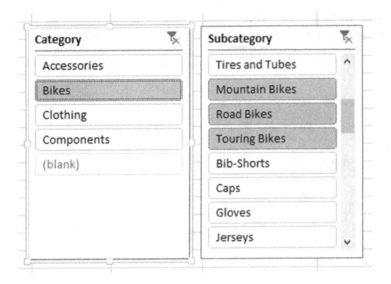

Figure 7-7. Creating cascading filters using slicers

Adding Visualizations to a Pivot Table

In order to help identify trends, outliers, and provide insight into the data, you can add many types of visualizations to a pivot table. These include conditional formatting, data bars, and trend lines. Figure 7-8 shows a pivot table with data bars and conditional formatting.

Row Labels ▼	Order Quantity	Sales Amount	Margin
⊞ Accessories	2740	$60,086.05	$17,312.40
⊞ Bikes	4669	$3,699,096.26	($502,489.41)
⊞ Clothing	4967	$129,921.56	($3,853.94)
⊞ Components	5680	$1,453,875.07	$66,463.69
Grand Total	18056	$5,342,978.94	($422,567.26)

Figure 7-8. Using conditional formating and databars

To create the visual formatting, select the data you want to format in the pivot table, and in the Home tab, click on the Conditional Formatting drop-down (see Figure 7-9). As you can see, you have a lot of options for creating conditional formatting. In Figure 7-8 there is a Highlight Cells Rule that displays negative numbers in red.

Figure 7-9. *Setting up conditional formatting*

Once you establish a rule, you can edit it by selecting the Manage Rules option and selecting the rule you want to edit. Figure 7-10 shows the various options you can set for a Data Bar formatting rule.

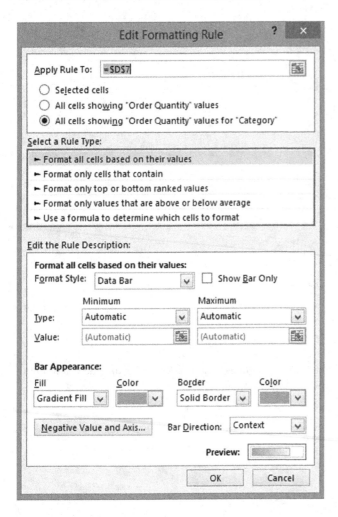

Figure 7-10. *Editing a Data Bar rule*

You can produce some interesting effects with the formatting rules. For example, the pivot table in Figure 7-11 shows a heat map used to quickly determine which months have good sales and which are bad.

Sum of OrderQuantity	Column Labe ☷				
Row Labels ▾	Australia	Canada	France	Germany	United Kingo
April	115	2861	628	541	750
August	415	5269	3252	1184	1350
December	901	3981	652	482	1505
February	110	2313	1444	504	562
January	103	1726	371	359	507
July	124	3794	890	756	1073
June	893	3827	625	427	1513
March	509	2428	376	286	1013
May	209	3824	2177	783	960
November	224	3885	2229	836	968
October	110	2848	659	615	829
September	1235	5005	1045	607	2163

Figure 7-11. *Creating a heat map with conditional formatting*

Another popular feature associated with pivot tables are spark lines. *Spark lines* are mini graphs that show the trend of a series of data. Figure 7-12 shows spark lines that display the sales trend across the four quarters of the year.

Year	2006	☷			
Sum of SalesAmount	Column Labels ▾				
Row Labels ▾	1	2	3	4	Sales Trend
Large	$1,512,840.61	$1,673,185.81	$4,031,239.79	$2,895,748.58	
Medium	$690,013.60	$685,873.20	$1,253,354.23	$822,995.20	
Small	$1,866,331.83	$1,794,761.41	$3,595,645.41	$3,322,439.98	

Figure 7-12. *Using spark lines to show trends*

To create a spark line, highlight the values in the pivot table that contain the data and select the Sparklines button on the Insert tab. You then select the location of the spark line (see Figure 7-13). You have to choose from a line, a column, or a win/loss spark line.

Figure 7-13. *Setting up a spark line*

Although adding visualizations to pivot tables can enhance your ability to analyze the data, many times the best way to spot trends and compare and contrast the data is through the use of charts and graphs. In the next section, you will see how charts and graphs are useful data analysis tools and how to add them to your analysis dashboards.

Working with Pivot Charts

Along with pivot tables, Excel has a robust set of charts and graphs available for you to use to analyze your data. Adding a pivot chart is very similar to adding a pivot table. On the Insert tab of Excel, select the PivotChart drop-down. You have the option of selecting a single PivotChart or a PivotChart and PivotTable that are tied together (see Figure 7-14).

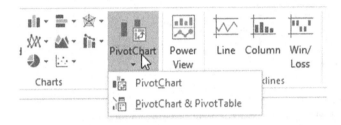

Figure 7-14. Adding a pivot chart

After selecting the pivot chart, you are presented with a window to select a data source and where you want to put the pivot chart (see Figure 7-15).

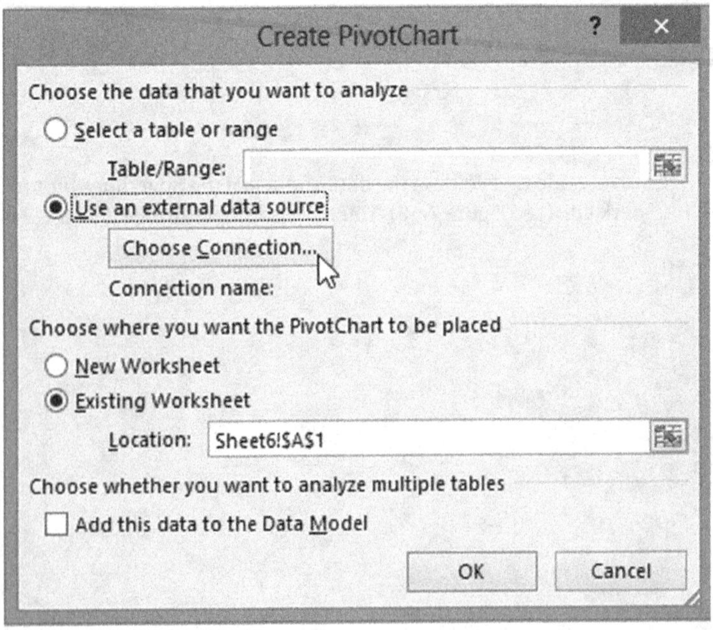

Figure 7-15. Selecting a data source

To select the Power Pivot model as the data source, choose to use an external connection and click the Choose Connection button. In the Existing Connections window, select the Tables tab and select the Tables In Workbook Data Model (see Figure 7-16).

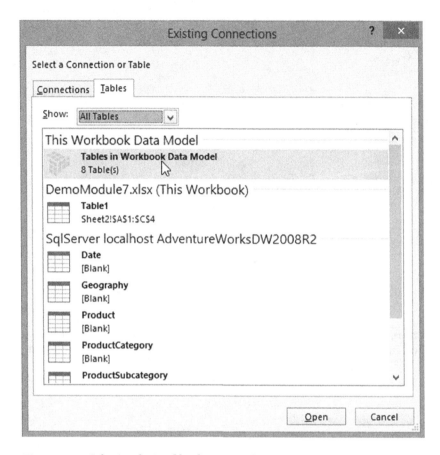

Figure 7-16. *Selecting the Workbook Data Model*

Once you select the data source, you are presented with a blank chart and the field selection box where you can drag and drop fields for the chart values and axis (see Figure 7-17).

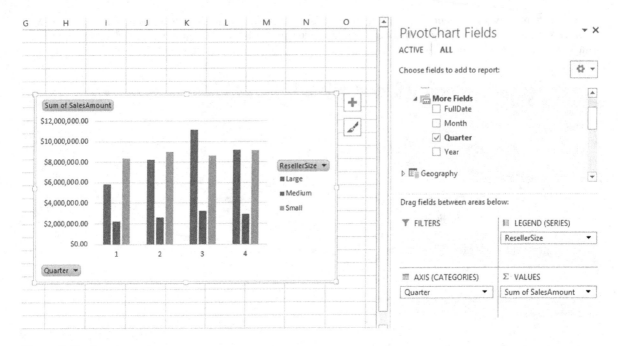

Figure 7-17. *Creating a chart*

By default, the chart is a column chart, but you have many different types of charts to choose from. If you click on the chart and select the PivotChart Tools Design tab, you can select the Change Chart Type button and choose from a variety of types (see Figure 7-18).

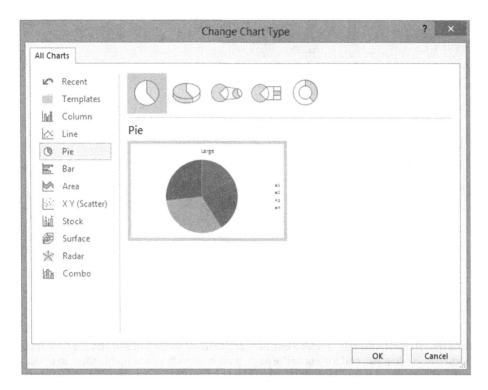

Figure 7-18. *Selecting a chart type*

Along with changing the chart type the PivotChart Tools tabs allow you a vast assortment of design and formatting options you can use to customize the look and feel of your charts and graphs. It is definitely worth your time to play around with the tools and create various graphs to gain a better idea of the various options available.

Using Multiple Charts and Tables

When creating pivot tables and charts to display and make sense of the data, you often want to create a dashboard that easily allows you to determine performance. You may be interested in sales performance, network performance, or assembly-line performance. Dashboards combine visual representations, such as key performance indicators (KPIs), graphs, and charts, into one holistic view of the process. Although they are not technically considered dashboard tools, you can create some very compelling data displays using Excel with Power Pivot tables and charts that can then be displayed and shared in SharePoint.

When adding multiple charts and tables to a dashboard, you may want to link them together so they represent the same data in different ways. You also will probably want to control them with the same slicers so that they stay in sync. The easiest way to do this is to add them using the Insert tab and selecting PivotChart & PivotTable (see Figure 7-19).

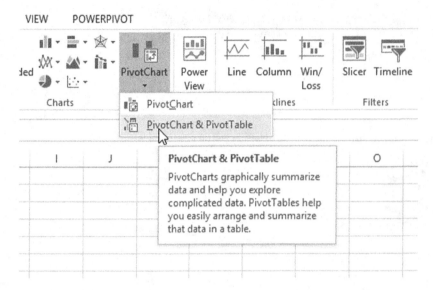

Figure 7-19. Adding a pivot chart and a related pivot table

Adding the pivot chart and pivot table in this way creates a link between them so that when you add a field to one, it adds the same field to the other. Also when you add a slicer to the page, it automatically hooks up the slicer to both the pivot table and the pivot chart. Figure 7-20 shows a simple dashboard consisting of a linked pivot table, pivot chart and slicer.

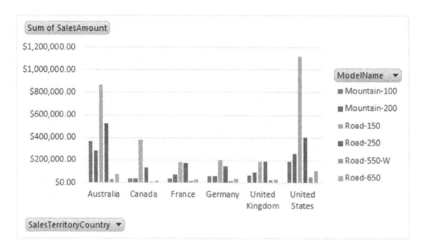

Sum of SalesAmount	Column Labels						
Row Labels	Mountain-100	Mountain-200	Road-150	Road-250	Road-550-W	Road-650	Grand Total
Australia	$365,748.92	$286,230.90	$865,941.34	$524,360.36	$30,013.13	$81,990.24	$2,154,284.88
Canada	$40,599.88	$39,111.44	$382,874.89	$134,122.46	$8,003.50	$16,890.21	$621,602.38
France	$37,199.89	$72,030.94	$182,491.77	$174,786.79	$18,007.88	$30,424.75	$514,942.01
Germany	$57,624.83	$55,638.15	$203,961.39	$150,527.81	$16,007.00	$37,471.66	$521,230.85
United Kingdom	$64,374.81	$94,727.27	$189,648.31	$187,876.16	$25,010.94	$29,949.37	$591,586.85
United States	$189,599.44	$259,570.30	$1,123,576.78	$399,924.04	$49,021.44	$105,004.55	$2,126,696.55
Grand Total	$755,147.77	$807,308.99	$2,948,494.48	$1,571,597.63	$146,063.88	$301,730.79	$6,530,343.53

Figure 7-20. *Creating a simple dashboard in Excel*

If you need to connect multiple charts together, open the Model Designer and select the PivotTable drop-down on the Home tab (see Figure 7-21). This also allows you to insert a flattened pivot table, which is useful for printing.

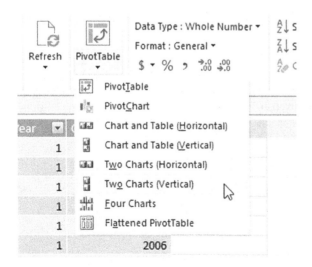

Figure 7-21. *Connecting multiple pivot charts*

Using Cube Functions

Using the built-in PivotChart and PivotTable layouts in Excel allows you to create compelling dashboards and provide great interfaces for browsing the data. There are times, however, when you may find yourself frustrated with some of the limitations inherent with these structures. For example, you cannot insert your own columns inside the pivot table to create a custom calculation. You may also want to display the data in a non-tabular format for a customized report. This is where the Excel cube functions are really useful.

The Excel cube functions allow you to connect directly to the Power Pivot data model without needing to use a pivot table. The cube functions are Excel functions (as opposed to DAX functions) and can be found on the Excel Formulas tab under the More Functions drop-down (see Figure 7-22).

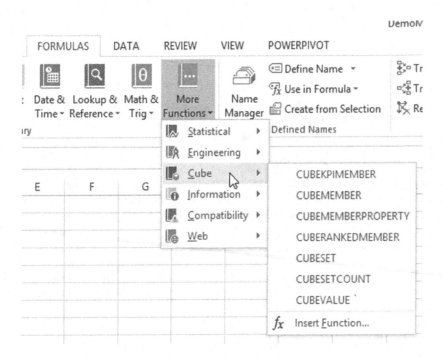

Figure 7-22. *Using cube functions to connect to the model*

The easiest way to see how these functions are used is to create a pivot table, and on the PivotTable Tools Analyze tab, select the OLAP Tools drop-down, and then select the Convert To Formulas option (see Figure 7-23).

Figure 7-23. *Converting from a pivot table to cube functions*

Figure 7-24 shows the table after the conversion to cube functions. It uses the CUBEMEMBER function to return a member or tuple (ordered list) from the cube and the CUBEVALUE function to return an aggregated value from the cube.

fx	=CUBEMEMBER("ThisWorkbookDataModel","[Product].[ProductCategory].[Category].&[Accessories]")						

B	C	D	E	F	G	H	I
Sum of SalesAmount	Column Labels						
Row Labels	AU	CA	DE	FR	GB	US	Grand Total
Accessories	23947.5301	118127.3489	35083.0651	48031.7274	42593.0284	303515.2279	571297.9278
Bikes	1323820.733	11636380.59	1543015.649	3560665.645	3405747.206	44832751.73	66302381.56
Clothing	42915.8039	378947.6336	71619.4348	128092.2217	118828.7978	1037436.947	1777840.839
Components	203651.3093	2244470.02	334269.888	870748.3407	711839.7945	7434097.306	11799076.66
Grand Total	1594335.377	14377925.6	1983988.037	4607537.935	4279008.827	53607801.21	80450596.98

Figure 7-24. *Using cube functions to retrieve values*

The following formula is used to return the column label for cell C3:

```
=CUBEMEMBER("ThisWorkbookDataModel","[Geography].[CountryRegionCode].&[AU]")
```

The first parameter is the name of the connection to the data model and the second parameter is the member expression.

The value in cell C4 is returned using the following formula:

```
=CUBEVALUE("ThisWorkbookDataModel",$B$2,$B4,C$3)
```

This formula uses cell references, but you can replace these with the cube functions contained in these cells:

```
=CUBEVALUE
(
    "ThisWorkbookDataModel",
    CUBEMEMBER("ThisWorkbookDataModel","[Measures].[Sum of SalesAmount]"),
    CUBEMEMBER("ThisWorkbookDataModel",
        "[Product].[ProductCategory].[Category].&[Accessories]"),
    CUBEMEMBER("ThisWorkbookDataModel",
        "[Geography].[CountryRegionCode].&[AU]")
)
```

Notice one of the parameters is the CUBEMEMBER function returning the aggregation you want the value of; the other parameters use the CUBEMEMBER to define the portion of the cube used in the aggregation.

Sales	US	CA	GB
Total	$53,607,801	$14,377,926	$4,279,009
Bikes	$44,832,752	$11,636,381	$3,405,747
Components	$7,434,097	$2,244,470	$711,840
Total	$52,266,849	$13,880,851	$4,117,587
Others			
Accessories	$303,515	$118,127	$42,593
Clothing	$1,037,437	$378,948	$118,829

Figure 7-25. *Rearranging the data*

You can now rearrange the values and labels to achieve the layout and formatting that you need (see Figure 7-25).

HANDS-ON LAB—CREATING THE BI INTERFACE IN EXCEL

In the following lab you will

- Add conditional formatting to a pivot table.

- Create a chart to help analyze data.

- Link together pivot tables and pivot charts.

- Use cube functions to display model data.

1. In the LabStarters folder, open the LabChapter7.xlsx file. This file contains inventory and sales data from the test AdventureWorksDW database.

2. In Excel Sheet1 insert a Power Pivot table using the PivotTable button on the Insert tab. Select the Use An External Data Source and click the Choose Connection button. On the Tables tab of the Existing Connections window, select Tables In Workbook Data Model (see Figure 7-26).

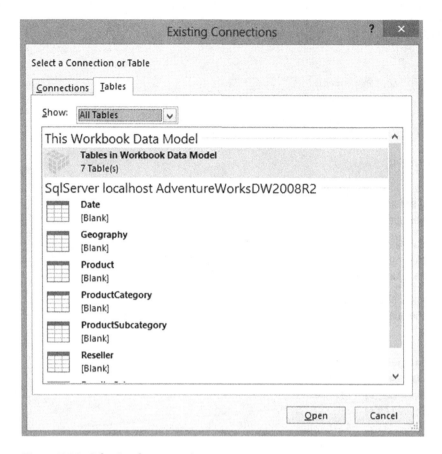

Figure 7-26. *Selecting the connection*

3. Add TotalQuantity, TotalSales, and TotalMargin from the ResellerSales table to the Values drop area in the Field List window. Add the Calendar hierarchy to Row Labels drop area.

4. Notice that some of the margins are negative. To bring attention to the negative values you are going to format them in red.

5. Select a TotalMargin cell in the pivot table. On the Home tab, click the Conditional Formatting drop down. Select the Highlight Cells ➤ Less Than option. Format the cells that are less than 0 with red text (see Figure 7-27).

Less Than	?	✕

Format cells that are LESS THAN:

0	📑	with	Red Text	∨

OK	Cancel

Figure 7-27. Setting conditional formatting

6. When finished you should see an icon next to the selected cell. Click it and select the All Cells Showing TotalMargin Values option.

7. Select one of the TotalSales cells. This time, select the Data Bars under the Conditional Formatting drop-down. Select one of the gradient styles. After selecting the Data Bar, you should see a small icon next to the values. Click it and select the All Cells Showing TotalSales Values.

8. Your Pivot table should look similar to Figure 7-28. Expand the years and notice the formatting shows up for the quarters, months, and years.

Row Labels ▾	TotalQuantity	TotalSales	TotalMargin
⊞ 2005	10835	$8,065,435.31	$328,927.08
⊞ 2006	58241	$24,144,429.65	$323,401.79
⊟ 2007	100172	$32,202,669.43	($168,557.73)
⊞ 1	12307	$5,266,343.51	$193,324.41
⊞ 2	19466	$6,733,903.82	$298,556.44
⊟ 3	39784	$10,926,196.09	($710,603.34)
July	9871	$2,665,650.54	($181,857.11)
August	15139	$4,212,971.51	($250,821.21)
September	14774	$4,047,574.04	($277,925.03)
⊞ 4	28615	$9,276,226.01	$50,164.75
⊞ 2008	45130	$16,038,062.60	($13,288.53)
Grand Total	**214378**	**$80,450,596.98**	**$470,482.60**

Figure 7-28. Adding data bars to the pivot table

9. Open sheet2 and on the Insert tab, select the PivotChart drop-down. From the drop-down, chose the pivot chart. Insert the chart on the current sheet using the Tables In Workbook Data Model connection.

10. In the Field List window, add the TotalSales from the ResellerSales table to the Values drop area and add the CountryRegionName from the Geography table to the Axis Fields drop area. You should see a column chart showing sales by country (see Figure 7-29).

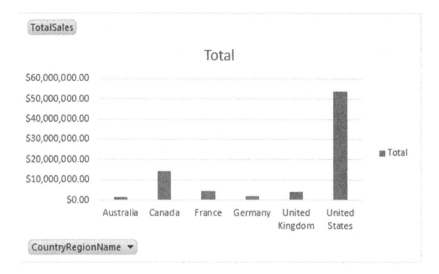

Figure 7-29. *Adding a column chartSelect the column chart. You should see the PivotChart Tools tabs. In the Design tab, you can change the chart colors, change the layout, and change the chart type*

11. On the Layout tab, you can work with changing the titles, legend, labels, and gridlines. The Format tab lets you format the shapes and text in the chart. The Analyze tab lets you show/hide the field buttons.

12. Rename the title of the chart to **Sales By Country**. Hide the field buttons and the legend. Remove the gridlines.

13. Right-click on the vertical axis and select Format Axis. Under Axis Options, change the Display Units to Millions. Under the Number node, change the Category to Currency with zero decimal places. Your chart should look similar to Figure 7-30.

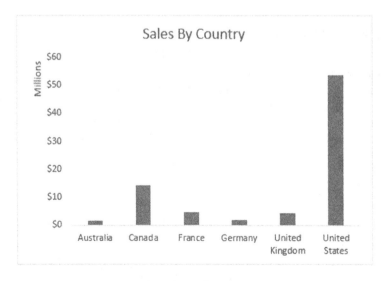

Figure 7-30. *Formatting the column chart*

14. Sometimes you want to see a data chart and a data table together. To do this, go to the Power Pivot Model Designer and on the Home tab, select the PivotTable drop-down. From the drop-down, chose the Chart And Table (Horizontal). Insert the chart and table on a new sheet.

15. Change the chart type to a pie chart. On the Field List window for the chart, add the TotalSales field to the Values drop area and the CountryRegionCode to the Axis Fields drop area.

16. Change the title of the chart to Sales By Country and remove the field buttons.

17. Change the Chart Layout on the Design tab to show values as currency with no decimals (see Figure 7-31).

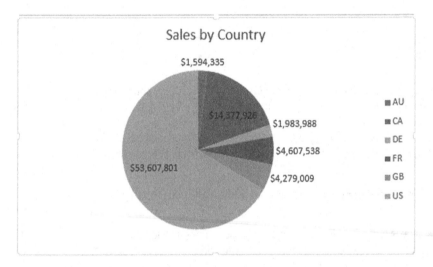

Figure 7-31. *Creating the sales pie chart*

18. Click on the pivot table to bring up its Field List window. Add the ResellerSales TotalSales to the Values drop area. Add the Product Subcategory to the Row Labels drop area.

19. With the pie chart selected, insert a slicer for the product category and one for the year (see Figure 7-32). Verify that the slicers filter the pie chart but not the pivot table.

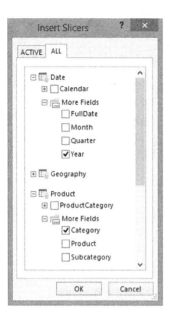

Figure 7-32. *Inserting the slicers*

20. Select the Year slicer and on the Slicer Tools Options tab, click the Report Connections button. Add the pivot table located on the same sheet as the pie chart. Repeat this for the category slicer.

21. Verify that the slicers filter both the chart and the pivot table. Your dashboard should look similar to Figure 7-33.

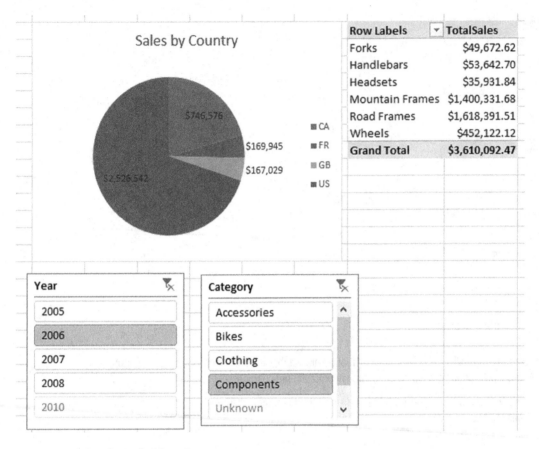

Row Labels ▼	TotalSales
Forks	$49,672.62
Handlebars	$53,642.70
Headsets	$35,931.84
Mountain Frames	$1,400,331.68
Road Frames	$1,618,391.51
Wheels	$452,122.12
Grand Total	**$3,610,092.47**

***Figure 7-33.** Creating a dashboard*

22. Add a new sheet to the workbook. You are going to use cube functions to calculate the top product and top reseller in total sales. The final result should look similar to Figure 7-34.

◢	A	B	C	D
1		TotalSales		
2		Top Reseller	Brakes and Gears	$877,107.19
3		Top Product	Mountain-200 Black, 38	$3,105,726.66

Figure 7-34.

23. Add the following code in B1 to select the TotalSales measure.

```
=CUBEMEMBER("ThisWorkbookDataModel","[Measures].[TotalSales]")
```

24. In B2, use the following function to get the set of resellers ordered by TotalSales descending. You will use this set to select the top reseller.

```
=CUBESET("ThisWorkbookDataModel",
    "[Reseller].[ResellerName].children","Top Reseller",2,B1)
```

25. In B3, use this function to get the set of products ordered by TotalSales descending.

```
=CUBESET("ThisWorkbookDataModel",
    "[Product].[Product].children","Top Products",2,B1)
```

26. In C2, use the CUBERANKEDMEMBER function to get the top reseller from the set returned by the function in B2.

```
=CUBERANKEDMEMBER("ThisWorkbookDataModel",B2,1)
```

27. In C3 use the CUBERANKEDMEMBER function to get the top product from the set returned by the function in B3.

```
=CUBERANKEDMEMBER("ThisWorkbookDataModel",B3,1)
```

28. In D2 use the CUBEVALUE function to get the total sales of the top reseller found in C2. Notice you have to concatenate the name of the reseller found in C2 to the [Reseller].[ResellerName] attribute in the Power Pivot model.

```
=CUBEVALUE("ThisWorkbookDataModel",
    "[Reseller].[ResellerName].&["& C2 &"]","[Measures].[TotalSales]")
```

29. Using a similar CUBEVALUE function, you can get the total sales value for the top product.

```
=CUBEVALUE("ThisWorkbookDataModel",
    "[Product].[Product].&[" &C3&"]","[Measures].[TotalSales]")
```

Summary

As you saw in this chapter, Excel is a feature-rich environment for creating dashboards using pivot tables and pivot charts. At this point, you should feel comfortable creating pivot tables and pivot charts using your workbook model as a data source. You also used Excel cube functions to query the model directly without needing to use a pivot table. Although this chapter covered the basics to get you started, you have a lot more to learn about Excel and how it can help you analyze your data. I encourage you to dig deeper into these features. The next chapter is the first of three in which you will look at another useful interface for your Power Pivot model. Power View provides a rich interactive interface for users to explore the data. You will first look at optimizing models for analysis in Power View, next you will create standard reports using Power View, after that, you will look at creating compelling interactive reports in Power View.

Building Interactive Reports and Dashboards with Power View

Optimizing Power Pivot Models for Power View

Power View is a worksheet type in Excel that lets users develop interactive visualizations that encourage ad-hoc exploration of the data. It is an ideal tool for users who are not Excel power users who want to explore and gain insight from the data. Since Power View visualizations are based on a Power Pivot model, you need to provide users with a solid model as a foundation for these visualizations. A good Power Pivot model tuned for use by Power View will make the difference between a great user experience and an extremely frustrating one. There are ways to optimize a Power Pivot model so that it facilitates better report creation in Power View. This chapter reviews these settings and shows how to create models that provide support for many Power View features.

After completing this chapter you will be able to

- Understand the types of visualizations available in Power View.

- Create basic visualizations in Power View.

- Set properties in the Power Pivot model to improve the Power View experience.

Note   For copies of color figures, go to Source Code/Downloads at http://www.apress.com/9781430264453.

Visualizing Data with Power View

As we saw in Chapter 7, you can create powerful data visualizations and perform in-depth data analysis using Excel pivot tables and charts. Chances are that if you are an Excel power user and perform detailed data analysis as part of your job function, these will be your tools of choice. On the other hand, if you need a tool that allows users to create quick and easy visualizations from your Power Pivot models, then Power View is a great option. You use Power View to create compelling dashboards that contain contextually linked visualizations that can be easily filtered, sorted, and drilled through. Power View reports can be hosted as a worksheet in Excel or in a SharePoint library. One added benefit is they can be exported to PowerPoint where they can be used for presentations while still retaining their interactivity. Figure 8-1 shows a sample of a Power View report with a linked chart and graph. When a bar is clicked on the chart, the graph is filtered by that country and year.

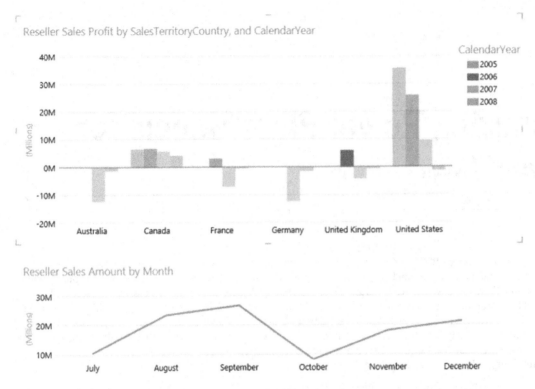

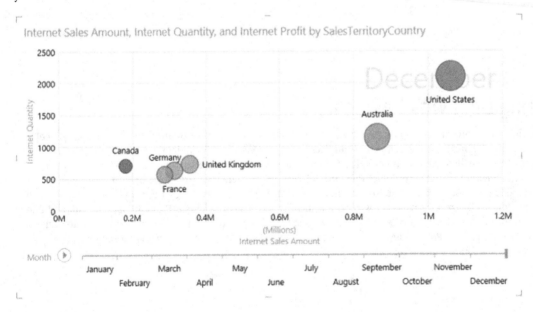

Figure 8-1. *An interactive chart and graph in Power View*

With Power View you can create the common visualizations such as tables, matrices, charts, and graphs. In addition, you can create bubble charts that include a time axis that reveals how the data changes over time (see Figure 8-2).

Figure 8-2. *Adding a play axis to a bubble chart*

Since Power View uses Bing Maps tiles, you can present your data on interactive maps that you can zoom in and pan down to street address level as you explore the data. Figure 8-3 shows a map of rainfall by county.

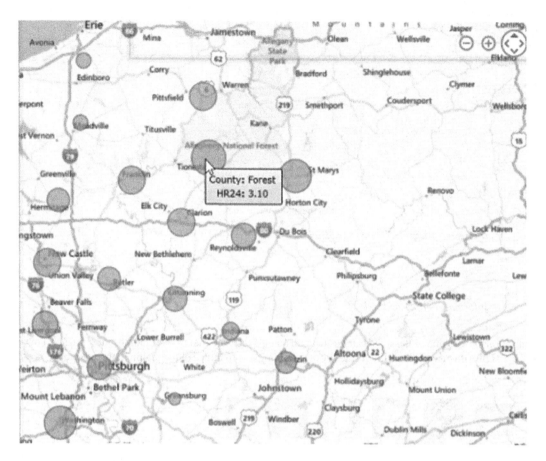

Figure 8-3. *Map of rainfall by county*

Two other data visualizations available in Power View are cards and tiles. *Cards* display the data from each row laid out in an index card style. For example, you can look at contact information for employees, as shown in Figure 8-4.

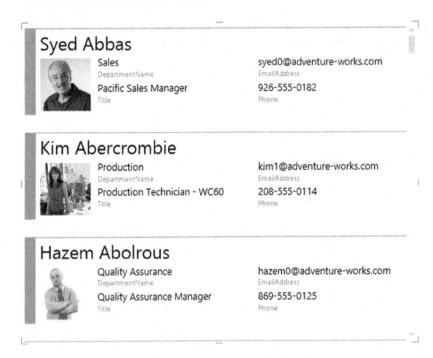

Figure 8-4. *Employee information in a card style*

A *tile* visualization allows you to interactively filter the data using a tab strip that can contain text and images. For example, Figure 8-5 shows the use of tiles to filter sales by region using a map image of the region in the tab strip.

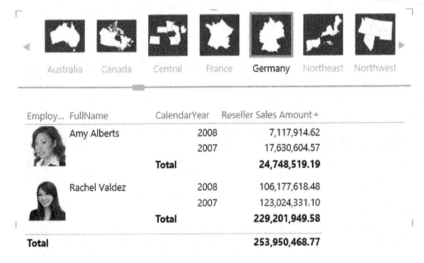

Figure 8-5. *Using tile images in Power View*

Now that you are familiar with some of the types of visualizations available in Power View, let's look at the process of creating some basic reports.

Creating a Basic Report

Power View reports are based on Power Pivot models in Excel. In order to create a report, open the Excel workbook that contains a model and on the Insert tab, click the Power View button (see Figure 8-6).

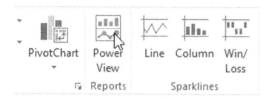

Figure 8-6. *Inserting a Power View report*

This will insert a new tab into the workbook and present you with the Power View design surface. The design has a Data Visualization area, a Filters area, and a Power View Fields window. The Power View Fields window contains the tables and fields of the Power Pivot model that are exposed to the client tools (see Figure 8-7).

Figure 8-7. *The Power View design surface*

One of the keys to creating visualizations in Power View is to begin with a table view, and then once you have the fields selected, you can switch the table view to one of the other data visualization types. If you expand the table nodes in the Power View Field List, you will see the available fields. If you want to create a bar chart showing sales by sales territory, first drag the desired fields to the Fields drop area. This will create a table view on the design surface. Selecting the table view then allows you to choose a different visualization type on the Design tab (see Figure 8-8).

Table
Bar Chart
Column Chart
Other Chart
Map
Tiles
Tile Type
Slicer
Switch Visualization
Tiles
Slicer
SalesTerritoryCountry
Reseller Sales Amount
Australia 204,074,928.22
Canada 1,840,374,476.35
France 589,764,855.68
Germany 253,950,468.77
United Kingdom 547,713,129.80
United States 6,861,798,554.91
Total 10,297,676,413.73

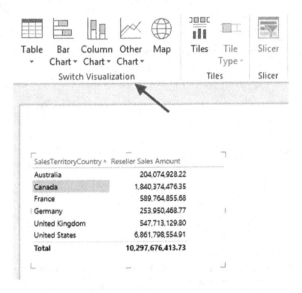

Figure 8-8. *Changing the visualization*

Once you switch the visualization, the drop areas under the Field List will change based on the visualization type. Figure 8-9 shows the drop areas for a bar chart. You may have to rearrange the fields and you can add additional fields to the drop area to get the visualization you want.

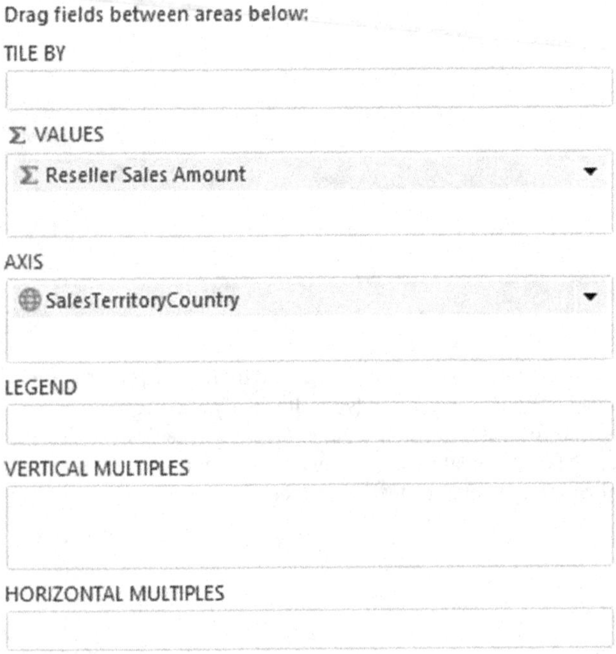

Drag fields between areas below:
TILE BY
Σ VALUES
Σ Reseller Sales Amount
AXIS
SalesTerritoryCountry
LEGEND
VERTICAL MULTIPLES
HORIZONTAL MULTIPLES

Figure 8-9. *The bar chart drop areas*

You can easily change visualizations from one type to another. For example, if you select the bar chart and select the other chart drop-down in the Design tab, you can switch it to a pie chart (see Figure 8-10).

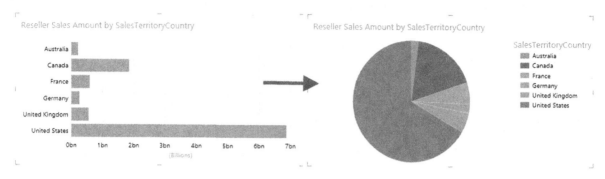

Figure 8-10. *Switching visualization types*

Now that you have seen how to create a basic visualization (you will look at creating more complex visualizations in Chapters 9 and 10), let's look at what you can do with the Power Pivot model to improve the designer and user experience in Power View.

Improving the Power View Experience

It is very important that users of your Power Pivot models have a pleasant experience as they build and explore the various visualizations in Power View. For example, you should only expose fields that users find meaningful. It is always a good idea to hide key values that are used to relate the tables in the model. To hide a column from the list of available fields in Power View, right click the column and select Hide From Client Tools (this will turn the column gray in the Model Designer). Figure 8-11 shows hiding a CustomerID field that has no business relevance.

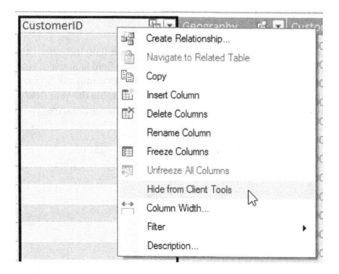

Figure 8-11. *Hiding fields from client tools*

If you look at the bottom of the pop-up menu in Figure 8-11, you will see that you can enter a description for the field. This description will show up when you hover over the field in Power View. This option is also available for measures created in the model and can be very useful for business users who need to understand how the measure is defined. Figure 8-12 shows the description displayed in Power View.

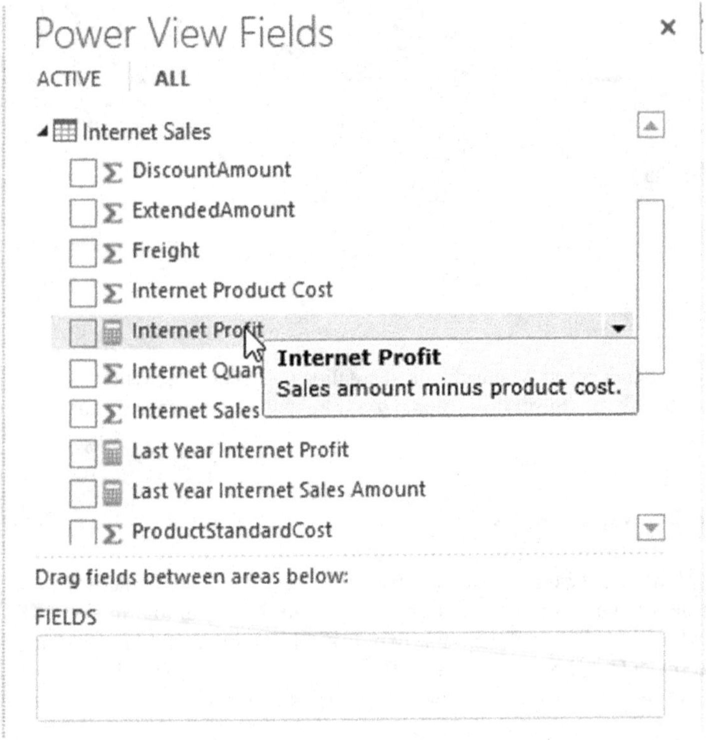

Figure 8-12. *Adding field descriptions improves the user experience*

As you look at the Field List in Figure 8-12, notice the icons in front of the fields. The calculator icon indicates that the field is a measure created in the Power Pivot model. The summation symbol indicates that the field is numeric and will be aggregated when dragged to the Fields drop area. By default the aggregate is a summation that may not be the aggregate needed. In some cases you do not want to aggregate a number; for example, in the date table the year field is not meant to be aggregated. You can control this behavior in the Power Pivot model by setting the Summarize By drop-down on the Advanced tab (see Figure 8-13).

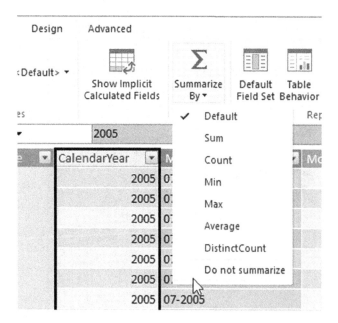

Figure 8-13. *Setting default summarizations for fields*

Along with setting field level properties, you can set some table level properties in the Power Pivot model that make creating reports in Power View easier. If you look at the Advanced tab for a table in the Power Pivot Model Designer, you will see a Default Field Set button (see Figure 8-13). Selecting this will allow you to designate the default field set for the table (see Figure 8-14). When set, this will allow the Power View user to quickly create a table by clicking the table node in the Power View Field List (see Figure 8-15).

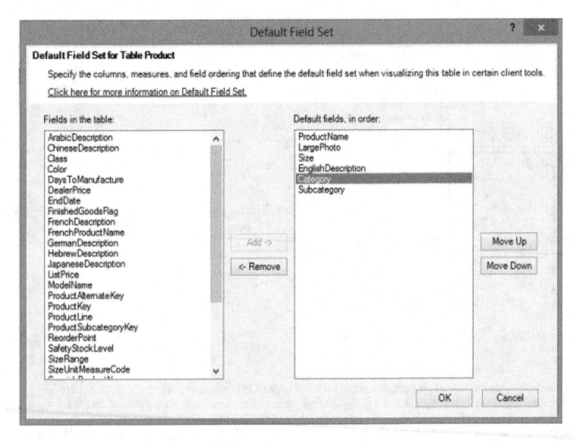

Figure 8-14. Setting default fields for a table

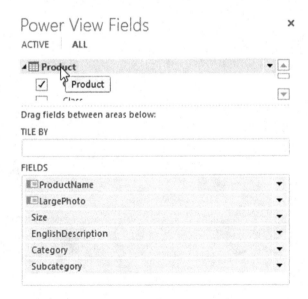

Figure 8-15. Using default fields in Power View

When you create visualizations in Power View, it groups items automatically depending on what fields are selected and the type of visualization selected. You can control how grouping is evaluated by setting the Table Behavior properties in the Power Pivot model. You can access the Table Behavior properties on the Advanced tab in the Model Designer (see Figure 8-13). When clicked, the Table Behavior button will display the Table Behavior settings window (see Figure 8-16).

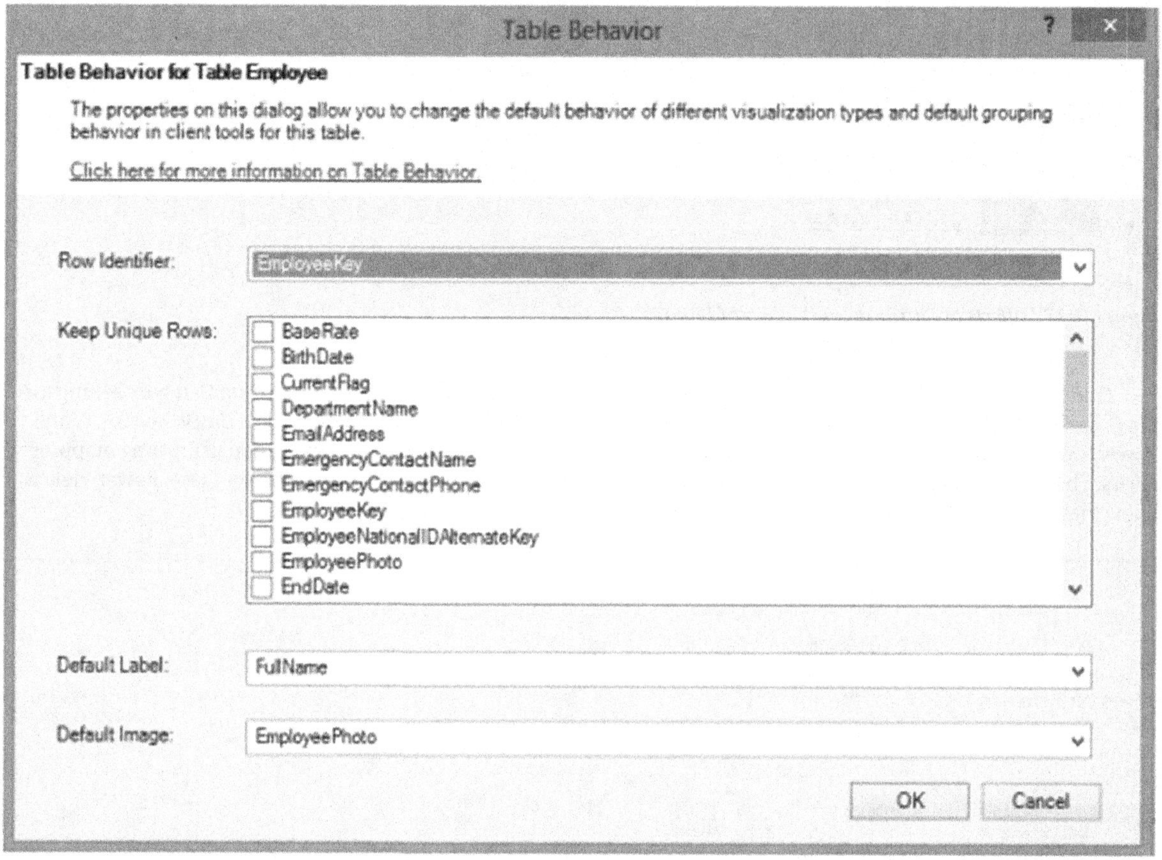

Figure 8-16. *Setting the table behavior*

The Table Behavior properties you can set for a table are the row identifier, any columns that indicate uniqueness, the default label, and the default image. The row identifier is used to indicate the field that uniquely identifies each row (often referred to as the primary key). This field needs to be unique and cannot be blank. Once the row identifier is set, you can choose which columns contain values that should remain unique. For example, you may have two employees with the same name and you do not want to group records of one employee with those of the other. The default label and default image are used in the Power View card and tile type visualizations, and when set, give a nicer formatting style. Figure 8-17 shows the same card with two different formats. The top card shows the format when the default label and image is set and the bottom card shows the format when they are not set.

Figure 8-17. *Effects of setting default label and image*

One last setting available on the Advanced tab of the Power Pivot Model Designer is the Data Category setting for the fields (see Figure 8-18). This comes into play for location types like City, Postal Code, and Country/Region. When Power View knows the column is a location type, it can use the field to implement a visualization using Bing mapping layers. The other data categories that are useful to set are the image and web URLs. When you set these, Power View will know these are hyperlinks and format them appropriately.

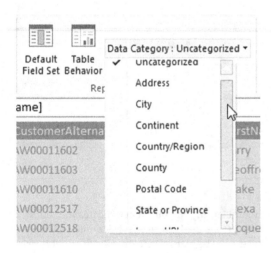

Figure 8-18. *Setting the data category for a field*

At this point you should have a good understanding of how the settings in the Power Pivot model affect the user experience in Power View. In the following lab, you will gain hands-on experience working with these properties.

HANDS-ON LAB—OPTIMIZING A POWER PIVOT MODEL FOR POWER VIEW

In the following lab you will

- Optimize a Power Pivot model for Power View.

- Create a table and a card visualization in Power View.

- Explore table view filtering.

1. In the LabStarters folder, open the LabChapter8.xlsx file. This file contains sales data from the test AdventureWorks database.

2. Select the Insert tab in Excel and click on the Power View button. This will insert a Power View report sheet in the workbook. In the Power View Fields window expand the Customer node and observe the Field List (see Figure 8-19).

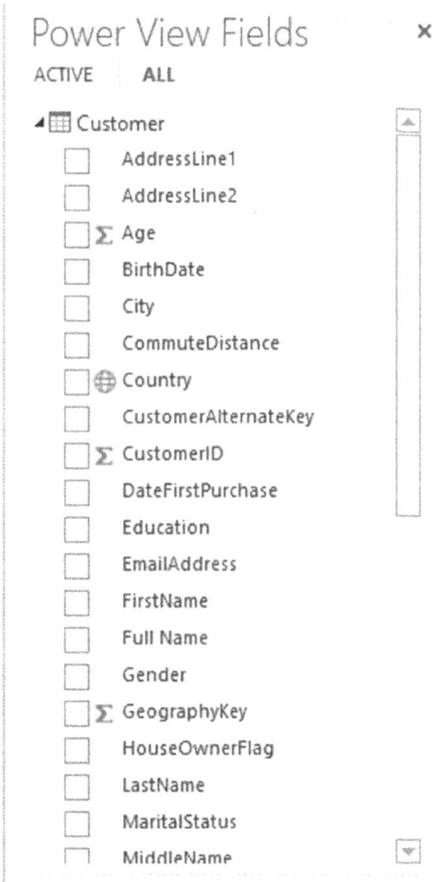

Power View Fields   ✕

ACTIVE   **ALL**

◢ ▦ Customer
- ☐   AddressLine1
- ☐   AddressLine2
- ☐ Σ Age
- ☐   BirthDate
- ☐   City
- ☐   CommuteDistance
- ☐ ⊕ Country
- ☐   CustomerAlternateKey
- ☐ Σ CustomerID
- ☐   DateFirstPurchase
- ☐   Education
- ☐   EmailAddress
- ☐   FirstName
- ☐   Full Name
- ☐   Gender
- ☐ Σ GeographyKey
- ☐   HouseOwnerFlag
- ☐   LastName
- ☐   MaritalStatus
- ☐   MiddleName

Figure 8-19. *Customer fields exposed to Power View*

3. Notice that the CustomerID, CustomerAlternateKey, and the GeographyKey are exposed to the users. Go to the Power Pivot model and hide these keys.

4. If you look at the Age field in Figure 8-19 you see a summation symbol in front of the field. This means it will sum up the ages if you drag this field to the drop area. To change this in the Power Pivot model, select the Age column, and on the Advanced tab under the Summarize By drop-down, select Do Not Summarize. Repeat this for the columns NumberCarsOwned, NumberChildrenAtHome, and TotalChildren.

5. If you look at the Country field in Figure 8-19, you see a globe icon in front of the field. This indicates this field is a location type field. To verify this, select the Country field in the Power Pivot model and select the Advanced tab. Notice the Data Category has been set to Country/Region (Suggested). The model used the name of the column to guess this setting.

6. Set the StateProvince and City columns to the appropriate data category. Go back to the Power View Field List and notice these fields now have globe icons.

7. In the Power View Field List expand the Date table. Notice that there are a lot of default summations that you do not want and there are a bunch of fields you do not want to show. Update the model so that the final Field List looks like Figure 8-20. Also set the MonthName column to be sorted by MonthNumberOfYear and add a Calendar and Fiscal hierarchy to the model.

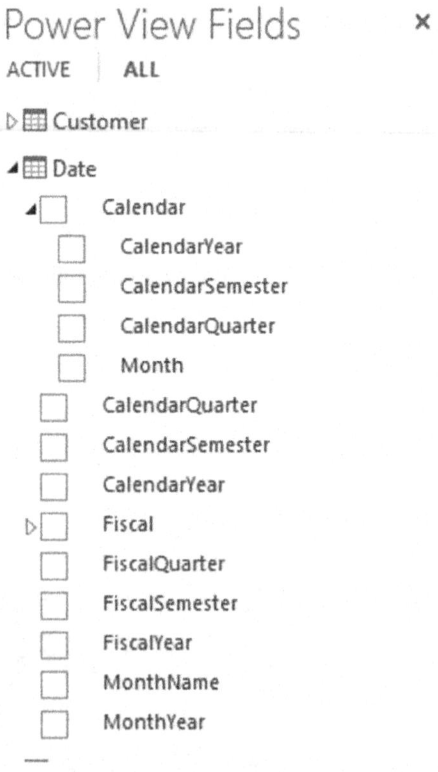

Power View Fields   ✕

ACTIVE   ALL

▷ ⊞ Customer

◢ ⊞ Date

   ◢ ☐   Calendar

       ☐   CalendarYear

       ☐   CalendarSemester

       ☐   CalendarQuarter

       ☐   Month

    ☐   CalendarQuarter

    ☐   CalendarSemester

    ☐   CalendarYear

   ▷ ☐   Fiscal

    ☐   FiscalQuarter

    ☐   FiscalSemester

    ☐   FiscalYear

    ☐   MonthName

    ☐   MonthYear

Figure 8-20. *Updated date fields*

8. Expand the Employee table in the Power View Field List. The Power Pivot model contains a photo of each employee, but it is not being recognized by Power View. To remedy this, go to the Power Pivot model, select the Employee table, and on the Advanced tab, select the Table Behavior button. In the Table Behavior settings window, set the Row Identifier to EmployeeKey. Set Keep Unique Rows to FullName. Set the Default Label to FullName and the Default Image to EmployeePhoto (see Figure 8-21).

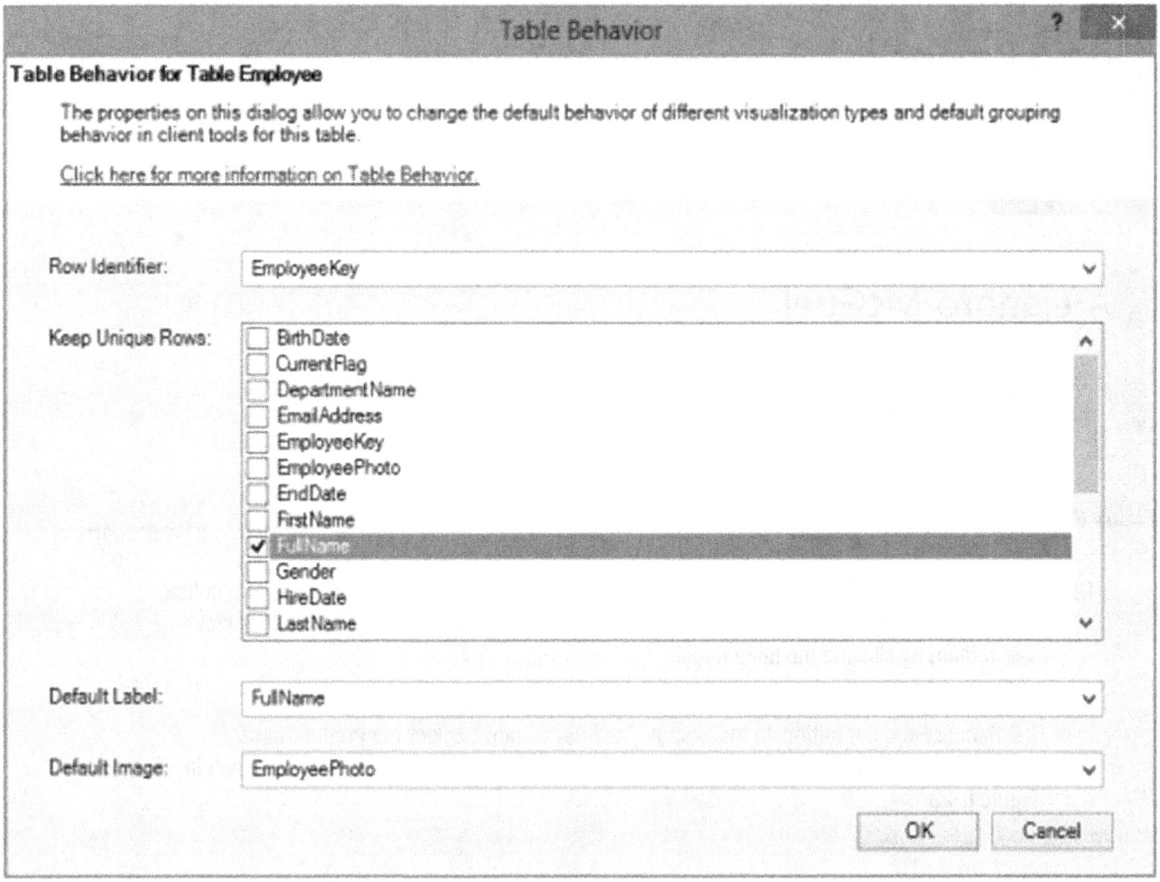

Figure 8-21. *Setting table behavior properties*

9. Go back to the Power View Field List and expand the Employee table. Notice you can now see the EmployeePhoto field. Also notice there is a new icon in front of the EmployeePhoto and FullName fields indicating these are default fields.

10. Drag and drop the FullName, EmployeePhoto, Title, and Phone to the Fields drop area below the Field List. Notice the table being built on the view surface.

11. Once you have a basic table built, you can convert it to another type of visualization. In the Design tab, select the Table drop-down and change the visualization to the Card type. You should end up with a visualization similar to Figure 8-22.

A. Scott Wright

Master Scheduler
Title

992-555-0194
Phone

Alan Brewer

Scheduling Assistant
Title

438-555-0172
Phone

Alejandro McGuel

Production Technician - WC40
Title

668-555-0130
Phone

Figure 8-22. *Creating employee cards*

12. Insert a new Power View sheet into the workbook. Expand the Product table node and notice the large number of fields. To help the users, you can set the default field set so they can select them by clicking the table node.

13. In the Power Pivot model, select the Product table and on the Advanced tab, click on the Default Field Set button. In the Default Field Set window, select the ProductName, ProductLine, Category, Subcategory, StandardCost, DealerPrice, and ListPrice, as shown in Figure 8-23.

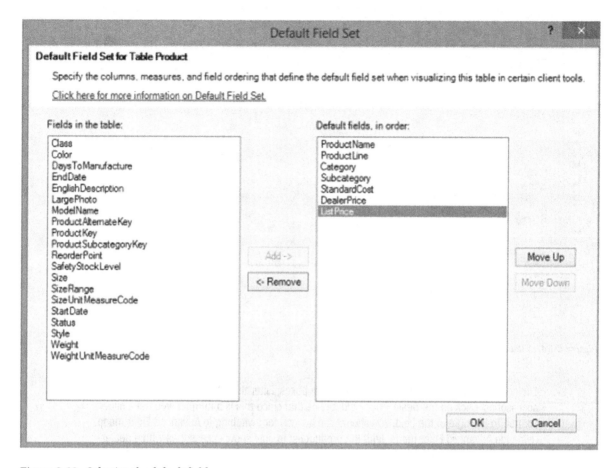

Figure 8-23. *Selecting the default fields*

14. Go back to the Power View sheet and click on the Product table in the Power View Field List. You should see a new table created consisting of the default fields you selected in step 13.

15. With the table selected, click on the Power View tab and notice that you can change the theme, font, and text size. Experiment with changing these settings. Add a title of Product List to the Power View sheet.

16. Notice that by clicking on the column header in the table you can sort by any of the columns ascending or descending. In the upper right corner of the table is a filter icon. Click on this to show the table filters (see Figure 8-24).

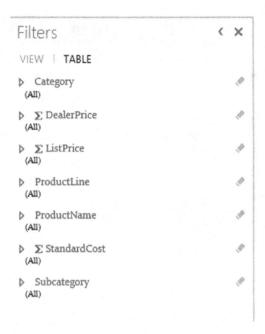

Figure 8-24. *Viewing table filters*

17. Click on the Category field to show the selection boxes. Filter the table to just show accessories. Click on the DealerPrice field; notice that since this is a number, you get a slider control. To the right of the field, you should see an icon for switching to Advanced Filter mode. Using the Advanced Filter mode, limit the product list to only show accessories with a dealer price greater than or equal to $25.

18. Experiment with changing and clearing the filters. When you're done, save your changes and exit Excel.

Summary

A good Power Pivot model tuned for use by Power View will make the difference between a great user experience and an extremely exasperating one. This chapter showed you how to optimize a Power Pivot model so that it facilitates better report creation in Power View. You saw how to set Table Behavior properties and column properties and how these settings affect the Power View experience. You also became familiar with creating cards and tables in Power View and how to filter and sort the tables. The next chapter delves deeper into the features of the Power View report designer. It shows how to create the fundamental visualization types along with the interaction features built into these visualizations. Cross view filtering, drill-down features, and slicers are discussed and demonstrated.

CHAPTER 9

Creating Standard Visualizations with Power View

In the last chapter you saw how important it is to create a Power Pivot model that works well with Power View. In this chapter you will investigate some of the standard visualizations used to create reports and dashboards. You will become familiar with the common features of the Power View designer. You will build standard visualizations such as column, bar, and pie charts. In addition, you will look at using a scatter chart and how to turn it into a bubble chart with a play axis. The final visualization you will investigate is how to use maps to analyze data geographically.

After completing this chapter you will be able to

- Create tables and matrices.
- Construct bar, column, and pie charts.
- Build line and scatter charts.
- Create map-based visualizations.

Note For copies of color figures, go to Source Code/Downloads at http://www.apress.com/9781430264453.

Creating Tables and Matrices

As you learned in the last chapter, all visualizations in Power View start off as a table and are then converted to another type of visualization. Although it is one of the most basic types of data visualization, a table is still one of the most useful ways to look at your data. This is especially true if you need to look up detailed information. Figure 9-1 shows a table displaying customer contact information.

Full Name	AddressLine1	City	StateProvince	Country	PhoneNumber
Aaron Adams	4116 Stanbridge Ct.	Downey	California	United States	417-555-0154
Aaron Alexander	5021 Rio Grande Drive	Kirkland	Washington	United States	548-555-0129
Aaron Allen	6695 Black Walnut Court	Sooke	British Columbia	Canada	648-555-0141
Aaron Baker	8054 Olivera Rd.	Renton	Washington	United States	488-555-0125
Aaron Bryant	2325 Candywood Ct	Redwood City	California	United States	754-555-0137
Aaron Butler	9761 Darnett Circle	Lebanon	Oregon	United States	466-555-0180
Aaron Campbell	3310 Harvey Way	Bellflower	California	United States	187-555-0177
Aaron Carter	3450 Rio Grande Dr.	Woodland Hills	California	United States	180-555-0167
Aaron Chen	4633 Jefferson Street	Los Angeles	California	United States	969-555-0160
Aaron Coleman	3393 Alpha Way	Santa Monica	California	United States	914-555-0128
Aaron Collins	6767 Stinson	Santa Cruz	California	United States	170-555-0177
Aaron Diaz	9413 Maria Vega Court	Melton	Victoria	Australia	1 (11) 500...
Aaron Edwards	663 Contra Loma Blvd.	Beverly Hills	California	United States	355-555-0115

Figure 9-1. *Customer contact information*

When you combine a table with the automatic filtering you get with Power View, this becomes a great way to look up customers based on their demographic data. When you select the table in the view, click on the Table tab in the Filters area (see Figure 9-2). The fields in the table will show up automatically in the table filter list. To add a field to the filter list that you want to filter on but do not want to show up in the table, just drag the field from the Power View Field List to the Filters area.

Figure 9-2. *Filtering a table*

Another way you can implement filtering for the table is using slicers. To create a slicer, first create a one-column table using the field you want to slice by. Select the table on the view surface and, in the Design tab, click on the Slicer button (see Figure 9-3).

Figure 9-3. *Creating a slicer*

Slicers will filter all data on the view—even other slicers. Figure 9-4 shows how the selection in a Country slicer limits what is shown in the StateProvince slicer.

Figure 9-4. *Filtering with slicers*

A matrix is similar to a table in that it contains rows and columns, but instead of showing detail level records, it aggregates data up by the fields displayed in the row and column headers. When you create a pivot table in Excel it is essentially a matrix. If the matrix contains a hierarchy, you can drill up and down through the hierarchy. To create a matrix, start with a table and then convert it to a matrix. Figure 9-5 shows a table created to show sales profit for the different types of resellers for each month.

BusinessType	Reseller Sales Profit	CalendarYear	CalendarSemester	CalendarQuarter	Month
Specialty Bike Shop	$212,586.00	2005	2	3	July
Specialty Bike Shop	$1,370,508.70	2005	2	3	August
Specialty Bike Shop	$696,521.77	2005	2	3	September
Specialty Bike Shop	$271,020.65	2005	2	4	October
Specialty Bike Shop	$1,924,803.56	2005	2	4	November
Specialty Bike Shop	$1,023,151.24	2005	2	4	December
Specialty Bike Shop	$505,052.90	2006	1	1	January
Specialty Bike Shop	$1,521,877.95	2006	1	1	February
Specialty Bike Shop	$1,166,848.26	2006	1	1	March
Specialty Bike Shop	$909,624.09	2006	1	2	April
Specialty Bike Shop	$1,334,939.74	2006	1	2	May
Specialty Bike Shop	($9,513,763.39)	2006	1	2	June
Specialty Bike Shop	$268,083.52	2006	2	3	July
Specialty Bike Shop	$2,952,383.04	2006	2	3	August
Specialty Bike Shop	$2,834,482.60	2006	2	3	September
Specialty Bike Shop	$348,372.21	2006	2	4	October

Figure 9-5. *Table showing reseller sales by type and month*

As you can see, a table is not the best way to display this type of information. It would be much easier to decipher the information in a matrix where you can compare totals and drill down or up through the year, quarter, and month. To change this to a matrix, select the table and, on the Design tab, select the Table drop-down and select Matrix (see Figure 9-6).

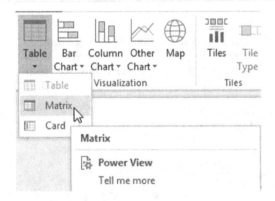

Figure 9-6. *Converting a table to a matrix*

As you can see in Figure 9-7, converting the table to a matrix added totals and subtotals.

BusinessType	CalendarYear ▲	CalendarSemester	CalendarQuarter	Month	Reseller Sales Profit
Specialty Bike Shop	2005	2	3	July	$212,586.00
				August	$1,370,508.70
				September	$696,521.77
				Total	$2,279,616.46
			4	October	$271,020.65
				November	$1,924,803.56
				December	$1,023,151.24
				Total	$3,218,975.45
			Total		$5,498,591.91
		Total			$5,498,591.91

Figure 9-7. Matrix containing totals and subtotals

If you look at the drop areas under the Field List, you should see a drop area for values, rows, and columns. To improve the look of the matrix, you can drag the BusinessType field to the Columns drop area. You can now easily compare the reseller types side by side (see Figure 9-8).

CalendarYear ▲	CalendarSemester	CalendarQuarter	Month	Specialty Bike Shop	Value Added Reseller	Warehouse	Total
2005	2	3	July	$212,586.00	$1,250,411.42	$717,282.39	$2,180,279.81
			August	$1,370,508.70	$2,003,003.75	$5,451,925.41	$8,825,437.86
			September	$696,521.77	$1,184,363.39	$5,468,098.30	$7,348,983.46
			Total	$2,279,616.46	$4,437,778.56	$11,637,306.11	$18,354,701.13
		4	October	$271,020.65	$2,429,595.96	$831,090.94	$3,531,707.55
			November	$1,924,803.56	$3,185,420.43	$6,163,078.99	$11,273,302.98
			December	$1,023,151.24	$1,369,984.64	$6,549,818.06	$8,942,953.95
			Total	$3,218,975.45	$6,985,001.02	$13,543,987.99	$23,747,964.47
		Total		$5,498,591.91	$11,422,779.58	$25,181,294.11	$42,102,665.60
	Total			$5,498,591.91	$11,422,779.58	$25,181,294.11	$42,102,665.60

Figure 9-8. Comparing reseller types by profit

To control totals and drilling for the matrix under the Design tab, use the Show Levels and Totals drop-downs (see Figure 9-9).

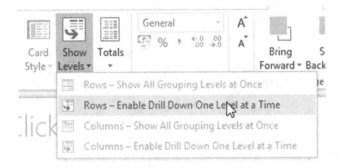

Figure 9-9. *Enabling drill-down for a matrix*

Once drill-down is enabled, the matrix collapses to only show the year level. When you click on a year, you will see an arrow icon that allows you to drill down to the next level in the calendar hierarchy (see Figure 9-10). As you drill down through the hierarchy, you will see another arrow that allows you to drill back up through the hierarchy.

CalendarYear ▲	Specialty Bike Shop	Value Added Reseller	Warehouse	Total
2005	$5,498,591.91	$11,422,779.58	$25,181,294.11	$42,102,665.60
2006	$4,915,357.61	$31,061,523.47	$5,418,547.89	$41,395,428.97
2007	($4,633,634.88)	$13,840,520.29	($30,782,275.34)	($21,575,389.93)
2008	($2,222,215.71)	$951,968.32	($430,684.03)	($1,700,931.42)
Total	$3,558,098.93	$57,276,791.67	($613,117.38)	$60,221,773.22

Figure 9-10. *Drilling down through a hierarchy*

In addition to wanting to see aggregated values in a matrix, you often want to show these values using a visual representation such as a bar, column, or pie chart. You will look at creating these next.

Constructing Bar, Column, and Pie Charts

Some of the most common data visualizations used to compare data are the bar, column, and pie charts. A bar chart and a column chart are very similar. The bar chart has horizontal bars where the x axis is the value of the measure whereas the y axis contains the categories you are comparing. For example, Figure 9-11 shows a bar chart comparing Internet sales by country.

Internet Sales Amount by Country

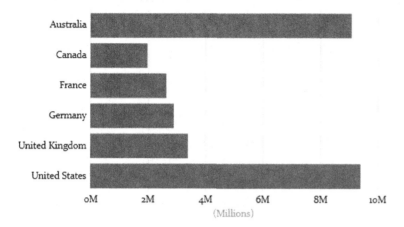

Figure 9-11. *Bar chart comparing sales by country*

The column chart switches the axes so that the measure amounts are on the y axis and the categories are on the x axis. For example, the bar chart in Figure 9-11 can just as easily be displayed as a column chart as shown in Figure 9-12.

Internet Sales Amount by Country

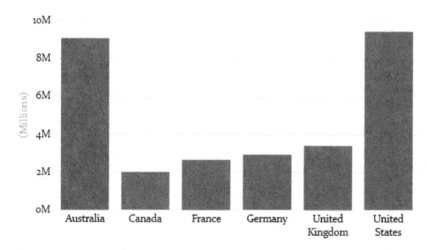

Figure 9-12. *A column chart comparing Internet sales by country*

There are three types of bar or column charts to choose from: stacked, 100% stacked, and clustered. Figure 9-12 is a stacked column chart that does not have a field for the legend. If you drag the Year field to the Legend drop area, it changes the visualization to the one shown in Figure 9-13. Notice the values for each year are stacked on top of each other.

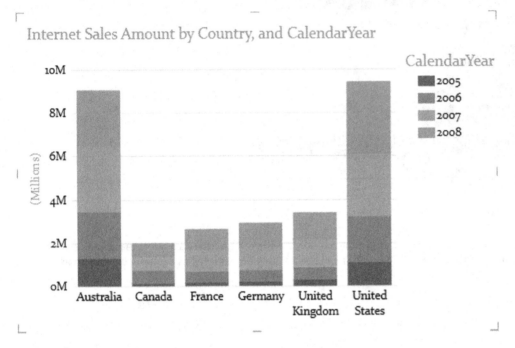

Figure 9-13. *Creating a stacked column chart*

Although the stacked column chart shows absolute values, you can change it to a 100% stacked chart to show relative values in terms of percentages. In Figure 9-14 the Country field is moved to the legend and the Year field is placed on the axis. It also has data labels set as Visible for easier comparisons.

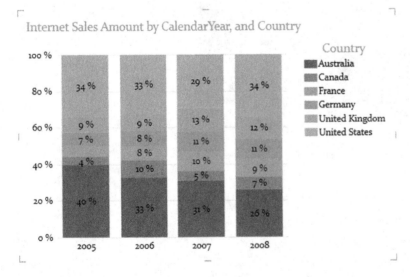

Figure 9-14. *Creating a 100% stacked column chart*

A clustered column chart moves the columns for the various countries side by side instead of stacking them on top of one another. Figure 9-15 shows the same information as Figure 9-13 does, but as a clustered column chart.

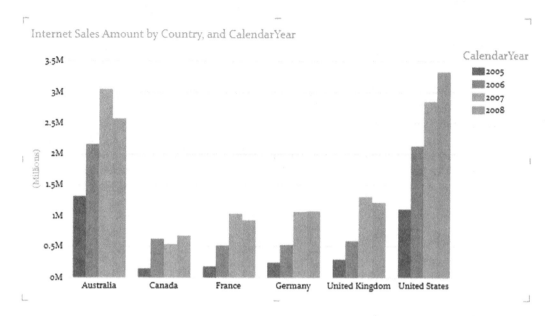

Figure 9-15. *Creating a clustered column chart*

Although you do not have much control over the layout of the charts, on the Design tab, you can control the title, legend, and data labels (see Figure 9-16).

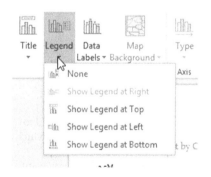

Figure 9-16. *Controlling the legend layout*

As with most visualizations, in Power View you get automatic filtering and sorting capabilities. For example, if you hover over the upper left corner of the chart in Figure 9-15, you get the option to change the sorting by Internet sales amount instead of country name (see Figure 9-17).

Internet Sales Amount by Country, and CalendarYear

3.5M

Figure 9-17. *Changing the sorting of a column chart*

Pie charts are similar to stacked column or stacked bar charts in that they allow you to compare the measures for members of a category and also the total for the category. Figure 9-18 shows a pie chart comparing sales of different types of resellers.

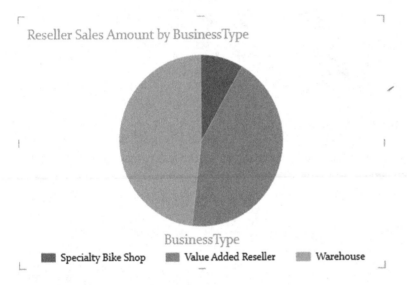

Figure 9-18. *Comparing data using a pie chart*

Just as with column and bar charts, you have very little control over the layout of the pie chart and are limited to the title and the positioning of the legend. At the time of this writing, pie charts do not even support data labels, which is truly unfortunate.

Although bar, column, and pie charts are great for comparing aggregated data for various categories, if you want to spot trends in the data, line and scatter charts are a better choice. You will investigate these types of charts next.

Building Line and Scatter Charts

A line chart is used to look at trends across equal periods. The periods are often time units consisting of hours, days, months, and so on. The time periods are plotted along the x axis and the measurement is plotted along the y axis. Figure 9-19 shows flight delays in minutes for the hours in the day. Each line represents a different carrier. Using this chart, you can easily spot trends throughout the day and compare carrier performance.

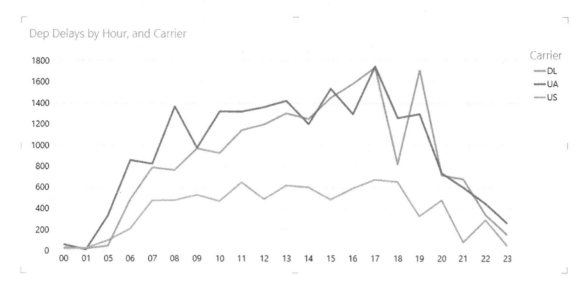

Figure 9-19. *Spotting trends using a line chart*

If you need to compare trending of two measures at the same time, you can use a scatter chart. Scatter charts plot one measure along the y axis and the other along the x axis. To create a scatter chart, create a table with a category field and two numeric fields—for example, reseller name (category), sales amount (numeric), and sales profit (numeric). After creating the table, switch the visualization to a scatter chart that is located under the Other Chart drop-down on the Design tab. Figure 9-20 shows the resulting scatter chart.

Figure 9-20. *Comparing data in a scatter chart*

Using the scatter chart you can easily spot trends and outliers that do not follow the trend.

If you look at the Field drop area for the scatter chart (see Figure 9-21), you see both a Size and a Color drop area. You can add another measure to the Size drop box and another category to the Color drop box.

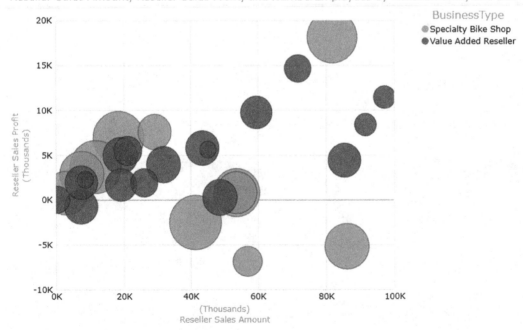

Figure 9-21. *Adding size and color to a scatter chart*

Once you add the size axis to the scatter chart, it becomes a bubble chart. Figure 9-22 shows a bubble chart where the size of the bubble represents the number of employees of the reseller and the color represents the reseller's business type.

Figure 9-22. *Comparing data in a bubble chart*

If you take a look at the drop area for the scatter chart, you should see another drop box labeled Play Axis. You can drop a time-based field in this box, which results in a play axis being placed below the scatter chart. The *play axis* allows you to look at how the measures vary over time. It allows you to play, pause, and retrace the changes as you perform your analysis. If you click on one of the bubbles in the chart, you can see a trace of the changes that occurred over the time period. Figure 9-23 shows a scatter chart that can be used to analyze how sales of products compare over time.

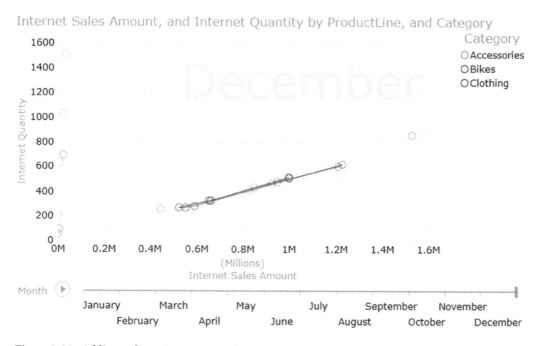

Figure 9-23. *Adding a play axis to a scatter chart*

In addition to the standard visualizations for comparing data, Power View allows you to look at data geographically using Bing Maps. You will see how to create map-based visualizations in the next section.

Creating Map-Based Visualizations

One of the nice features of Power View is that it can use Bing Maps tiles to create visualizations. If your data contains a geographic field such as city, state/province, and country, it is very easy to incorporate the data into a map. You can tell whether a field can be geolocated by a globe icon in the Field List (see Figure 9-24).

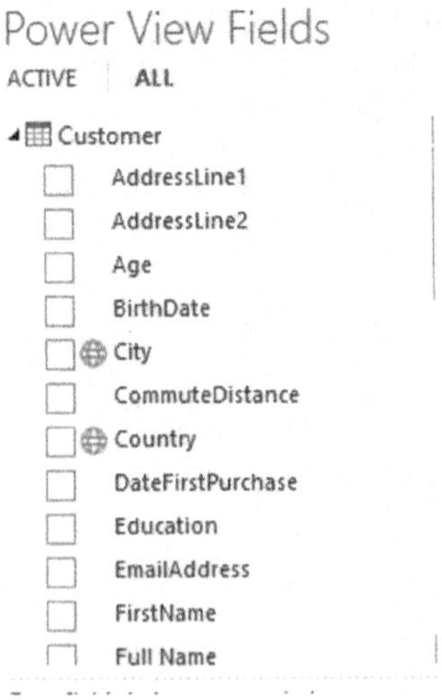

Power View Fields

ACTIVE   **ALL**

▲ ▦ Customer
- ☐   AddressLine1
- ☐   AddressLine2
- ☐   Age
- ☐   BirthDate
- ☐ ⊕ City
- ☐   CommuteDistance
- ☐ ⊕ Country
- ☐   DateFirstPurchase
- ☐   Education
- ☐   EmailAddress
- ☐   FirstName
- ☐   Full Name

Figure 9-24. *The globe icon indicates fields that can be mapped*

To create the map, first create a table with the geospatial field and the measure you want to see on the map. Once you have the table created, you can switch it to a map. The locations show up on the map as bubbles whose size indicates the value of the measure. Figure 9-25 shows sales by city where the map is zoomed in to the San Francisco, California area.

Internet Sales Amount by City

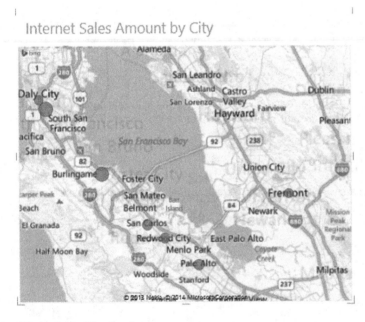

Figure 9-25. *Viewing data on a map*

If you look at the field drop areas of the map, you should see Longitude and Latitude drop boxes; this allows you to create precise location points on the map. There is also a color drop area where you can drop a category field. This will convert the bubbles on the map into pie charts showing each category (see Figure 9-26).

Figure 9-26. *Adding a category to the map*

Now that you have seen how to create the various visualizations available in Power View, it is time to get some hands-on experience creating a few.

HANDS-ON LAB—CREATING STANDARD VISUALIZATIONS IN POWER VIEW

In the following lab you will

- Create a bar, column, and pie chart.

- Create a line and scatter graph.

- Create a map-based visualization.

1. In the LabStarters folder, open the LabChapter9.xlsx file. This file contains sales data from the test AdventureWorks database.

2. Select the Insert tab in Excel and click on the Power View button. This will insert a Power View report sheet in the workbook.

3. Create a table that lists sales by territory or country and reseller sales.

4. With the table selected on the Power View sheet, switch the visualization to a clustered bar chart. Resize the chart. It should look similar to Figure 9-27.

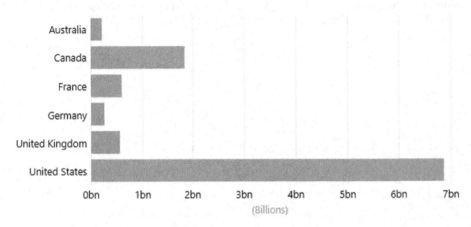

Figure 9-27. *Creating a bar chart*

5. With the bar chart selected, drag and drop the Reseller Business Type to the Legend drop box. The chart now displays a bar for each business type grouped by country.

6. Switch the chart to a 100% stacked bar chart. Under the Layout tab, change the setting to show the data labels. The chart should look like Figure 9-28.

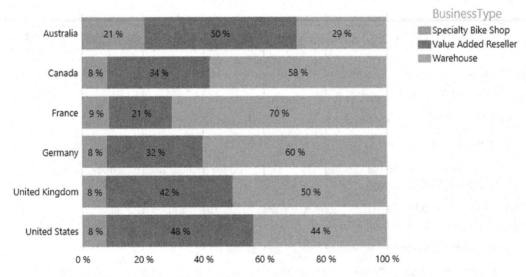

Figure 9-28. *Creating a 100% stacked bar chart*

7. On the Power View tab, click on the Power View button to insert a new Power View sheet. Create a stacked column chart that shows reseller sales profit by year and category. Your chart should look similar to Figure 9-29.

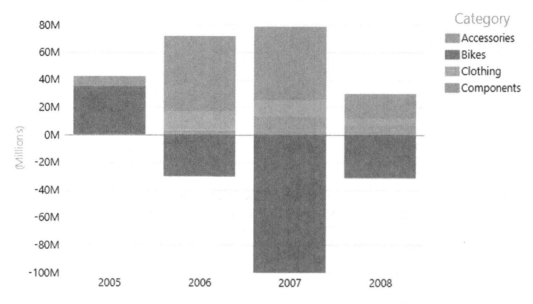

Figure 9-29. *Creating a stacked column chart*

8. Add a new Power View sheet. On this sheet, create a table that shows department names and average vacation hours. You will need to change the vacation hours from Sum to Average in the Fields drop area.

9. Switch the visualization to a pie chart. Under the chart Filters area, limit the chart to the Information Services, Marketing, Purchasing, and Sales departments. The chart should look similar to Figure 9-30.

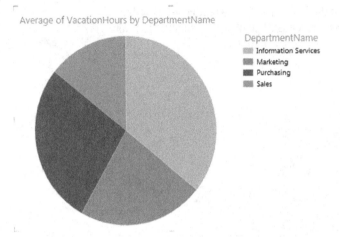

Average of VacationHours by DepartmentName

Figure 9-30. *Creating a pie chart*

10. To create a line chart, add a new Power View sheet and create a table containing month name and Internet sales amount. Switch the visualization to a line chart. Add the customer's country to the Legend drop area. The final chart should look like Figure 9-31. Notice the United States and Australia have peaks whereas the others are pretty steady.

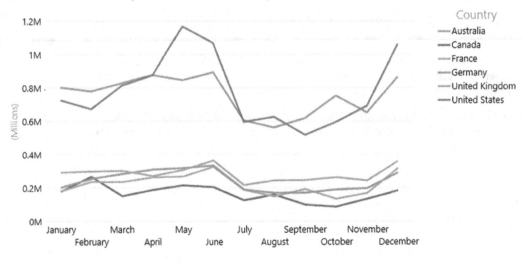

Internet Sales Amount by MonthName, and Country

Figure 9-31. *Comparing data in a line chart*

11. To create a scatter chart, add a new Power View sheet and create a table containing ResellerName, ResellerSalesProfit, and ResellerSales. Change the table to a scatter chart. Add the business type to the Color drop box.

12. Drag the SalesTerritoryCountry to the Chart Filters area and limit the chart so it will just show Germany. Create a play axis using the MonthYear. Using the play axis, determine who, when, and how much for the greatest profit loss. You should end up with a visualization similar to what appears in Figure 9-32.

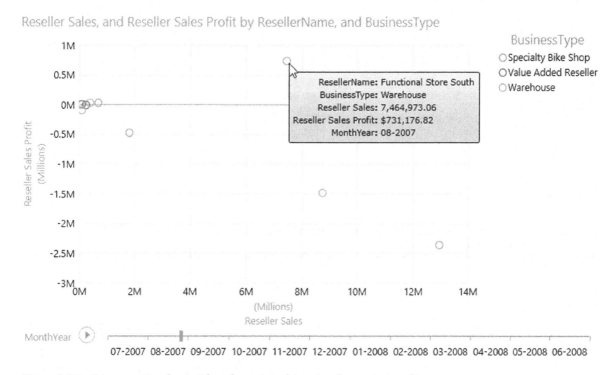

Figure 9-32. *Using a scatter chart with a play axis to determine the greatest profit*

13. To create a map-based visualization, insert a new Power View sheet into the workbook. Create a table using the customer FullName and customer StateProvince. Switch the table to a map and drag the Full Name field from the Color drop box to the Size drop box and change the aggregation to Distinct Count.

14. Drag the HouseOwnerFlag to the Color drop box. Zoom in to the western United States; your map should look similar to Figure 9-33.

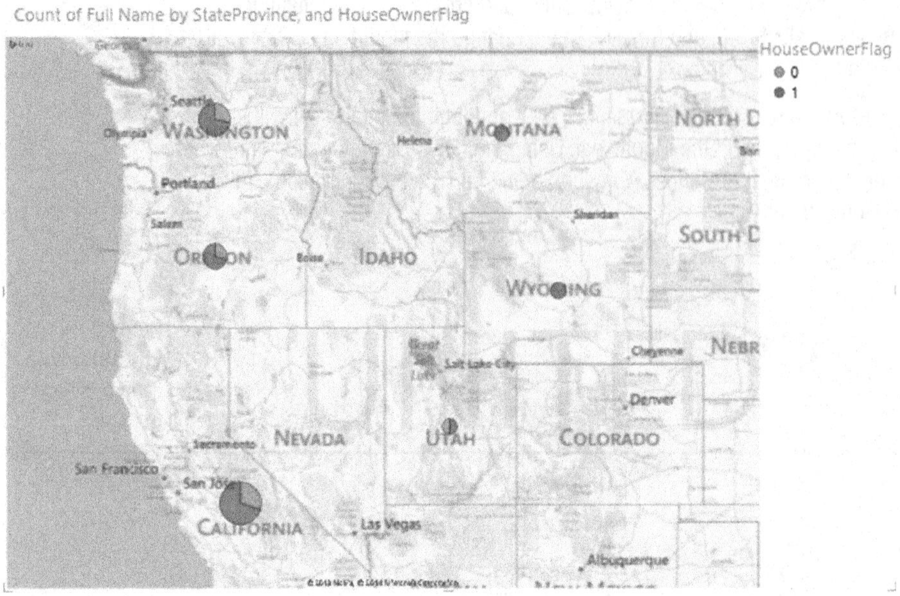

Count of Full Name by StateProvince, and HouseOwnerFlag

Figure 9-33. *Mapping the number of customers*

15. Experiment with mapping other fields and zooming to different areas of the map. When done, save your changes and exit Excel.

Summary

In this chapter you have seen how to create the various visualizations in Power View. You created the standard column, bar, and pie charts. You looked at line and scatter charts and how you create bubble charts and add a play axis to look at trends over time. In addition, you saw how to present measures tied to a geospatial field on a map. At this point, you should be comfortable creating the various visualizations in Power View. Up to this point, you have created each of the visualizations as a standalone chart or graph. One of the strengths of Power View is its ability to tie these visualizations together to create interactive dashboards. You will explore this in the next chapter.

■ ■ ■

Creating Interactive Dashboards with Power View

In the last chapter, you investigated some of the standard visualizations used to create reports and dashboards. In this chapter, you will combine these visualizations so they work together to form interactive dashboards. Interactive dashboards differ from a traditional dashboard by extending the user experience from passive to active. You can perform filtering, drill up or down through different levels of detail, and discover associations between the various metrics. You will also look at how you can group the data using tiles and create filters for the groups and views as a whole. In addition, you will look at how you can include images to enhance the dashboard experience.

After completing this chapter you will be able to

- Link visualizations in Power View.

- Use tiles to organize data.

- Filter groups and views.

- Expose dashboards to consumers.

■ **Note** For copies of color figures, go to Source Code/Downloads at http://www.apress.com/9781430264453.

Linking Visualizations in Power View

One of the strengths of Power View is that if the Power Pivot model contains a link between the data used to create the various visualizations, Power View will use the relationship to implement interactive filtering. *Interactive filtering* is when the process of filtering one visualization automatically filters a related visualization. For example, Figure 10-1 shows a bar chart that displays sales for the different product categories from the Adventure Works sample database.

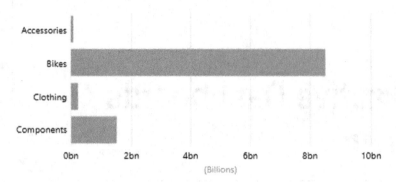

Figure 10-1. *Reseller sales by category*

To this view, you can add a column chart that shows various countries' sales, as shown in Figure 10-2.

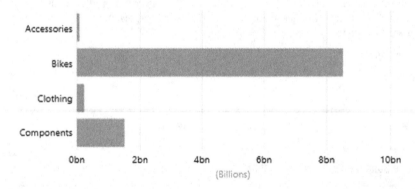

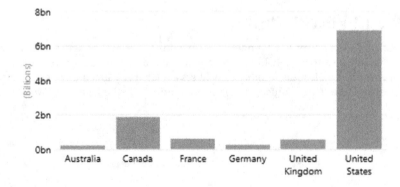

Figure 10-2. *Adding related visualizations to the same view*

Since the Sales table is related to the SalesTerritory table and the Product table, if you select one of the Product category bars, it will highlight the bar chart to show sales for that category (see Figure 10-3).

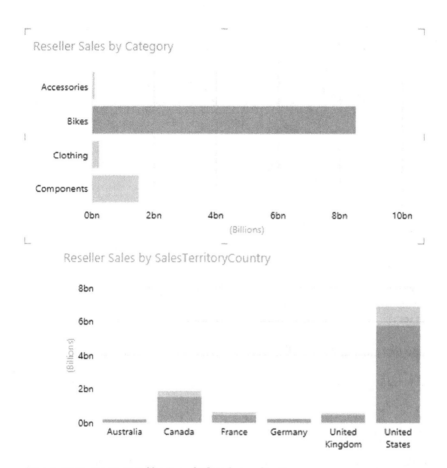

Figure 10-3. *Interactive filtering of related visualizations*

The filtering works both ways so you can click on one of the columns in the lower chart and it will filter the top chart to show sales for that country. This interactive filtering works for most types of visualizations available in Power View. Figure 10-4 shows a bubble chart and a table. When you click on a bubble the table is filtered to show the detail records that make up the bubble values.

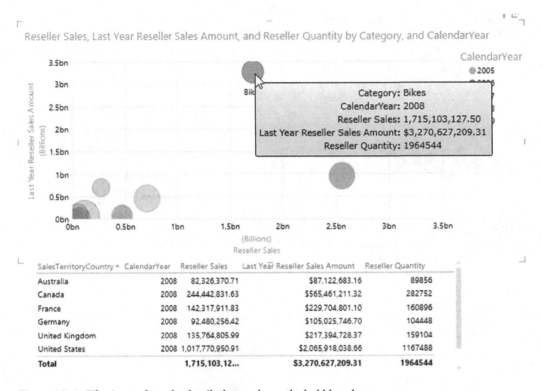

Reseller Sales, Last Year Reseller Sales Amount, and Reseller Quantity by Category, and CalendarYear

SalesTerritoryCountry ▲	CalendarYear	Reseller Sales	Last Year Reseller Sales Amount	Reseller Quantity
Australia	2008	82,326,370.71	$87,122,683.16	89856
Canada	2008	244,442,831.63	$565,461,211.32	282752
France	2008	142,317,911.83	$229,704,801.10	160896
Germany	2008	92,480,256.42	$105,025,746.70	104448
United Kingdom	2008	135,764,805.99	$217,394,728.37	159104
United States	2008	1,017,770,950.91	$2,065,918,038.66	1167488
Total		1,715,103,12...	$3,270,627,209.31	1964544

Figure 10-4. *Filtering to show the details that make up the bubble values*

Now that you understand how visualizations interact with each other, you are ready to see how you can group visualizations using tiles.

Using Tiles to Organize the Data

In the last section you saw how visualizations placed on the same view interact with each other. Another way to group visualizations together is to use tiles. First create a table containing the grouping criteria. For example, you may want to organize sales figures by sales regions. To do so, first create a table using the sales territory image, then change it to a tile type of visualization. You will see a visualization similar to the one in Figure 10-5.

Figure 10-5. *Creating a tile group*

In Figure 10-5, notice that the sales territory image is in both the Title field and the Details area. You can remove the field from the Details area and add data related to the sales territory from the Power Pivot model. For example, you can add the sales people assigned to the territory, their photo, their sales, and the sales year. This will create a table in the Details section of the tiles (see Figure 10-6).

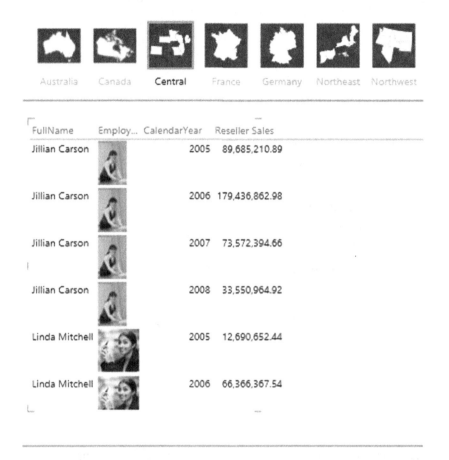

Figure 10-6. *Creating a table inside a tile*

You can change the detail visualization to another type—for example, a matrix. When you click on the various tiles, the details are filtered by the tile group (see Figure 10-7).

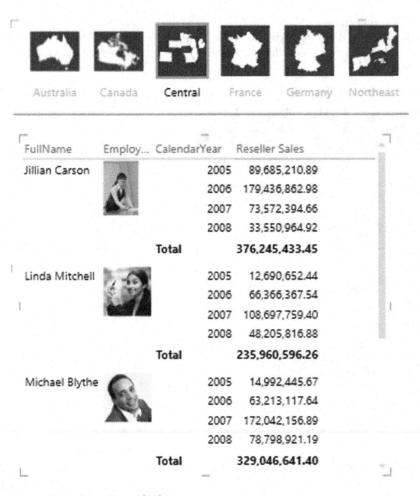

Figure 10-7. Grouping with tiles

If you click on the blank area of the tile's Detail section, you can build another visualization. For example, Figure 10-8 shows a matrix and a column chart that are both filtered by the tile chosen.

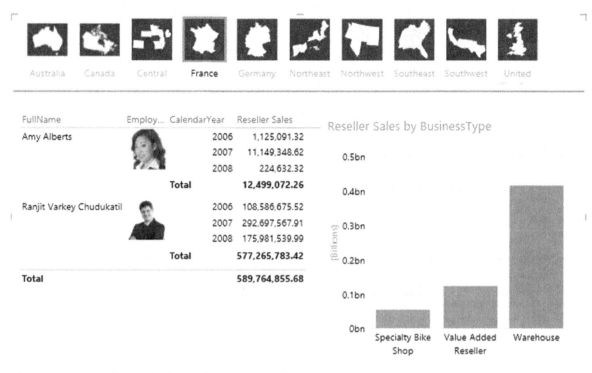

Figure 10-8. *Controlling multiple visualizations with tiles*

After grouping visualizations, make sure you understand how filtering affects visualizations grouped in tiles and on the view. You will look at this next.

Filtering Groups and Views

When you place multiple visualizations on the same view, you have the option of filtering the entire view (page) or the individual visualizations that make up the view. Figure 10-9 shows the Filters area where you can toggle between the View and the Chart tab. The View tab is for applying filters to all the visualizations on the page whereas the Chart tab will apply the filters to just the individual visualization (a chart, in this instance).

Figure 10-9. *Filtering the chart or view*

By default the visualization filter contains the fields that make up the visualization and these fields cannot be removed. You can, however, add additional fields to the filters from the Field List. When you first click on the View tab in the Filters area, there are no fields listed. To filter the values in the view, add fields from the Field List that are related to the fields contained in the visualizations on the view.

All filters have a list mode in which the values are displayed as a checkbox list (see Figure 10-10).

Figure 10-10. *Using a filter pick list*

You can also switch to advanced filtering mode by selecting the arrow to the right of the field name. The type of advanced filtering controls exposed in Power View depends on the data type of the filter. Figure 10-11 shows the advanced filtering controls exposed for a date field.

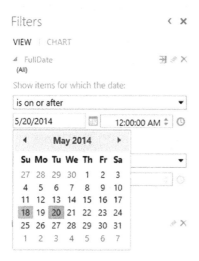

Figure 10-11. *Advanced filtering by date*

Figure 10-12 shows the options you get when advanced filtering is used with a text-based field.

Figure 10-12. *Advanced filtering using a text-based field*

Another way of filtering a view is using a slicer. Slicers are nice for users since they are part of the view. The downside to slicers is that they are limited to a pick list and do not expose the advanced filtering mentioned previously. Combining grouping with tiles and slicers can create different sets of filters. Figure 10-13 shows the same chart in a tile group and outside the tile group. Both charts are filtered by the CalendarYear slicer because they are located on the same view. The chart in the tile group is further filtered by the sales territory because it is part of the tile group.

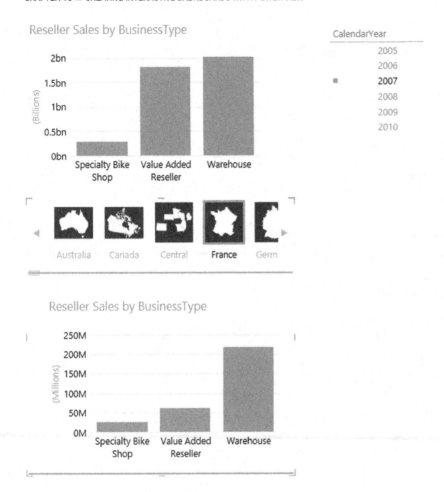

Figure 10-13. *Filtering with slicers and tiles*

Once you have built the dashboard it is time to expose it to users. You will briefly review your options in the following section.

Exposing the Dashboard

After constructing an interactive dashboard, the next step is to expose the dashboard to others, such as business analysts and managers, who want to explore the data. Since the Power Pivot model and the Power View visualizations that make up the dashboard are a self-contained unit, you can just share copies of the Excel file with consumers. However, this is not an ideal way to manage the dashboards and will soon become unwieldy. A better way of managing the dashboards is to host them in a SharePoint site. You can host them in an on-premise SharePoint Server 2013 or the cloud-based Office 365 SharePoint Server.

The cloud-based Office 365 solution has some very compelling features that make it an excellent hosting site for your Power BI solutions. These features include Power BI sites where users can share, view, and interact with Power View dashboards. It also includes a Power BI admin center where you can secure, monitor, and automate the data refresh of your dashboards. I recommend you take a look at the Office 365 capabilities if you need to implement a solution for creating and distributing a large number of views to a large number of users. Figure 10-14 shows a Power View dashboard in an Office 365 Power BI site.

Olympic Greats

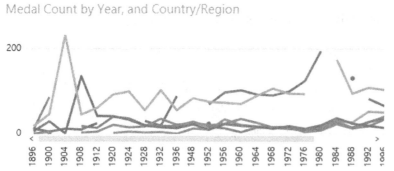

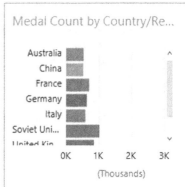

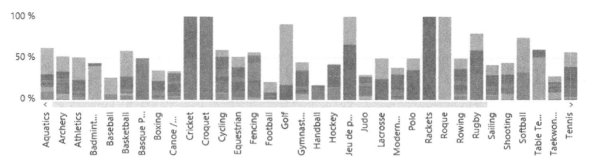

Figure 10-14. *Exposing a Power View dashboard on a Power BI site*

One thing to remember is that Power View was originally created for interactive data exploration. Although it is evolving into a pretty decent dashboarding tool, it is not the best choice for producing static reports that require printing. When you print the Power View page it is essentially just printing a screenshot.

Now that you have seen how to create interactive dashboards with Power View, it is time to get some hands-on experience creating one.

HANDS-ON LAB—CREATING A DASHBOARD IN POWER VIEW

In the following lab you will

- Create an interactive dashboard using Power View.

- Group visualizations with tiles.

1. In the LabStarters folder, open the LabChapter10.xlsx file. This file contains sales data from the test AdventureWorks database.

2. Select the Insert tab in Excel and click on the Power View button. This will insert a Power View sheet in the workbook. You will build a dashboard on this sheet.

3. Change the title of the dashboard to **Reseller Sales Analysis**.

4. Create a table that lists CalendarYears and convert it to a slicer. Select the year 2006 in the slicer to limit the data.

5. Click on a blank area of the design surface to create a new visualization. Select the MonthName from the Date table and the Reseller Sales Profit from the Reseller Sales table. Convert the table to a line chart and resize the chart. Add the Category from the Product table to the Legend drop area of the line chart.

6. Create a clustered bar chart using the BusinessType from the Reseller table and the Last Year Reseller Sales Amount and the Reseller Sales from the Reseller Sales table.

7. Rearrange the visualizations so the dashboard looks similar to Figure 10-15.

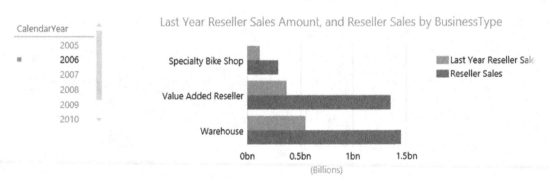

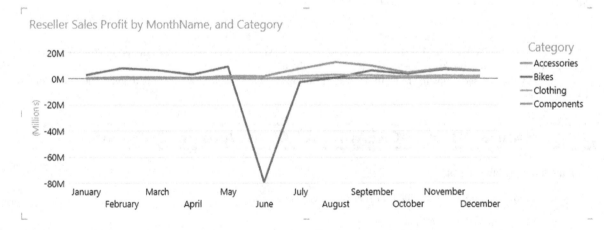

Figure 10-15. *The reseller sales analysis dashboard*

8. Test the interaction of the dashboard by changing the year in the slicer, selecting a reseller type in the bar chart, and selecting a category line in the line chart. Notice how this affects the charts in the dashboard. You can clear the filter on a chart by clicking on a blank area of the chart (see Figure 10-16).

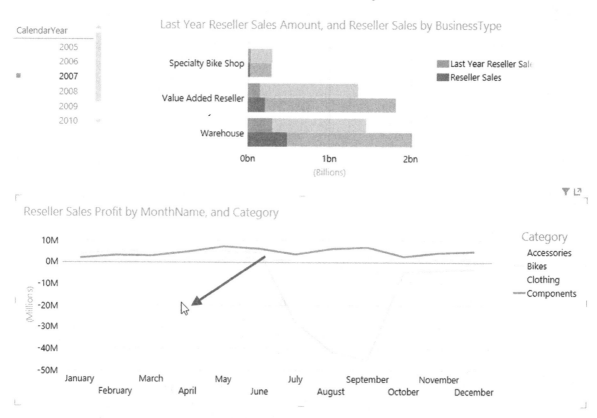

Figure 10-16. *Clearing the interactive filters*

9. Add a new Power View sheet. Title this dashboard **Sales Performance**.

10. Create a table of EmployeePhotos from the Employee table. Change the table to Tiles by selecting Tiles from the Design tab.

11. Drag the DepartmentName from the Employee table to the Filters area. Filter the view to only show sales department employees. Resize the Tile area to take up most of the view (see Figure 10-17).

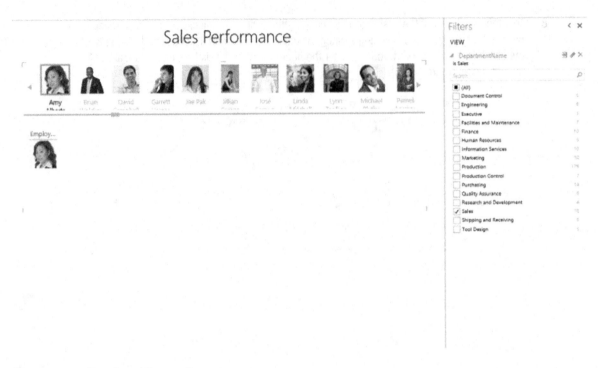

Figure 10-17. *Creating a tile grouping*

12. Delete the employee image that is sitting below the tiles.

13. Select an empty area inside the Tile box and click Reseller Quantity in the Reseller Sales table from the Field Selection pane. Select Reseller Quantity in the Reseller Sales table from the Field Selection pane. Next, select the SalesTerritoryImage and SalesTerritoryRegion from the Sales Territory table. Finally, select the Category from the Product table.

14. Convert the table to a matrix and drag CalendarYear from the Date table to the Column Groups of the matrix. Resize the matrix so that it takes up about half of the Tile area (see Figure 10-18). You can decrease the text size in the Design tab to get it to fit.

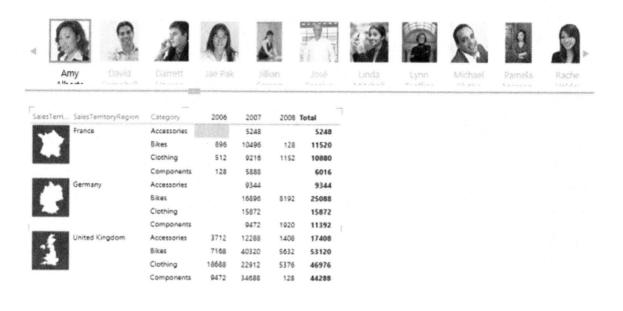

Sales Performance

Figure 10-18. *Adding a matrix to the Tile area*

15. To create a column chart, select an empty area inside the Tile box and click. Select the Category from the Product table, the Reseller Sales from the Reseller Sales table, and the CalendarYear from the Date table. Change the table created to a 100% Stacked Column chart. Resize the chart so that it looks similar to Figure 10-19.

Figure 10-19. *Adding a Stacked Column chart to the dashboard*

16. Select different sales persons and notice the data is filtered to just their sales. Also click on a section of the column chart and notice how it filters the matrix data.

17. Explore interacting with the two dashboards you have created.

18. You may want to explore changing the theme and adding a background image to your dashboard. You can also add a company logo and a standard disclaimer, which are common requirements for most company dashboards. When you are finished, save and exit Excel.

Summary

In this chapter you have seen how to combine the various visualizations in Power View to create interactive dashboards. You also saw how you can use tiles to group other visualizations on the dashboards. Although you did not explore deploying a dashboard to SharePoint, this would be the logical next step. SharePoint, either in the cloud with Office 365 or on-premises with SharePoint 2013, enables great features for collaborating and managing self-service BI. In the next chapter, you will look at another useful Excel add-in to use in your self-service BI arsenal. Power Query provides an easy-to-use interface for discovering and transforming data for use in your Power Pivot models. It also contains tools to clean and shape data such as removing duplicates, replacing values, and grouping data.

Exploring and Presenting Data with Power Query and Power Map

CHAPTER 11

███

Data Discovery with Power Query

Although Power Pivot provides many types of connections you can use to query data, there are times when you need to manipulate the data before loading it into the model. This process is commonly known as tttthe transform part of the ETL (extract, transform, and load) process. This is where Power Query really shines and is a very useful part of your BI arsenal. Power Query provides an easy-to-use interface for discovering and transforming data. It contains tools to clean and shape data such as removing duplicates, replacing values, and grouping data. In addition, it supports a vast array of data sources both structured and unstructured, such as relational databases, web pages, and Hadoop, just to name a few. Once the data is extracted and transformed, you can then easily load it into a Power Pivot model.

After completing this chapter you will be able to

- Discover and import data from various sources.

- Cleanse data.

- Merge, shape, and filter data.

- Group and aggregate data.

- Insert calculated columns.

Discovering and Importing Data

Traditionally, if you needed to combine and transform data from various disparate data sources, you would rely on the IT department to stage the data for you using a tool such as SQL Server Integration Services (SSIS). This can often be a long, drawn-out effort of data discovery, cleansing, and conforming the data to a relational structure. Although this type of formal effort is needed to load and conform data for the corporate operational data store, there are many times when you just want to add data to your Power Pivot model from a variety of sources in a quick, intuitive, and agile manner. To support this effort, you can use Power Query, a free add-in to Excel, as your self-service BI ETL tool. Once you have downloaded and installed the latest version of Power Query, you will see a new Power Query tab in Excel (see Figure 11-1).

Figure 11-1. *The new Power Query tab*

If you look at the Get External Data area of the tab, you can see the variety of data sources available to you. You can get data from the web, files, databases, and a variety of other sources (see Figure 11-2).

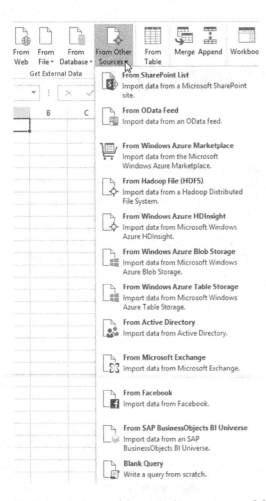

Figure 11-2. *Some of the many data sources available in Power Query*

The type of connection will dictate what information you need to supply to gain access to the data source. For example, a web source requires a URL whereas a CSV file requires the file path. Once you connect to a data source, the Query Editor window will launch, displaying a sample of the data. For example, Figure 11-3 shows flight delay data contained in a CSV file.

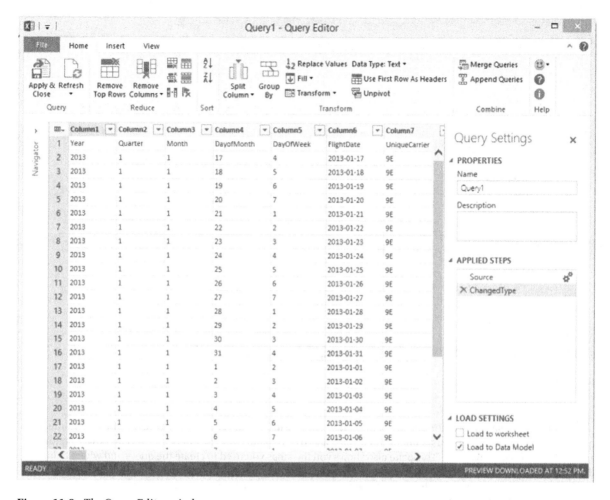

Figure 11-3. *The Query Editor window*

If you select a data source with multiple tables, you will see a Navigator pane displayed in Excel. Figure 11-4 shows the Navigator pane displayed when you connect to an Access source. After you select a table, the Query Editor will display with the sample data.

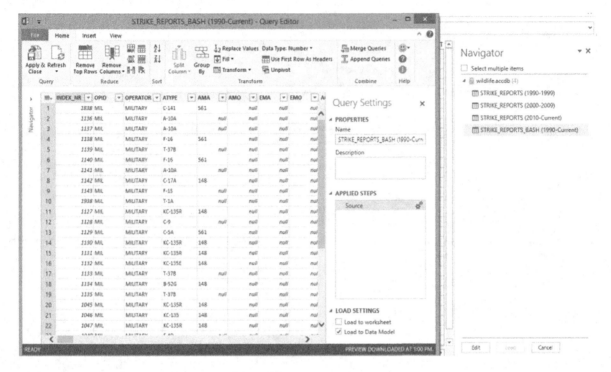

Figure 11-4. *Using the Navigator pane to select a table*

If you look at the Query Settings pane of the Query Editor window, you can see you have the ability to name the query and add a description. This is important if you want to reuse and share the queries you create (these features are available in Office 365 only). This pane also shows you the steps you used to create the query and where to load the data. You have the option of loading the data to a worksheet or to the Power Pivot data model.

Once you have connected to the data source, the next step is to transform, cleanse, and filter the data before importing it into the data model.

Transforming, Cleansing, and Filtering Data

After connecting to the data source you are ready to transform and clean the data. This is an important step and will largely determine how well the data will support your analysis effort. Some common transformations you will perform are removing duplicates, replacing values, removing error values, and changing data types. For example, in Figure 11-5 the FlightDate column is a Text data type in the source CSV file, but you want it to be a Date column in your model.

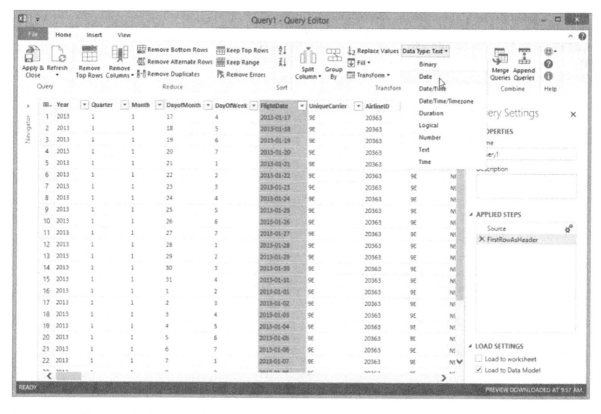

Figure 11-5. *Changing the data type of a column*

Often you need to replace values from a source system so that they sync together in your model. For example, a carrier listed as VX in the CSV file has a value of VG in your existing data. You can easily replace these values as the data is imported by selecting the column and then selecting the Replace Values transformation in the menu. This launches a window in which you can enter the values to find and what to replace them with (see Figure 11-6).

Replace Values

Replace one value with another in the selected columns.

Value To Find

> VX

Replace With

> VG

☑ Match entire cell contents

Figure 11-6. *Replacing values in a column*

When loading data from a source, another common requirement is filtering out unnecessary columns and rows. To remove columns, simply select the columns and select the Remove Columns button on the Home tab. If you only need a few columns, you can also select the columns you want to keep and then select the Remove Other Columns option. You can filter out rows by selecting the drop-down beside the column name and entering a filter condition (see Figure 11-7).

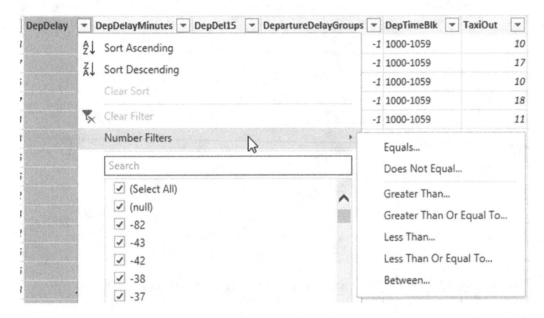

Figure 11-7. *Filtering rows*

As you apply the data transformations and filtering, the Query Editor lists the steps you have applied. This allows you to organize and track the changes you make to the data. You can rename, rearrange, and remove steps by right clicking the step in the list (see Figure 11-8).

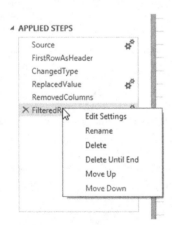

Figure 11-8. *Managing the query steps*

After cleansing and transforming the data, you may need to combine data from several sources into one table in your data model or expand data contained in a column.

Merging and Shaping Data

There are times when you may need to merge data from several tables and/or sources before you load the data into the model—for example, if you have codes in a table that link to another look-up table that contains the full value for the field. One way to deal with this is to import both tables into your model and create a link between the tables in the Power Pivot model. Another option is to merge the tables together before importing the data. For example, in the flight data you saw earlier, there is a UniqueCarrier column that contains carrier codes. You can merge these with another CSV file that contains the carrier codes and the carrier name. First create and save a query for each set of data with the Query Editor. For the look-up table, you can uncheck the Load to worksheet and Load to Data Model checkboxes which you do not need because the data will be loaded after the merge. Next open the main query and select the Merge button on the Home tab. This will launch the Merge window (see Figure 11-9) where you select the look-up query and the columns that link the data together.

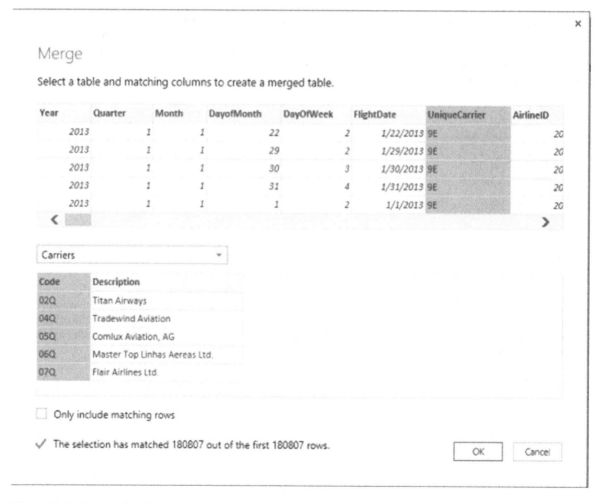

Figure 11-9. Merging data from two queries

Once you merge the queries you can choose which columns to merge (see Figure 11-10). Once the columns are merged you will probably want to rename the columns in the main query.

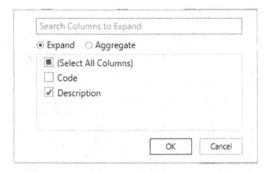

Figure 11-10. *Choosing columns to merge*

Along with merging data from look-up tables, you may also need to append data from two different sources. For example, say you have flight data for each year separated into different source files or tables and want to combine multiple years into the same table. In this case, you would create two similar queries, each using a different source. First open one of the queries in the Query Editor and select the Append Queries button on the Home tab. You can then select the other query as the table to append (see Figure 11-11).

Figure 11-11. *Appending two querries*

Sometimes a source may provide you with data in a column that needs to be split up among several columns. For example, you may need to split the city and state, or the first name and last name. To do this, select the column in the Query Editor and on the Home tab, choose Split Column. You can either split the column by a delimiter or by the number of characters (see Figure 11-12).

Split a column by delimiter

Specify the delimiter used to split the text column.

Select or enter delimiter

Comma	▼

Split

○ At the left-most delimiter

○ At the right-most delimiter

◉ At each occurrence of the delimiter

◢ Hide advanced options

Number of columns to split into

2

Figure 11-12. Spliting a column using a delimiter

Another scenario you may run into is when the data source contains data that is not in tabular form, but rather in a matrix, as in Figure 11-13.

	1/1/2013	1/2/2013	1/3/2013	1/4/2013	1/5/2013	1/6/2013	1/7/2013	1/8/2013	1/9/2013	1/10/2013	1/11/2013
American Airlines Inc.	72	24	8	88	-6	25	121	135	69	-40	-20
Delta Air Lines Inc.	-13	-12	-22	-18	-7	163	-7	-20	-24	-20	74
ExpressJet Airlines Inc.	463	1503	1571	1394	598	587	242	577	-112	239	544
JetBlue Airways	119	37	68	21	83	113	-3	74	-26	13	-11
Mesa Airlines Inc.	-53	131	364	115	-86	18	-11	23	103	322	302
Pinnacle Airlines Inc.	0	-25	22	-18	-13	63	44	-30	-21	-23	33
SkyWest Airlines Inc.	33	-10	0	51	33	10	-11	-9	22	-9	-2
Southwest Airlines Co.	-14	30	181	17	38	4	664	36	14	42	55
United Air Lines Inc.	473	692	1423	1385	509	581	419	274	298	452	290
Virgin America	-20	35	-1	14	-14	7	0	6	-6	-31	-21

Figure 11-13. Using a matrix as a data source

In order to import this data into the data model, you will need to unpivot the data to get it in a tabular form. In the Query Editor, select the columns that need to be unpivoted (see Figure 11-14).

⊞▾		▼ 1/1/2013	▼ 1/2/2013	▼ 1/3/2013	▼ 1/4/2013	▼ 1/5/2013	▼
1	American Airlines Inc.	72	24	8	88	-6	
2	Delta Air Lines Inc.	-13	-12	-22	-18	-7	
3	ExpressJet Airlines Inc.	463	1503	1571	1394	598	
4	JetBlue Airways	119	37	68	21	83	
5	Mesa Airlines Inc.	-53	131	364	115	-86	
6	Pinnacle Airlines Inc.	0	-25	22	-18	-13	
7	SkyWest Airlines Inc.	33	-10	0	51	33	
8	Southwest Airlines Co.	-14	30	181	17	38	
9	United Air Lines Inc.	473	692	1423	1385	509	
10	Virgin America	-20	35	-1	14	-14	

Figure 11-14. Selecting columns to unpivot

225

On the Home tab, select the Unpivot transform. Once the data is unpivoted, you will get an Attribute column from the original column headers and a Value column (see Figure 11-15). You should rename these columns before importing the data.

		Attribute	Value
1	American Airlines Inc.	1/1/2013	72
2	American Airlines Inc.	1/2/2013	24
3	American Airlines Inc.	1/3/2013	8
4	American Airlines Inc.	1/4/2013	88
5	American Airlines Inc.	1/5/2013	-6
6	American Airlines Inc.	1/6/2013	25
7	American Airlines Inc.	1/7/2013	121
8	American Airlines Inc.	1/8/2013	135
9	American Airlines Inc.	1/9/2013	69
10	American Airlines Inc.	1/10/2013	-40
11	American Airlines Inc.	1/11/2013	-20
12	Delta Air Lines Inc.	1/1/2013	-13
13	Delta Air Lines Inc.	1/2/2013	-12
14	Delta Air Lines Inc.	1/3/2013	-22
15	Delta Air Lines Inc.	1/4/2013	-18
16	Delta Air Lines Inc.	1/5/2013	-7
17	Delta Air Lines Inc.	1/6/2013	163
18	Delta Air Lines Inc.	1/7/2013	-7
19	Delta Air Lines Inc.	1/8/2013	-20
20	Delta Air Lines Inc.	1/9/2013	-24

Figure 11-15. *Resulting rows from the unpivot transformation*

As you bring data into the model, you often do not need the detail level data; instead, you need an aggregate value at a higher level—for example, product level sales or monthly sales. Using Power Query, you can easily group and aggregate the data before importing it.

Grouping and Aggregating Data

The need to group and aggregate data is a common scenario you may run into when you are importing raw data. For example, you may need to roll the data up by month or sales territory depending on the analysis you need. To aggregate and group the data in the Query Editor, select the column you want to group by and select the Group By transform in the Home tab. You are presented with a Group By window (see Figure 11-16).

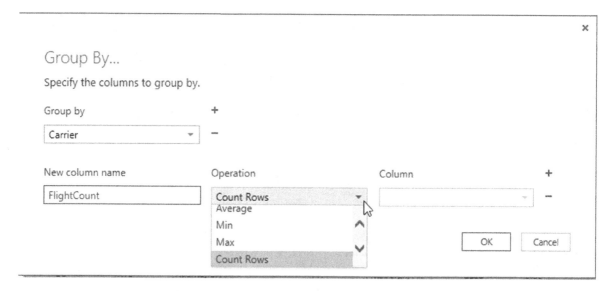

Figure 11-16. *Grouping data in Power Query*

You can group by multiple columns and aggregate multiple columns using the standard aggregate functions. Figure 11-17 shows some of the results from grouping by origin and carrier and aggregating the average and maximum departure delays.

▦▾	Origin ▾	Carrier ▾	FlightCount ▾	MaxDelay ▾	AveDelay ▾
1	MSP	DL	2196	700	27.369308
2	ATL	DL	11016	820	21.364833
3	DEN	DL	378	655	34.23545
4	JFK	DL	734	599	28.100817
5	MOT	DL	11	40	12
6	DTW	DL	2020	582	26.605446
7	RDU	DL	173	566	30.364162
8	SFO	DL	299	307	29.471572
9	LAS	DL	473	508	26.17759
10	MIA	DL	339	333	26.613569
11	PBI	DL	232	798	32.047414
12	MKE	DL	190	344	22.331579
13	PDX	DL	111	690	40.981982
14	SLC	DL	1450	687	32.016552
15	SDF	DL	85	566	41.941176
16	CVG	DL	254	327	20.133858
17	SNA	DL	99	373	32.838384
18	LAX	DL	964	447	22.482365
19	ELP	DL	40	157	29.725

Figure 11-17. *Grouping and aggregating flight data*

The final requirement you may run into as you import data using Power Query is inserting a calculated column. This is a little more advanced because you need to write code, as you will see in the next section.

Inserting Calculated Columns

Up until now you were able to build and execute queries using the visual interfaces provided by Power Query. Behind the scene, however, the Power Query Editor was creating a file used to execute the query. This file is written in a new language called M. As you have seen, you can get a lot of functionality out of Power Query without ever having to know about M or learn how it works. Nevertheless, at the very least, you should know it is there and that it is what gets executed when you run the query. If you navigate to the View tab in the Query Editor, you will see an option to open the Advanced Editor, which will display the M code used to build the query (see Figure 11-18).

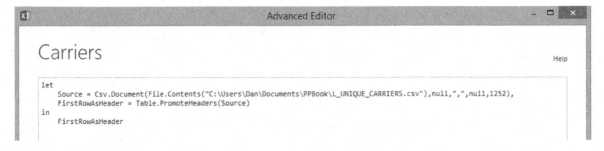

Figure 11-18. *Building a query with M*

You can use the Advanced Editor to write the query directly with M, thereby exposing some advanced data processing not exposed in the visual interface tools.

If you want to insert a calculated column into the query, you need to use the M functions. On the Insert tab of the Query Editor you can duplicate columns, insert an index column, merge columns, and insert a custom column. When you select the Insert A Custom Column option, you are presented with a Insert Custom Column editor where you insert the M function used to create the column (see Figure 11-19).

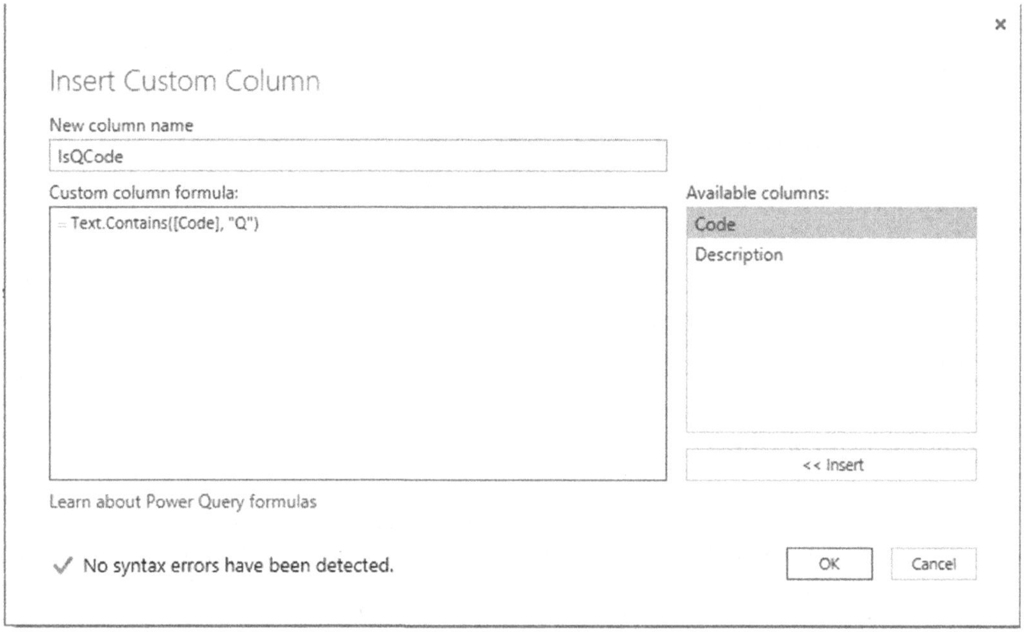

Figure 11-19. *Creating columns using M formulas*

Figure 11-20 shows the results of the query with the custom column added.

⊞▾	Code	▾	Description	▾	IsQCode	▾
1	02Q		Titan Airways		TRUE	
2	04Q		Tradewind Aviation		TRUE	
3	05Q		Comlux Aviation, AG		TRUE	
4	06Q		Master Top Linhas Aereas Ltd.		TRUE	
5	07Q		Flair Airlines Ltd.		TRUE	
6	09Q		Swift Air, LLC		TRUE	
7	0BQ		DCA		TRUE	
8	0CQ		ACM AIR CHARTER GmbH		TRUE	
9	0GQ		Inter Island Airways, d/b/a Inter Island Air		TRUE	
10	0HQ		Polar Airlines de Mexico d/b/a Nova Air		TRUE	
11	0J		JetClub AG		FALSE	
12	0JQ		Vision Airlines		TRUE	
13	0KQ		Mokulele Flight Services, Inc.		TRUE	
14	0LQ		Metropix UK, LLP.		TRUE	
15	0MQ		Multi-Aero, Inc. d/b/a Air Choice One		TRUE	
16	0OQ		Open Skies		TRUE	
17	0Q		Flying Service N.V.		TRUE	

Figure 11-20. *Displaying the results of the query*

So, if you need to create columns using Power Query before inserting the data into the Power Pivot model, you use M formulas. If you create the columns after importing the data into the Power Pivot model you use DAX formulas.

Now that you have seen how Power Query works, it is time to get some hands-on experience using it to import data. In order to complete this lab it is assumed you have installed the latest Power Query add-in.

HANDS-ON LAB—IMPORTING AND SHAPING DATA WITH POWER QUERY

In the following lab you will

- Create a query to import data.

- Filter and transform data.

- Append and shape data.

- Group and aggregate data.

    1. In the LabStarters folder, open the LabChapter11.xlsx file. This file contains a basic Power Pivot model that you will add to using Power Query.

    2. Select the Power Query tab in Excel. Under the Get External Data, select from File and choose the From CSV option. Navigate to the FlightPerformance_2012_10.csv in the LabStarters folder. You should see the Query Editor window with airline delay data, as in Figure 11-21.

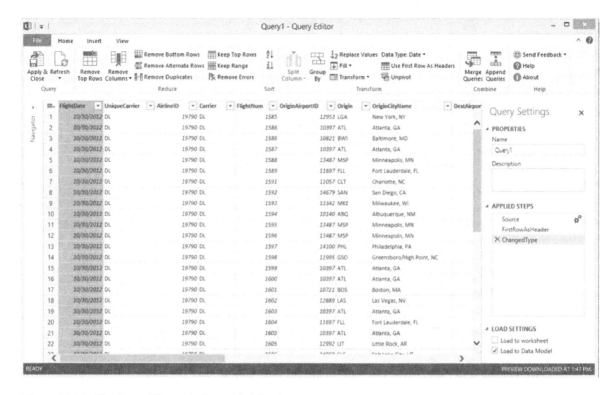

Figure 11-21. *The Query Editor window with delay data*

3. In the Query Settings pane, rename the query to **FlightDelays** and uncheck the Load To Data Model.

4. In the Applied Steps list, if the Query Editor did not automatically add the transform to set the first row as headers, add it now.

5. Check the types of each column to see if the Query Editor updated the FlightDate to a Date data type and the number type columns to a Number data type. If it did not, change them now.

6. Remove the UniqueCarrier, FlightNum, AirTime, Flights, and Distance columns.

7. Filter the data so that it only pulls rows that have a flight departure delay of greater than 15 minutes.

8. Select Apply & Close to save the query.

9. Complete steps 2-8 for the `FlightPerformance_2012_11.csv` file, except this time, name the query **FlightDelays2**.

10. You should now have two workbook queries, as shown in Figure 11-22.

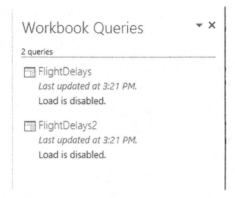

Figure 11-22. *Current workbook queries*

11. Double click on the FlightDelays query to open it back up in the Query Editor.

12. Select the Append Queries option in the Combine section of the Home tab. Append the FlightDelays2 query to the FlightDelays query.

13. Select the OriginCityName column and split it into two columns named OriginCity and OriginState using the comma. Do the same for the DestCityName column.

14. Replace West Palm Beach/Palm Beach in the City columns with just Palm Beach.

15. Check the Load To Data Model Load setting and click the Apply & Close button.

16. Open the Power Pivot model and verify that the table was loaded.

17. Select the Power Query tab in Excel. Under Get External Data, select From File and choose the From CSV option. Navigate to the FlightPerformance_2012_12.csv in the LabStarters folder.

18. In the Query Settings pane, rename the query to **DelaySummary** and uncheck Load To Data Model.

19. Keep the Carrier, Origin, and DepDelay columns and remove the rest.

20. Filter out delays that are less than 15 minutes.

21. Find the average delay and max delay grouping by the origin and carrier (see Figure 11-23).

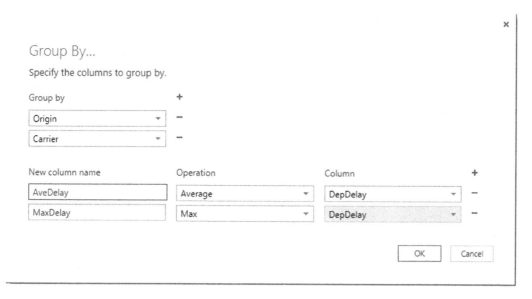

Figure 11-23. *Grouping by origin and carrier*

22. Click the Apply & Close button to save the query.

23. Add a query called **Carriers** that gets the code and description from the Carriers.csv file.

24. Open the DelaySummary query and select the Merge Queries option on the Home tab. Using the Carriers query, merge the Description column matching the Carrier column in the DelaySummary query with the Code column in the Carriers query (see Figure 11-24).

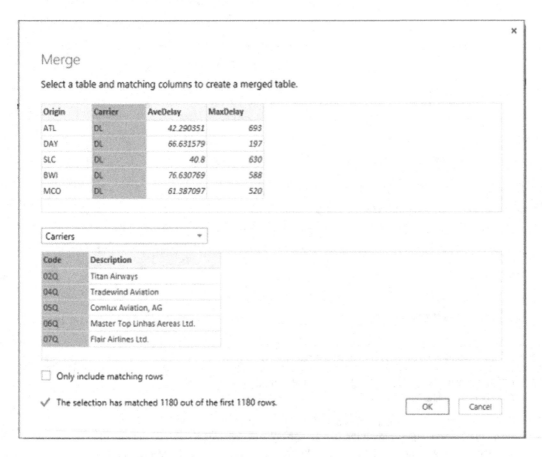

Figure 11-24. Merging data from two queries

25. Rename the Carrier column to **CarrierCode** and the Description column to **Carrier**.

26. When you are done, under the Load Settings, check the Load To Data Model checkbox and then click the Apply & Close button on the Home tab.

27. When done, open the Power Pivot model and verify that the table was added to the model.

Summary

Power Query is a very useful tool you can use to get data from many different types of sources. In this chapter, you learned how to use Power Query to shape, cleanse, and transform data using intuitive interfaces without having to use code. Power Query builds the code for you but does not hide it from you. If you need to alter or enhance the code, you can use the Advanced Editor view. Although this chapter only touched on the M query language, as you gain experience using Power Query, you may want to investigate the M coding language more in depth.

In the next chapter, Chapter 12, you will look at another useful Excel add-in to use in your self-service BI arsenal. Power Map greatly increases the mapping visualizations available to you. It can produce 3D visualizations by plotting up to a million data points in the form of columns, heat maps, and bubble charts on top of a Bing map. If the data is time stamped, it can also produce interactive views displaying how the data changes over space and time.

■ ■ ■

Geospatial Analysis with Power Map

Power Map is an Excel add-in that provides you with a powerful set of tools to help you visualize and gain insight into large sets of data that have a geocoded component. It can help you produce 3D visualizations by plotting up to a million data points in the form of column, heat, and bubble maps on top of a Bing map. If the data is time stamped, it can also produce interactive views that display how the data changes over space and time. In this chapter, you will learn to create compelling and unique visual representations using Power Map.

After completing this chapter you will be able to

- Prepare the data for mapping.

- Create a map-based graph.

- Create heat and region maps.

- Add multiple layers to a map.

- Analyze changes over time.

- Create a tour.

■ **Note**   For copies of color figures, go to Source Code/Downloads at http://www.apress.com/9781430264453.

Preparing Data for Mapping

As with any successful data analysis effort, it is paramount that you properly prepare your data to support the effort. Power Map can use one of two sources of data for the maps: an Excel table or a table contained in a Power Pivot data model. The primary requirement for the table is that it contains unique rows. It must also contain location data, which can be in the form of a Latitude/Longitude pair, although this is not a requirement. You can use address fields instead, such as Street, City, Country/Region, Zip Code/Postal Code, and State/Province, which can be geolocated by Bing. You may need to use a combination of columns to get an accurate mapping. For example, many cities with the same name are located in various states and countries.

In addition to the geolocation columns, the table rows also need to contain the measures that you want to plot on the map. A measure needs to be one of the numeric data types, such as integer for counts and money/decimal for sales. If you want to compare how the data changed over time, the final requirement is that each row must contain a date or time field. Figure 12-1 shows a table in a Power Pivot data model that contains information about airplane bird-strike incidents. Since the table includes airport location information along with bird-strike information, you can use it as the source for a Power Map. Remember that although this data can be mapped down to the longitude and latitude level, you can use any of the location fields to map the data. For example, if you did not have the Longitude and Latitude fields, you could still map the data using the City or State fields.

INCIDENT_DATE	TIME_OF_DAY	SPECIES	City	STATE	Country	Latitude	Longitude
5/8/2010 12:00:00 AM	Night	Unknown ...	Sacra...	CA	United Sta...	38.695417	-121.590778
7/21/2010 12:00:00 AM	Night	Unknown ...	Sacra...	CA	United Sta...	38.695417	-121.590778
9/9/2010 12:00:00 AM	Night	Unknown ...	Sacra...	CA	United Sta...	38.695417	-121.590778
9/26/2010 12:00:00 AM	Night	Unknown ...	Sacra...	CA	United Sta...	38.695417	-121.590778
12/27/2010 12:00:00 ...	Night	Unknown ...	Sacra...	CA	United Sta...	38.695417	-121.590778
6/1/2010 12:00:00 AM	Night	Unknown ...	Buffalo	NY	United Sta...	42.940525	-78.732167
10/12/2010 12:00:00 ...	Night	Unknown ...	Buffalo	NY	United Sta...	42.940525	-78.732167
2/1/2010 12:00:00 AM	Night	Unknown ...	Orlando	FL	United Sta...	28.429394	-81.308994
4/4/2010 12:00:00 AM	Night	Unknown ...	Portla...	OR	United Sta...	45.588722	-122.5975
4/2/2010 12:00:00 AM	Night	Unknown ...	Phoenix	AZ	United Sta...	33.434278	-112.011583

Figure 12-1. *Bird-strike data containing location information for use in Power Map*

If you need to get the map data from an external source and shape it to use it in a Power Map, remember from the last chapter that Power Query is an excellent tool for this purpose. Once the data is properly prepared, you are ready to create the map.

Creating a Map-Based Graph

To launch Power Map, go to the Insert tab in Excel, click on the Map drop-down, and select Launch Power Map. If this is the first map you have created in the Excel workbook, this will launch the Power Map interface where you design and view your maps (See Figure 12-2).

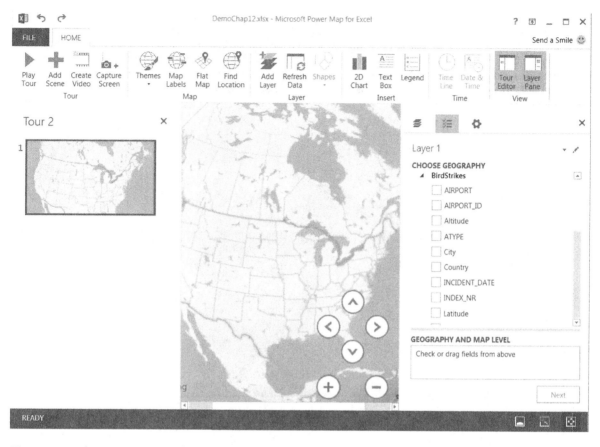

Figure 12-2. *The Power Map interface*

There are three panes available in the Power Map interface. The one on the left is the Tour Editor. This is where you can add various views of the map as scenes and then use these to create a video tour of the data. The center pane is the map where the data is plotted. You can interact with the map by panning and zooming to see the data from different perspectives. The pane on the right is the Layer Pane where you create the data layers that get plotted on the map. Each layer represents a set of data that you want to add or remove from the map. You can show or hide the Tour Editor and Layer Pane by toggling the buttons in the View section of the Home tab (see Figure 12-3).

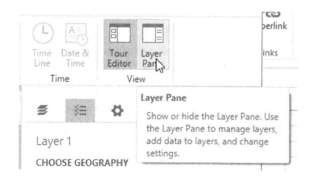

Figure 12-3. *Showing/hiding the panes*

To begin creating a map you use the Layer Pane to create a layer. A layer represents a specific data set. You can create multiple layers and overlay them on top of each other. For example, you can create one layer that shows stream levels and another that shows rainfall amounts and then place the Rainfall layer on top of the Stream Level layer.

Once you have selected the data for the layer, you are ready to incorporate it into a map. In the Choose Geography area of the Layer Pane, select the geography fields you want to plot on the map. These can be fields such as City, State, or Latitude/Longitude. Once you select the geography fields, you will see the locations plotted on the map (see Figure 12-4).

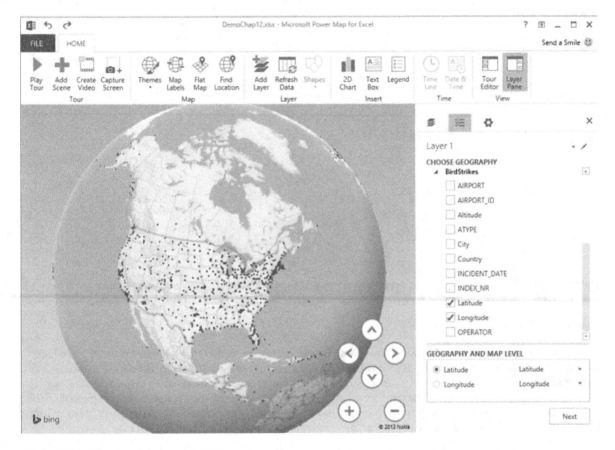

Figure 12-4. Selecting the geography fields

The next step is to select the type of graph you want to create in the layer. You can select a stacked column, clustered column, or bubble graph. In addition you can also create a heat or region map. When you first create a map, the stacked column graph is selected by default. Once you select the type of graph, you then add the fields to the various sections. For example, the stacked column needs a field for the Category area. You can also add a field for the Height and Time areas. If you do not add a field for Height, then the row count for each of the category values is used. Figure 12-5 shows the phase of flight selected as the Category and the resulting stacked column graph, which shows the number of bird strikes for each phase at the various airports.

Figure 12-5. *Creating a stacked column map*

You can easily change from a stacked column map to a clustered column map depending on which one displays your data better.

A bubble map is similar to a column map except that it uses bubbles and pie wedges to show the data. For example, the bubble map in Figure 12-6 shows the number of bird strikes by the time of the day.

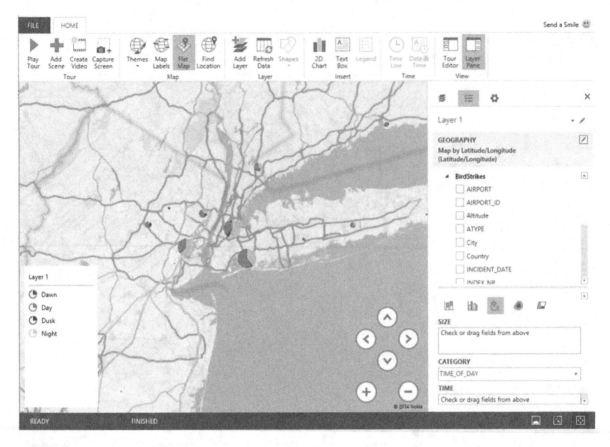

Figure 12-6. *Creating a bubble map*

As you have seen, the processes involved in creating the stacked column, clustered column, and bubble maps are very similar. Two addition types of maps that are similar to each other are the heat and region maps. You will take a look at these next.

Creating Heat and Region Maps

One interesting type of map available in Power Map is the heat map. Heat maps transform the data into color gradients. Higher values are depicted by darker shades whereas lower values are depicted by lighter shades. Although not all data lends itself to be represented by a heat map, for certain types of data, this type of map is very effective. Anytime you want to analyze the relative intensity of a value, a heat map is a good choice. For example, weather data such as temperature and rainfall amounts are typically depicted using heat maps (see Figure 12-7).

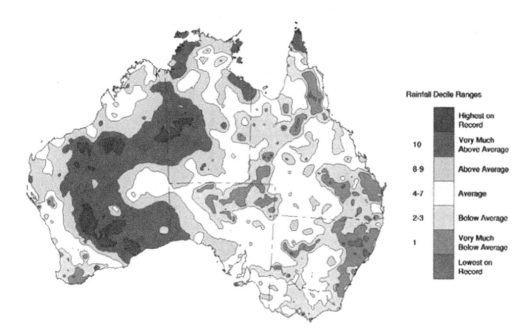

Figure 12-7. *Rainfall deficit heat map (Source: National Agricultural Monitoring System [NAMS])*

Creating heat maps in Power Map is not much different than creating a stacked column map. First select a table that has the geolocation data and the values you want to compare. After you select the geography fields, you can change the visualization to a heat map and select the value field you want to plot. If you do not select a value field, it will plot the row counts. Figure 12-8 shows a heat map depicting narcotics-related crime in a city neighborhood. The darker red represents higher crime areas.

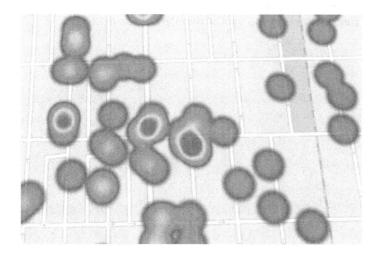

Figure 12-8. *A heat map depicting crime rates*

Another type of map that is similar to a heat map is the region map. A region map shows defined geographic areas such as countries, states, counties, and zip codes. It then color-codes the regions to compare value fields. A common type of region map is an election results map. Figure 12-9 shows an example of an election result by county. Red indicates a Republican majority and blue indicates a Democrat majority. The darker the shade, the greater the margin.

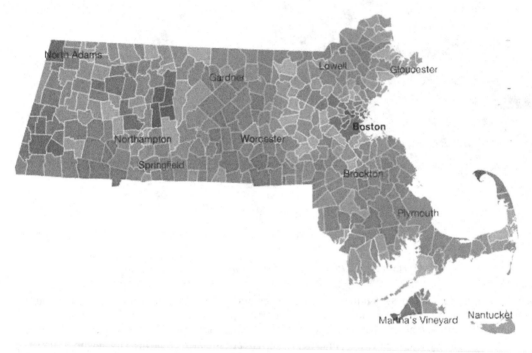

Figure 12-9. *Election results on a region map*

To create a region map, select the region field in the source table as the geography field and then switch the visualization to region. Then select the fields that contain the values you want on the map (see Figure 12-10).

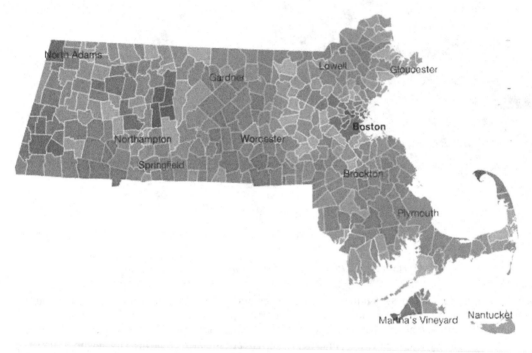

Figure 12-10. *Selecting values for the region map*

Each region will show the color of the value field that is greater. By selecting the layer options under the Settings tab, you can change the color, opacity, and color scale of the value fields shown on the map (see Figure 12-11).

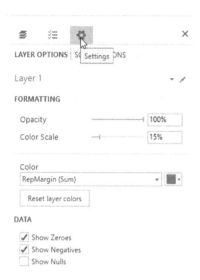

Figure 12-11. *Adjusting the color settings of a region map*

In this case, you can adjust the color so that Democrat margins show up in blue and Republican margins show up in red (see Figure 12-12).

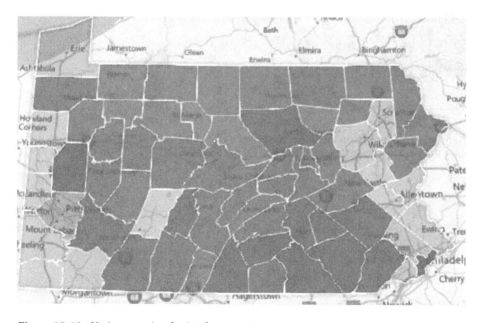

Figure 12-12. *Voting margins depicted on a region map*

Now that you have seen how you create the various types of maps, you may want to add multiple layers to a map. You will look at how this is done next.

Adding Multiple Layers to a Power Map

One of the many great features of Power Map is that you can use it to create multiple layers, each with its own visualization. You can then add and remove the various layers to create rich presentations.

To add another layer to the map, click the Add Layer button on the Home tab in the Power Map designer. After that, the process is the same as what you did earlier when you added your first layer to the map. Figure 12-13 shows the previous voting results layer and an added layer that shows a bubble map depicting the race (white and other) breakdown of the counties.

Figure 12-13. *Overlaying multiple layers in Power Map*

To control which layers appear or are hidden on the map, select the Layer Manager tab in the Layer Pane. In the Layer list, you can hide or show the layer by clicking the eye icon (see Figure 12-14).

Figure 12-14. Hiding and showing layers

As you can see, it is very easy to add multiple layers to a map.

Another feature of Power Map that all map visualizations have in common is the ability to show changes over a period of time. You will look at how to add this feature to a map next.

Analyzing Changes over Time

Another great feature of Power Map is that you can use it to view how changes in data occur over time. For example, say you are interested in tracking a hurricane's position and wind speed. Since the data has a date-time field, you can just drag this to the Time drop-down on the Field List tab in the Layer Pane (see Figure 12-15).

Figure 12-15. Adding a time field

Once you add a time field, a timeline player is automatically added to the map layer. Figure 12-16 shows a heat map depicting wind speeds as a hurricane travels up the coast. Using the play axis, you can view its location over time as it travels.

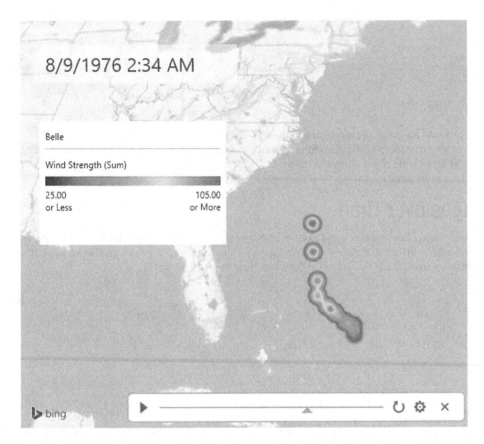

Figure 12-16. *Tracing the path and windspeed of a hurricane using the play axis*

One last unique feature of Power Map is the ability to record a tour that can pan and zoom through scenes. You can then play back the tour and also export it as an MP4 video. You will look at how to create a tour next.

Creating a Tour

With Power Map, you can tell a story with your data using tours. *Tours* are the top-level object in the Power Map hierarchy. Tours consist of one or more scenes; *scenes* are like a snapshot of your data that shows the data in a unique way. For example, Figures 12-17 and 12-18 show the same map viewed with different perspectives. You can create scenes using these two perspectives and add them to a tour to zoom from a view of the entire United States down to just the Northeastern states.

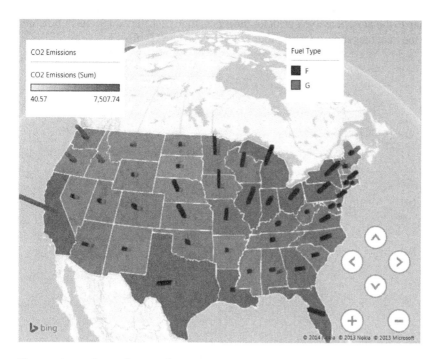

Figure 12-17. *Scene showing the entire United States*

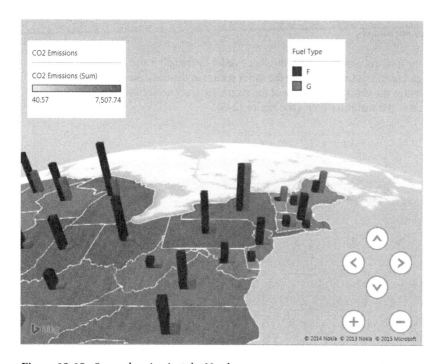

Figure 12-18. *Scene showing just the Northeastern states*

To capture a scene, adjust the map to the perspective you want for the scene; then click the Add Scene button on the toolbar. As you add the scenes to the tour, they show up in the Tour Editor (see Figure 12-19).

Figure 12-19. *The Tour Editor with scenes added*

Once you have added scenes to the tour, you can rearrange the scene order by dragging and dropping the scenes in the Tour Editor. You can also change a scene without affecting the other scenes in the tour. You can add or remove map layers, change the theme, and change the visual perspective of the scene. Each scene also has scene options that allow you to change the scene duration and transition effects (see Figure 12-20).

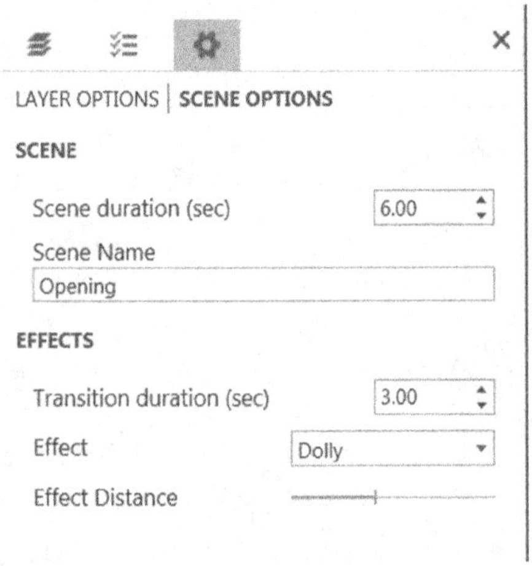

Figure 12-20. *Setting scene options*

Once you have created the scenes and set their transition effects, you can play the tour by clicking the Play Tour button on the Home tab (see Figure 12-19). After your tour is created, you can export the tour as an MP4 video to share with others and even attach a sound track to the tour (see Figure 12-21).

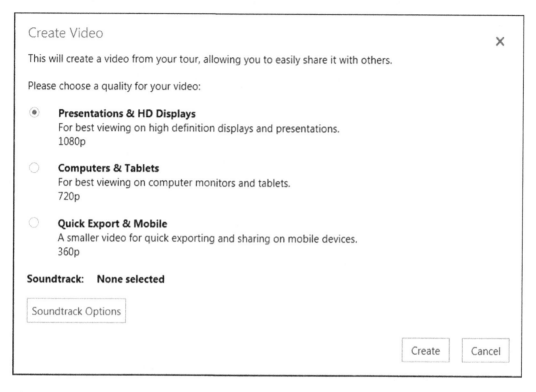

Figure 12-21. Exporting a tour as an MP4 video file

Now that you have seen the various features of Power Map, it is time to get some hands-on experience using it to map some data. In order to complete this lab, you will need to have installed the latest Power Map add-in.

HANDS-ON LAB—CREATING MAP VISUALIZATIONS IN POWER MAP

In the following lab you will

- Create a column map.

- Create a region map.

- Create a multilayer map.

- Create a heat map with a time axis.

1. In the LabStarters folder, open the LabChapter12.xlsx file. This file contains power plant and emission data that you will use to create visualizations in Power Map.

2. On the Insert tab in Excel, select the Map drop-down and then launch Power Map. You should see the Power Map designer and the tables in the Layer Panel (see Figure 12-22).

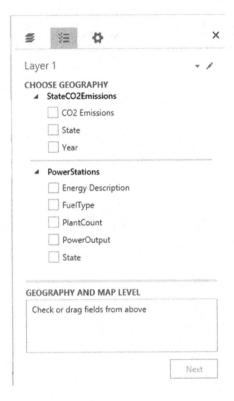

Figure 12-22. *The tables listed in the Layer Panel*

3. Rename the layer to **Fuel Type** and select the State field in the PowerStations table as the geography. Click on the Next button.

4. Add the PlantCount field to the Height drop box and the FuelType field to the Category drop box. Switch the map to a clustered column and zoom in to the Northeastern United States. You should see two columns on each state: one representing fossil fuel plants and the other representing green energy sources.

5. On the Settings tab of the Layer Pane, change the color of the fossil fuel column to black and the green energy column to green. You can also adjust the height and thickness of the columns. The final map should look similar to Figure 12-23.

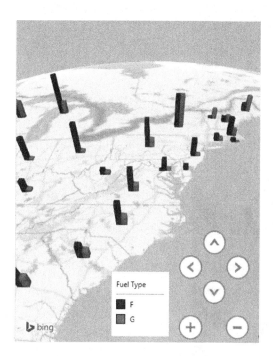

Figure 12-23. *Clustered columns showing the number of power plants for each state*

6. On the Layer Manager tab in the Layer Pane, add another layer named **CO2 Emissions**. Use the State field in the StateCO2Emissions table as the geography field.

7. Change the map type to Region and select CO2 Emissions as the value field.

8. On the Settings tab of the Layer Pane, change the color of the regions to blue. Adjust the color scale to zero so you can see small differences between the states values.

9. You should now have two layers in the same map as shown in Figure 12-24. You can show and hide the various layers on the map using the Layer Manager tab in the Layer Pane.

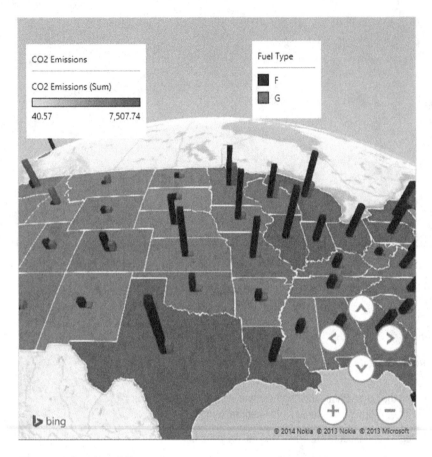

Figure 12-24. *A multilayer map*

10. Save and close the Excel workbook.

11. In the `LabStarters` folder, open the `LabChapter12_2.xlsx` file. This file contains hurricane data that you will use to create a heat map and timeline in Power Map.

12. Launch Power Map and create a layer named **Sandy**. Using the HurricaneSandy data add the Latitude and Longitude fields to the Geography drop box.

13. Change the map to a heat map and select Wind Strength as the value field and DateTime as the time field.

14. You should see a heat map as in Figure 12-25. Notice how the wind speed was greatest when it hit land. Using the play axis, push the Play button to watch the hurricane trace its path over time.

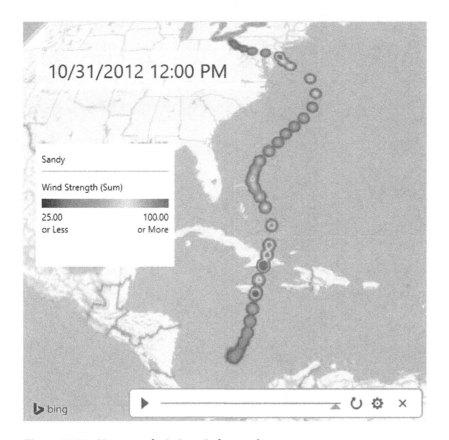

10/31/2012 12:00 PM

Sandy

Wind Strength (Sum)

25.00
or Less

100.00
or More

Figure 12-25. *Heat map depicting wind strength*

15. When you are done save and close Excel.

Summary

As you have seen in this chapter, Power Map is a powerful Excel add-in that provides a set of tools to help you visualize and gain insight into data that has a geography component. You can produce excellent 3D visualizations by plotting data in the form of columns on top of a Bing map. In addition, if the data has a date or time component, you can use Power Map to visualize data changes over time. You also saw how to create heat and region maps that, for certain types of data sets, are great ways to visualize and discover insights into the data. Another great feature of Power Map is its ability to overlay various data layers on the same map, which allows you to compare data that is linked together through a locational component.

Remember, currently Power Map is a work in progress and new features are being added to it on a regular basis. Make sure you are working with the latest release to take advantage of these features.

In the next chapter you will look at one of the most interesting aspects of BI analysis: predictive analytics. Predictive analytics allow you to extract information from your historical data and use it to predict future behavior and trends. Excel provides a set of data mining tools that make predictive analytics easy to implement. Using these tools you can perform advanced data analysis such as forecasting, clustering, and associations. Chapter 13 introduces you to these tools and shows you how to implement some common data mining models in order to gain powerful insight into your data.

CHAPTER 13

Mining Your Data with Excel

One of the most underutilized areas of business intelligence is data mining or *predictive analytics* as it is often referred to. This is due to the fact that traditional data mining uses a set of complex algorithms, and the tools often require you to be an expert in these algorithms to be able to implement them. Although it is not part of the official Microsoft self-service BI toolset, the set of table analysis tools Microsoft offers for Excel allows you to use data mining algorithms but hide much of the complexity associated with implementing them. Using these table analysis tools for Excel, you can perform advanced data analysis such as forecasting, clustering, and associations. This chapter shows you how to use these tools to implement some common data mining models and gain powerful insight into your data. I should mention, however, that to implement the table analysis tools, you need to be able to connect to an instance of SQL Server Analysis Server (SSAS), which provides the engine to run the algorithms.

After completing this chapter you will be able to

- Identify the table analysis tools available in Excel.

- Analyze key influencers.

- Identify data groups.

- Forecasting future trends.

- Use shopping basket analysis.

Table Analysis Tools in Excel

Data mining is the process of using historical data to discover patterns and develop predictions for future trends. Some common examples of data mining are market basket analysis, marketing effectiveness, and forecasting. *Market basket analysis* looks at historical data and determines which products are often associated with each other in a purchase. Using this information, you can make recommendations as to which products should be marketed together. *Marketing effectiveness* analyzes historical marketing campaigns and can be used to target customers for future campaigns. *Forecasting* allows you to predict the future from historical trends in the data. For example, you can make sales predictions based on sales trends from the past five years. This can help you plan stocking levels for the upcoming season.

To install the table analysis tools for Excel, go to the download page (www.microsoft.com/en-us/download/details.aspx?id=35578). Make sure you select the correct version for your Office installation (x86 or x64). Once you've downloaded the package, double-click on the SQL_AS_DMAddin.msi file to launch the installer. In the Feature Selection window, leave the default selection of Table Analysis Tools For Excel and Server Configuration Utility (see Figure 13-1).

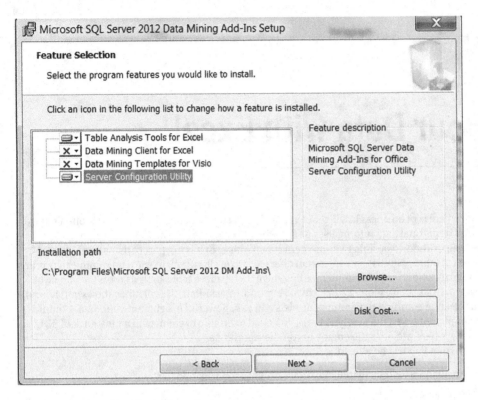

Figure 13-1. *Installing the table analysis tools*

Once you install the data mining tools for Excel, you will see a new tab when you select an Excel table. The Table Tools Analyze tab contains a set of tools to help you data mine the data contained in a table (see Figure 13-2).

Figure 13-2. *Table analysis tools on the Table Tools Analyze tab*

The first thing you should notice is that there is no connection listed. In order for these tools to work, you need to connect to an instance of SSAS. To create a connection, click on the Connection button. In the Analysis Services Connections window, click the New button. In the Connect To Analysis Services window (see Figure 13-3) enter the values to connect to an instance of SSAS. Your values will be determined by your instance of SSAS.

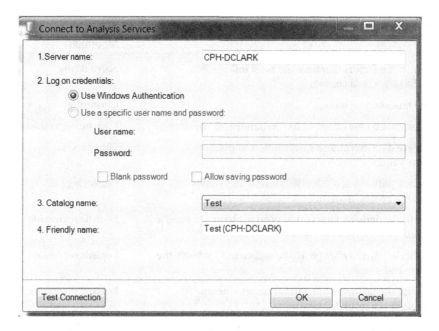

Figure 13-3. *Connecting to an SSAS instance*

Once the connection is added, you should see it listed in the table analysis tools in the connection area (see Figure 13-4).

Figure 13-4. *The table analysis tools with an active SSAS connection*

Each of these tools uses a well-known data mining algorithm and analyzes the data distribution and data types of your data. Using these tools shields you from the complexity of implementing the algorithm. Table 13-1 summarizes each of the available tools, when you should use them and the type of algorithm used.

Table 13-1. Summary of the Available Table Analysis Tools

Tool	Use	Algorithm
Analyze Key Influencers	Identify the factors that have the most influence on the target data column.	Naïve Bayes
Detect Categories	Find groupings of data.	Clustering
Fill From Example	Recommend new values based on patterns in the data.	Logistic regression
Forecast	Analyze data that changes over time and predict future values.	Time series
Highlight Exceptions	Analyze patterns in a table of data and find values that don't fit the pattern.	Clustering
Goal Seek Scenario	Identify underlying factors that need to change to meet a target.	Logistic regression
What-If Scenario	Predict whether a change will be sufficient to achieve the desired outcome.	Logistic regression
Prediction Calculator	Analyze the factors leading to the target outcome and predict a result for new inputs.	Logistic regression
Shopping Basket Analysis	Identify patterns that can be used in cross-selling or upselling.	Association

Now that you have seen the breadth of the tools available to you, it is time to look at some of them in more detail.

Analyzing Key Influencers

Using the Analyze Key Influencers tool, you can determine which factors have the most influence on an outcome. For example, you have a data table that contains attributes of customers and a column that indicates whether they bought a bike or not (see Figure 13-5).

Education	Occupation	Home Owner	Cars	Commute Distance	Region	Age	Purchased Bike
Bachelors	Skilled Manual	Yes	0	0-1 Miles	Europe	42	No
Partial College	Clerical	Yes	1	0-1 Miles	Europe	43	No
Partial College	Professional	No	2	2-5 Miles	Europe	60	No
Bachelors	Professional	Yes	1	5-10 Miles	Pacific	41	Yes
Bachelors	Clerical	No	0	0-1 Miles	Europe	36	Yes
Partial College	Manual	Yes	0	1-2 Miles	Europe	50	No
High School	Management	Yes	4	0-1 Miles	Pacific	33	Yes
Bachelors	Skilled Manual	Yes	0	0-1 Miles	Europe	43	Yes
Partial High School	Clerical	Yes	2	5-10 Miles	Pacific	58	No
Partial College	Manual	Yes	1	0-1 Miles	Europe	48	Yes
High School	Skilled Manual	No	2	1-2 Miles	Pacific	54	Yes
Bachelors	Professional	No	4	10+ Miles	Pacific	36	No
Partial College	Professional	Yes	4	0-1 Miles	Europe	55	No

Figure 13-5. Customer attributes

To determine the key factors influencing whether a client purchased a bike, select the table, and then in the Table Analysis Tools tab, select Analyze Key Influencers. You are presented with a column selection dialog box. First choose the column that contains the outcome you want to analyze (see Figure 13-6).

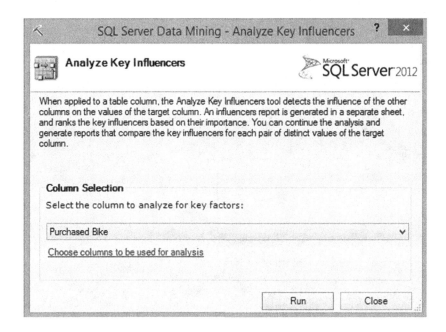

Figure 13-6. *Selecting the outcome field*

Next click on the link to choose the columns you want to use for analysis (see Figure 13-7).

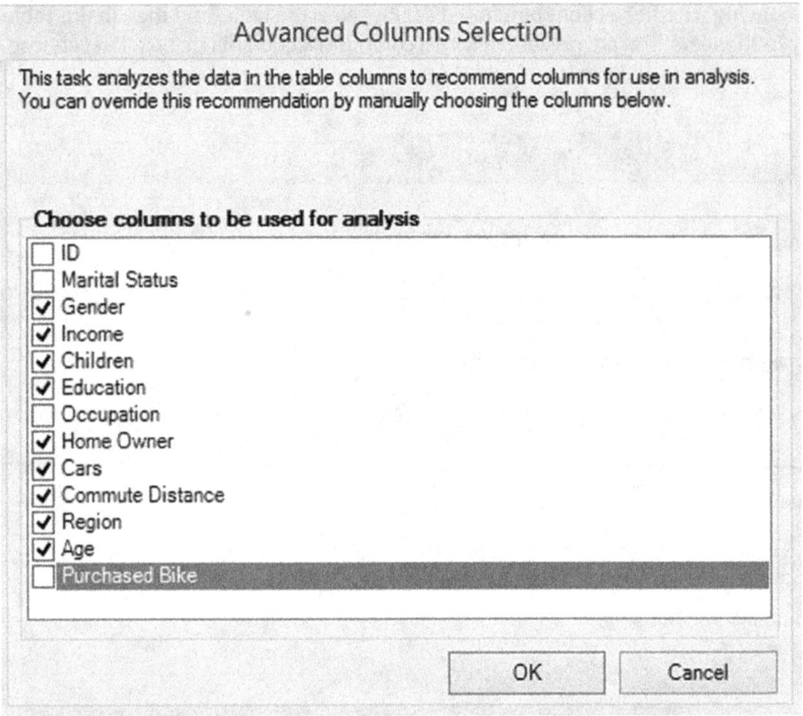

Figure 13-7. *Selecting the influencer fields*

After selecting the fields to analyze, select OK to close the Advanced Columns Selection window. In the Analyze Key Influencers window, select Run to start the analysis (see Figure 13-6).

When the Analyze Key Influencers tool analyzes the data, it first stores key information about the distribution of your data. Next it creates a model using the Microsoft Naïve Bayes algorithm and SSAS. Then it creates predictions that correlate each column of data with the specified outcome. Finally, it uses the confidence score for each of the predictions to identify the factors that are the most influential in producing the targeted outcome.

After it finishes its analysis, the Analyze Key Influencers tool creates a report on a new worksheet that lists the key influencers ordered by confidence scores (see Figure 13-8).

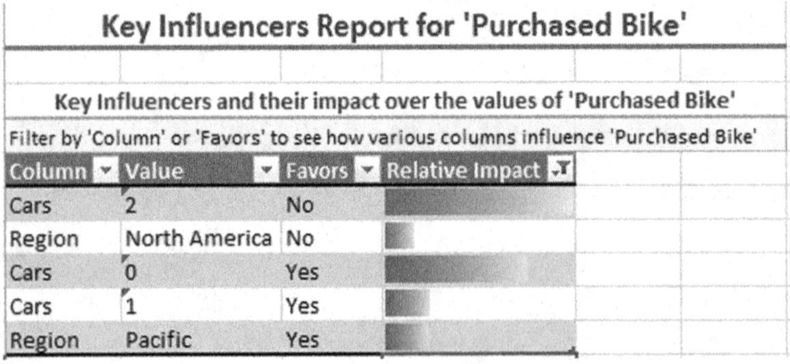
Key Influencers Report for 'Purchased Bike'

Key Influencers and their impact over the values of 'Purchased Bike'

Filter by 'Column' or 'Favors' to see how various columns influence 'Purchased Bike'

Column	Value	Favors	Relative Impact
Cars	2	No	
Region	North America	No	
Cars	0	Yes	
Cars	1	Yes	
Region	Pacific	Yes	

Figure 13-8. *Results of a key influencer analysis*

As you can see from the report, clearly the number of cars has an influence on bike buying.

Along with determining what factors influence the bike buyers, you may want to see what types of customers you are appealing to. What are the predominate groups? Are they young? Do they own a home? In the next section, you will look at using the Detect Categories tool and clustering to answer these questions.

Identifying Data Groups

Detecting different categories that your data falls into is an important analysis you perform on the data. This can be useful for many different scenarios; for example, you need to know what groups your customers fall into so that you can target your marketing for the different groups. Another reason to take a close look at categories is so you can determine outliers that do not fit in any group. This way, if you need to, you can filter out the outliers from your data set so they do not skew your results. Finding outliers is also a common pattern for detecting possible fraud.

To identify the various market segments of customers buying bikes, first select a table that contains customer demographics and a column that indicates if they purchased a bike. In the Table Tools Analyze tab select the Detect Categories tool. This launches a window where you select the fields to use and how many categories to create (see Figure 13-9). Do not select columns that have distinct values, such as ID fields, because these are not appropriate for grouping analysis.

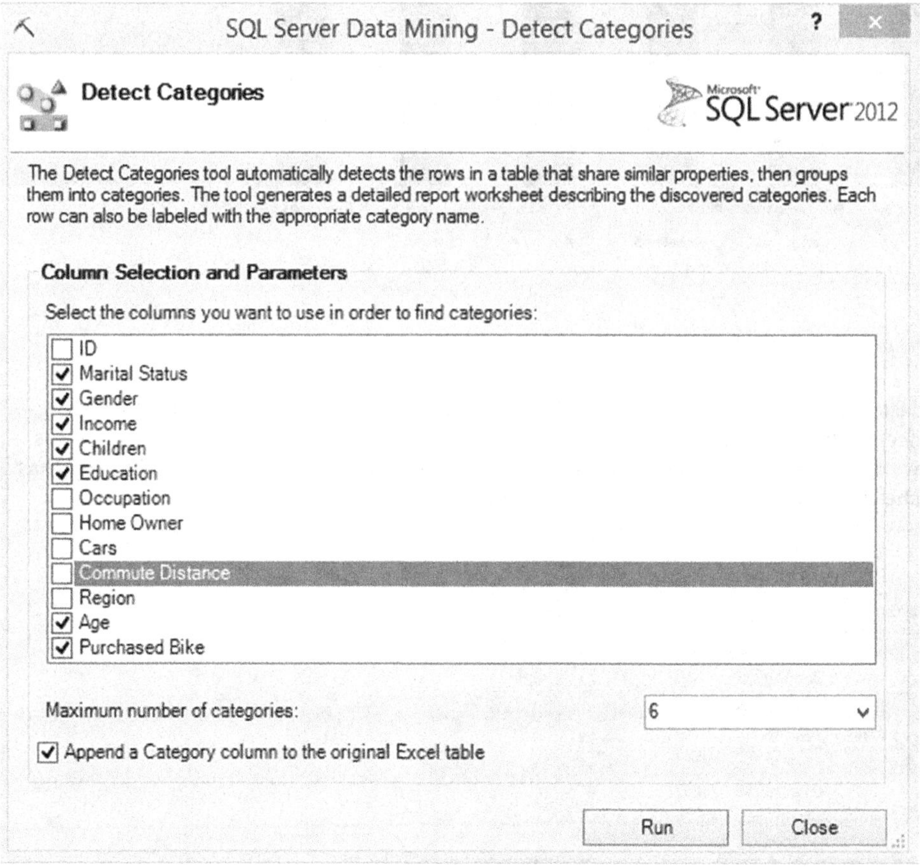

Figure 13-9. *Selecting the group attribute fields*

Once you run the Detect Categories tool, the data is analyzed using a cluster analysis algorithm. You can have the tool append a Category field to the data table. After the tool is finished, you will see a new worksheet displaying the results. On the worksheet is a graph that shows the population of each category for the chosen field (see Figure 13-10). Since you are interested in categories for customers who purchased bikes, you should set the column of the graph to that field.

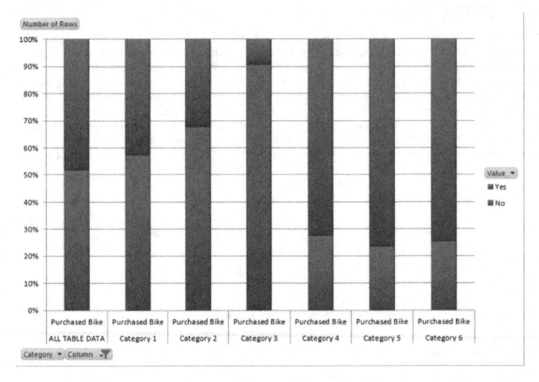

Figure 13-10. *Viewing the population graph*

As you can see, the customer segments associated with Categories 4, 5, and 6 are most likely to be bike buyers.

On this same worksheet is a table you can use to investigate the attributes of the rows that make up the various groups. Figure 13-11 shows the characteristics that make up Category 6. As you can see, the majority of the group has no children, earned a bachelor's degree, and is in the 37-46 age group.

Category Characteristics			
Filter the table by 'Category' to see the characteristics of different categories.			
Category	Column	Value	Relative Importance
Category 6	Children	0	
Category 6	Education	Bachelors	
Category 6	Age	Low:37 - 46	
Category 6	Purchased Bike	Yes	
Category 6	Marital Status	Single	
Category 6	Income	Low:39050 - 71062	
Category 6	Income	Medium:71062 - 97111	
Category 6	Age	Very Low:< 37	

Figure 13-11. *Reviewing group characteristics*

Along with the Detect Categories tool, the Highlight Exceptions tool also performs a clustering algorithm on the data. In this case, it is looking for data that does not fit in with the rest of the data. This information comes in handy when you need to clean up a data set before you perform some of the other analyses on the data. Remember, any time you perform data analysis on a set of data, you need to ensure that any outliers do not skew your results.

When you run the Highlight Exceptions tool, you are presented with a window in which to select the columns you want to analyze (see Figure 13-12).

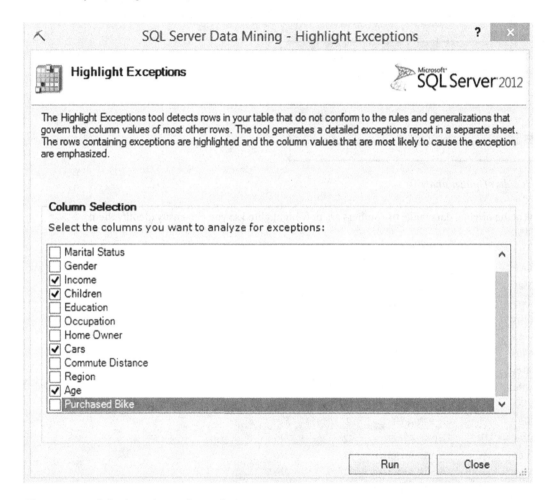

Figure 13-12. *Selecting columns for analysis*

After you run the tool, you are presented with a results table that shows the number of outliers found. You can also adjust the threshold to pick up more or fewer exceptions (see Figure 13-13).

The outlier cells are highlighted in the original table.

Exception threshold (more or fewer exceptions)	75

Column	Outliers
Income	0
Children	0
Cars	0
Age	2
Purchased Bike	0
Total	2

Figure 13-13. *Results of outlier analysis*

Take a look at the original data table; the outliers are now highlighted so you can easily identify them (see Figure 13-14).

Cars	Commute Distance	Region	Age	Purchased Bike
2	2-5 Miles	North America	55	Yes
0	0-1 Miles	North America	48	No
3	0-1 Miles	North America	45	Yes
1	0-1 Miles	Pacific	42	Yes
2	10+ Miles	North America	63	No
2	10+ Miles	North America	54	Yes
2	5-10 Miles	North America	73	Yes
0	2-5 Miles	North America	36	Yes
1	2-5 Miles	North America	2	Yes
0	1-2 Miles	North America	42	No
0	1-2 Miles	North America	31	No
2	0-1 Miles	North America	41	No
0	10+ Miles	North America	58	No

Figure 13-14. *Highlinghting the outlier rows found*

One area of data mining that is becoming increasingly important when you are trying to run an efficient business and reduce overhead is forecasting. You will look at this next.

Forecasting Future Trends

The Forecast tool allows you to predict future trends by looking at past trends. It uses a time series algorithm to predict future values. Running the tool opens a window where you chose the columns to predict, the time series column, and the number of time periods to predict (see Figure 13-15).

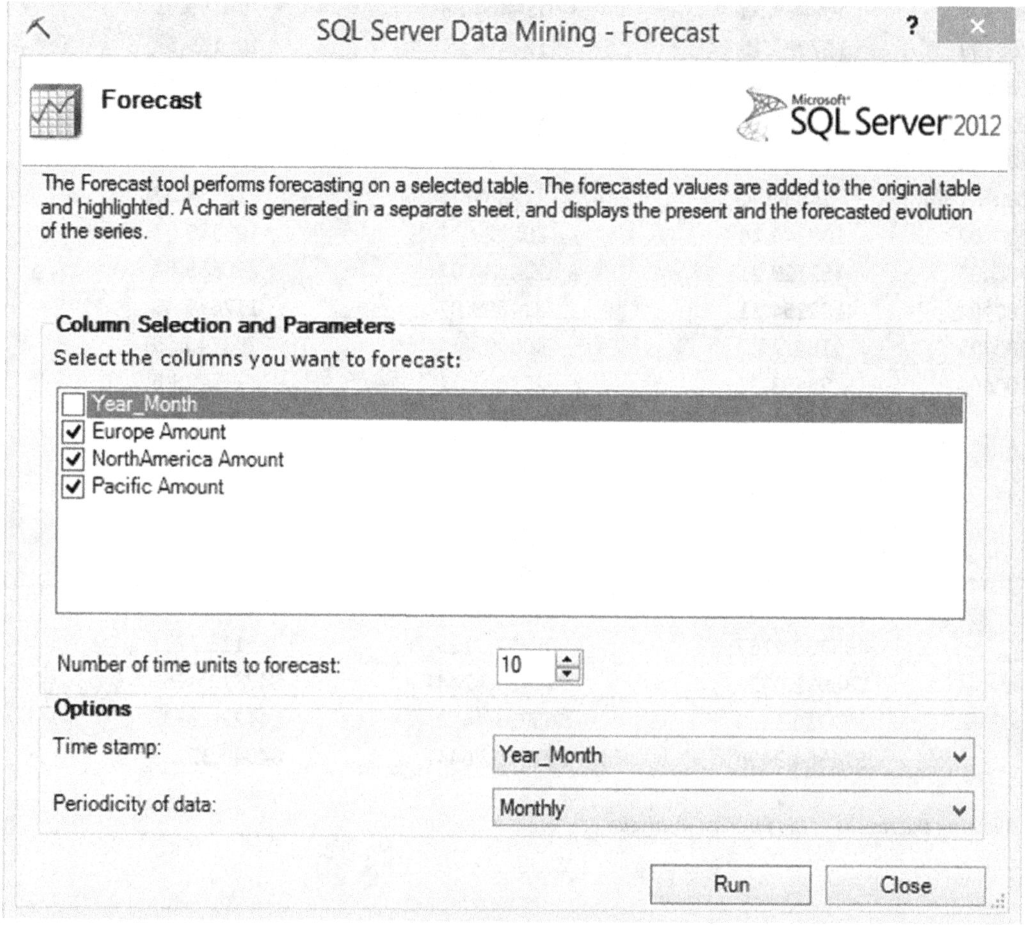

Figure 13-15. *Choosing the forecast parameters*

When the tool finishes running, the predicted values are placed at the end of the historical data and highlighted for review (see Figure 13-16).

Year/Month	Europe Amount	NorthAmerica Amount	Pacific Amount
200307	85489.63	135979.41	124579.46
200308	108439.53	154464.33	16139.93
200309	127024.45	124454.46	106169.54
200310	115449.5	138474.4	113029.51
200311	117644.49	182154.21	115374.5
200312	228304.01	311473.65	11524.95
200401	138349.4	212389.08	110734.52
200402	198344.14	205329.11	108539.53
200403	182129.21	214584.07	110859.52
200404	182254.21	214609.07	117619.49
200405	184774.2	405993.24	103849.55
200406	295483.72	297803.71	115249.5
	294331.324	405860.906	85701.6478
	353348.2333	449248.0423	85885.22423
	381638.0471	378704.0362	85918.73182
	371602.6967	434349.4848	85834.37076
	379592.4817	502464.2818	85658.65469
	559383.1098	704862.3261	85413.35197
	435760.4267	556791.7125	85116.2751
	538512.0337	541486.4244	84781.94255
	507780.3529	565725.7411	84422.13332
	514564.3496	571595.7644	84046.35133

Figure 13-16. *Viewing the results of the forecast analysis*

In addition, a new work sheet is inserted that shows a linear graph of historical trends and future predictions. The historical values are plotted using a solid line and the future predictions a graphed with a dashed line (see Figure 13-17).

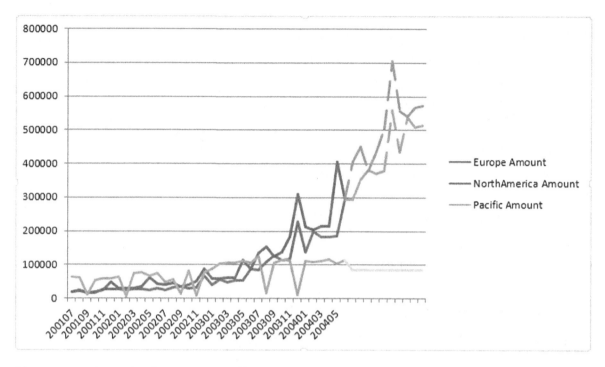

Figure 13-17. *The graphical representation of future trends*

Along with forecasting, another popular type of data mining is shopping basket analysis. You will look at this next.

Using Shopping Basket Analysis

The Shopping Basket Analysis tool uses the Association algorithm to find associations between the data. Traditionally this has been used to analyze customers' purchasing patterns and is useful when making recommendations for upselling other items. When you analyze data using the Shopping Basket Analysis tool, make sure the data has a key that organizes it into groupings—for example, an order number (see Figure 13-18).

Order Number	Category	Product	Product Price
SO61269	Helmets	Sport-100	53.99
SO61269	Jerseys	Long-Sleeve Logo Jersey	49.99
SO61270	Fenders	Fender Set - Mountain	21.98
SO61271	Tires and Tubes	LL Road Tire	21.49
SO61271	Tires and Tubes	Patch kit	564.99
SO61272	Tires and Tubes	Mountain Tire Tube	4.99
SO61272	Tires and Tubes	Patch kit	564.99
SO61273	Bottles and Cages	Water Bottle	4.99
SO61274	Caps	Cycling Cap	8.99
SO61274	Shorts	Women's Mountain Shorts	69.99
SO61275	Helmets	Sport-100	53.99
SO61276	Jerseys	Short-Sleeve Classic Jersey	539.99
SO61276	Caps	Cycling Cap	8.99
SO61277	Mountain Bikes	Mountain-500	539.99
SO61277	Jerseys	Short-Sleeve Classic Jersey	539.99
SO61277	Caps	Cycling Cap	8.99

Figure 13-18. *The order number is used to group transactions*

When you select the Shopping Basket Analysis tool, you are presented with a Column Selection window where you select the Transaction ID, Item, and Item Value columns (see Figure 13-19).

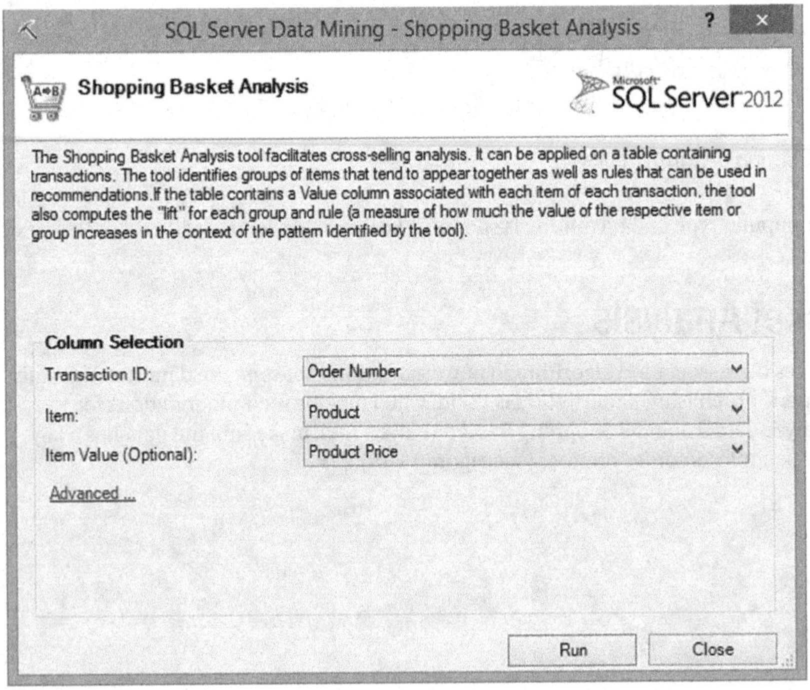

Figure 13-19. *Selecting the columns for analysis*

Selecting the Advanced link opens up a window that allows you to adjust the sensitivity of the algorithm (see Figure 13-20). Increasing the Minimum Support and Minimum Rule Probability parameters will decrease the number of items in your results but increase the significance of your results.

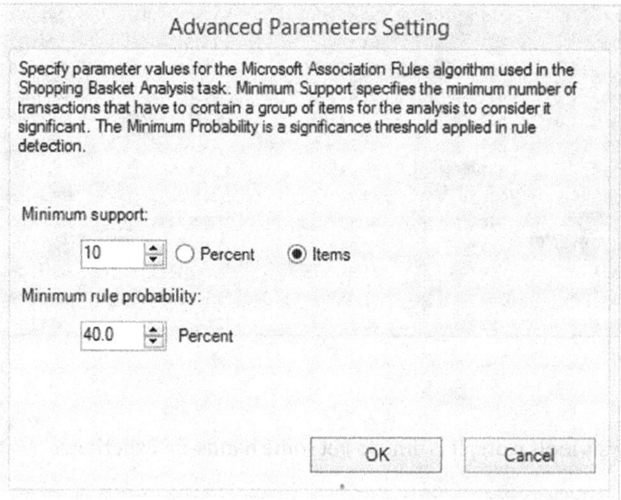

Advanced Parameters Setting

Specify parameter values for the Microsoft Association Rules algorithm used in the Shopping Basket Analysis task. Minimum Support specifies the minimum number of transactions that have to contain a group of items for the analysis to consider it significant. The Minimum Probability is a significance threshold applied in rule detection.

Minimum support:

10 ○ Percent ● Items

Minimum rule probability:

40.0 Percent

OK   Cancel

Figure 13-20. Specifying minimum parameter values

After you run the analysis two new worksheets are inserted. The first one, Shopping Basket Bundled Item, shows the items that are found bundled together as well as the bundle size, number of sales, the average value of the sales, and the overall value of the bundle (see Figure 13-21).

Bundle of items	Bundle size	Number of sales	Average Value Per Sale	Overall value of Bundle
Fender Set - Mountain, Mountain-200	2	438	2341.97	1025782.86
Mountain Bottle Cage, Mountain-200	2	430	2329.98	1001891.4
Mountain-200, Sport-100	2	407	2373.98	966209.86
Touring-1000, Sport-100	2	344	2438.06	838692.64
Mountain Bottle Cage, Mountain-200, Water Bottle	3	344	2334.97	803229.68
Mountain-200, Water Bottle	2	344	2324.98	799793.12
HL Mountain Tire, Mountain-200	2	314	2354.99	739466.86
Mountain-200, Patch kit	2	209	2884.98	602960.82
Touring-1000, Road Bottle Cage	2	216	2393.06	516900.96
Road-350-W, Sport-100	2	206	2497.34	514452.04

Figure 13-21. The results of the analysis showing bundled items sold

The second worksheet, Shopping Basket Recommendations, lists recommendations for products that have a high probability of being sold together. For example, if a customer buys a road bottle cage, you should recommend that they also buy a water bottle (see Figure 13-22). This worksheet also contains statistics like the percent of linked sales and the average value of the recommendation.

Selected Item	Recommendation	Sales of Selected Items	Linked Sales	% of linked sales	Average value of recommendation	Overall value of linked sales
Road Bottle Cage	Water Bottle	1005	897	89.25 %	4.453761194	4476.03
Touring Tire	Touring Tire Tube	582	507	87.11 %	4.346958763	2529.93
Mountain Bottle Cage	Water Bottle	1201	998	83.10 %	4.146561199	4980.02
HL Road Tire	Road Tire Tube	463	326	70.41 %	6.329892009	2930.74
ML Road Tire	Road Tire Tube	533	363	68.11 %	6.122645403	3263.37
HL Mountain Tire	Mountain Tire Tube	816	552	67.65 %	3.375588235	2754.48
ML Mountain Tire	Mountain Tire Tube	661	435	65.81 %	3.283888048	2170.65
Touring Tire Tube	Touring Tire	897	507	56.52 %	16.38565217	14697.93
LL Mountain Tire	Mountain Tire Tube	499	277	55.51 %	2.77	1382.23
LL Road Tire	Road Tire Tube	608	334	54.93 %	4.938585526	3002.66
Road-550-W	Sport-100	618	264	42.72 %	23.06368932	14253.36
Touring-1000	Sport-100	811	344	42.42 %	22.90081381	18572.56
Mountain Tire Tube	Sport-100	1782	749	42.03 %	22.69276655	40438.51
All-Purpose Bike Stand	Patch kit	130	54	41.54 %	234.6881538	30509.46
Half-Finger Gloves	Sport-100	849	352	41.46 %	22.38454653	19004.48
Touring-2000	Sport-100	211	86	40.76 %	22.00540284	4643.14

Figure 13-22. Recommendations for cross selling items

Now that you have seen how the various table analysis tools work, it is time to get some hands-on experience using a few of the tools.

HANDS-ON LAB—USING THE TABLE ANALYSIS TOOLS IN EXCEL

In the following lab you will

- Determine the key influencers for owning a home.

- Detect the various customer groups.

- Perform a shopping basket analysis on purchased products.

- Forecast pollution emissions.

1. In the LabStarters folder, open the LabChapter13.xlsx file. This file contains sample customer data. You will perform data mining on this data using the table analysis tools.

2. On the Influencers worksheet, click anywhere on the data table to show the Table Tools Analyze tab. On this tab, select the Analyze Key Influencers button. In the Column Selection window, select the Home Owner column to analyze for key factors.

3. Select the following columns to be used for analysis: Marital Status, Gender, Income, Children, Education, Occupation, Cars, Commute Distance, and Age. Run the analysis and when the Discrimination Reporting window (see Figure 13-23) appears, you can close it because there are only two values to compare and they have already been added to the report.

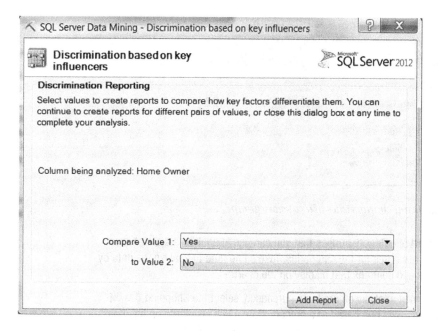

Figure 13-23. *Choosing values to compare*

4. In the Key Influencers report, notice that of the columns analyzed, marital status was the key influencer. The number of children and commute distance are also influencers, however. Just as interesting is the fact that education and age are not key influencers. This might be an area you want to investigate further especially because it may be a result of not having a large enough sample size.

5. To detect the various groups of customers, select the Categories worksheet. Click anywhere on the table and then select the Detect Categories tool on the Table Tools Analyze tab.

6. In the Detect Categories tool, select the Marital Status, Gender, Income, Children, Education, Occupation, and Age checkboxes, and then click the Run button.

7. On the Categories worksheet, notice there are six categories. Use the Category Characteristics table to determine the characteristics most important to each group (see Figure 13-24). You can rename the categories; for example, Category 1 is dominated by low income and you could rename it to reflect this.

Category Characteristics			
Filter the table by 'Category' to see the characteristics of different categories.			
Category	Column	Value	Relative Importance
Category 1	Income	Low:39050 - 71062	
Category 1	Occupation	Skilled Manual	
Category 1	Age	Very Low:< 37	
Category 1	Children	0	
Category 1	Age	Low:37 - 46	
Category 1	Education	Bachelors	
Category 1	Education	Graduate Degree	
Category 1	Children	1	

Figure 13-24. *Determining the significant charateristics of a category group*

8. Below the table is a chart of category profiles that you can use to analyze the distribution of values of the various attributes for the categories. Take some time to analyze the data by changing the categories and columns that display on the chart.

9. To perform shopping basket analysis on products purchased, select the Shopping Basket Worksheet. This contains items purchased at a grocery store. Click anywhere on the data table and select the Shopping Basket Analysis tool on the Table Tools Analyze tab.

10. On the Shopping Basket Analysis window, select the Order ID column for the Transaction ID. For the Item, select the Item column and leave the Item Value set to No Value Column.

11. Select the Advanced link, and in the Advanced Parameters Setting window, change Minimum Support to 20 items and Minimum Rule Probability to 50%.

12. Run the analysis and in the Shopping Basket Recommendations table, notice that 60% of the time a customer buys milk when they purchase cereal (see Figure 13-25).

Shopping Basket Recommendations					
Selected Item	Recommendation	Sales of Selected Items	Linked Sales	% of linked sales	Importance
cereals	whole milk	45	27	60.00 %	0.37
rice	whole milk	57	30	52.63 %	0.32

Figure 13-25. *Viewing the cross-selling recommendations*

13. To perform forecasting, select the Forecast tab, which contains pollutant emissions for several states from 2000 to 2010. Click anywhere on the data table and select the Forecast tool on the Table Tools Analyze tab.

14. In the Forecast window, select the State columns for forecasting. Set Time Stamp to Year and the Periodicity Of Data to Yearly (see Figure 13-26).

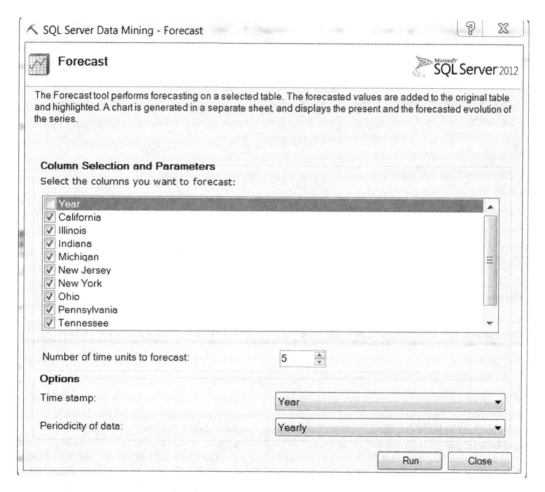

Figure 13-26. *Selecting the forecasting attributes*

15. Run the forecast. You will now see a forecasting graph that shows the forecast as dashed line extensions to the actual values (see Figure 13-27).

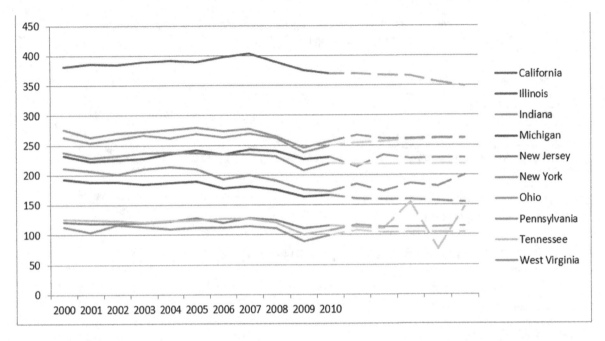

Figure 13-27. *The resulting forecast graph*

16. When you are done experimenting with the table analysis tools, save and close the Excel workbook.

Summary

Although data mining is one of the most underutilized areas of business intelligence, with the help of Excel's table analysis tools it does not have to be. Although data mining uses a set of complex algorithms and the traditional tools often require you to be an expert in such algorithms to be able to implement them, when you use the table analysis tools, Excel hides much of the complexity from you. This chapter showed you how to use these tools to perform advanced data analysis such as forecasting, clustering, and associations. You are now able to utilize these tools to gain more insight into your data. Remember to look beyond the specific examples and learn to apply the patterns in a variety of situations.

At the time of this writing, Microsoft is moving its data mining efforts into Microsoft Azure ML (Machine Learning) and has not been investing in any upgrades to Excel's data mining tools. This is unfortunate because Azure ML is a cloud-only—based system and is a little advanced for the typical business analyst. On the bright side, several third-party vendors (such as XLMiner and Predixion) are stepping up and offering their own data mining add-in tools for Excel. These tools are very similar to the look and feel of the table analysis tools covered in this chapter and I think you will find using these tools to be an easy transition.

In Chapter 14, you will look at two realistic case studies to solidify the concepts of the previous chapters. By working through these case studies, you will be able to gauge which areas you have mastered and which you need to study further. In addition, you will look at some common patterns associated with data analysis and how to implement these using the tools covered in this book.

CHAPTER 14

■ ■ ■

Creating a Complete Solution

In the previous chapters, you gained experience working with each of the pieces of Microsoft's self-service BI tool set. You used Power Pivot, Power View, Power Query, Power Map, and the Excel table analysis tools. This chapter provides you with several use cases to solidify the concepts of the previous chapters. By working through these use cases, you will gauge which areas you have mastered and which you need to spend more time studying. Since this is sort of like your final exam, I have deliberately not included step-by-step instructions like I did for the previous exercises. Instead, I have given you general directions that should be sufficient to get you started. If you get stuck, refer back to the previous chapters to remind yourself of how to accomplish the task.

This chapter contains the following use cases:

- Reseller Sales analysis
- Sales Quota analysis
- Sensor analysis

Use Case 1: Reseller Sales Analysis

In this scenario, you work for a bike equipment company and have been asked to analyze the sales data. You need to build a dashboard to compare same-store sales growth from one month to the next. An added constraint is that you only want to compare resellers who have been open for at least a year when you make the comparison.

Load the Data

Create a new Excel workbook named StoreSalesAnalysis.xlsx. In the Chapter14Labs folder, find the UseCase1 folder, which contains a StoreSales.accdb Access database. This database houses the sales data you need to analyze. Using this as a data source, import the data tables and columns listed in Table 14-1.

Table 14-1. *Store Sales Tables and Columns to Import*

Source Table	Friendly Name	Columns
dbo_DimDate	Date	DateKey, FullDateAlternateKey, EnglishMonthName, MonthNumberOfYear, CalendarQuarter, CalendarYear
dbo_DimGeography	Location	GeographyKey,City, StateProvinceCode, StateProvinceName, CountryRegionCode, EnglishCountryRegionName, PostalCode
dbo_DimProduct	Product	ProductKey, ProductSubcategoryKey, EnglishProductName, StandardCost, ListPrice, DealerPrice, LargePhoto
dbo_DimProductCategory	Category	ProductCategoryKey, EnglishProductCategoryName
dbo_DimProductSubcategory	Subcategory	ProductSubcategoryKey, EnglishProductSubcategoryName, ProductCategoryKey
dbo_DimReseller	Reseller	ResellerKey, GeographyKey, BusinessType, ResellerName, YearOpened
dbo_FactResellerSales	ResellerSales	ProductKey, ResellerKey, OrderDateKey, SalesOrderNumber, SalesOrderLineNumber, OrderQuantity, UnitPrice, ExtendedAmount, TotalProductCost, SalesAmount

Create the Model

After importing the tables, create the table relationships using the appropriate keys. Your model should now look similar to Figure 14-1.

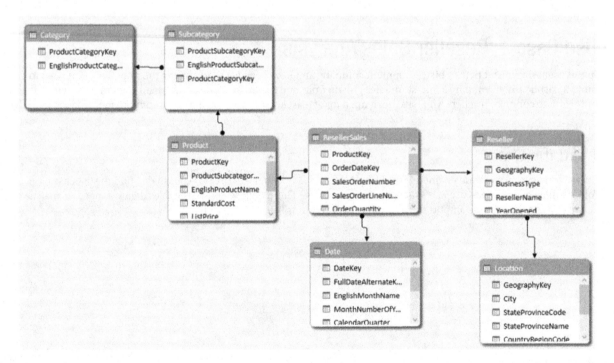

Figure 14-1. *Store sales model*

Rename the table columns and show or hide the columns from client tools according to the information listed in Table 14-2.

Table 14-2. *Table and Column Properties*

Table	Column	New Name	Hide from Client
Date	DateKey	—	X
	FullDateAlternateKey	Full Date	
	EnglishMonthName	Month	
	MonthNumberOfYear	Month Number	X
	CalendarQuarter	Calendar Quarter	
	CalendarYear	Calendar Year	
Product	ProductKey	—	X
	SubcategoryKey	—	X
	StandardCost	Standard Cost	
	ListPrice	List Price	
	DealerPrice	Dealer Price	
	LargePhoto	Product Photo	
Reseller	ResellerKey	—	X
	GeographyKey	—	X
	BusinessType	Reseller Type	
	ResellerName	Reseller Name	
	YearOpened	Year Opened	
Location	GeographyKey	—	X
	StateProvinceCode	State Province Code	
	StateProvinceName	State Province	
	CountryRegionCode	Country Code	
	EnglishCountryRegionName	Country	
ResellerSales	ProductKey	—	X
	ResellerKey	—	X
	OrderDateKey	—	X
	SalesOrderNumber	Order Number	
	SalesOrderLineNumber	Order Line Number	
	OrderQuantity	Quantity	
	UnitPrice	Unit Price	
	ExtendedAmount	Extended Amount	
	TotalProductCost	Product Cost	
	SalesAmount	Sales Amount	

In the Date table, create a calendar hierarchy of Year - Quarter - Month. Mark the table as the Date table with the Full Date column as the key. Sort the Month column by the Month Number column. Format the Full Date column to only show the date and not the time.

Create Calculated Columns

Using the DAX RELATED function, create a calculated column in the Product table for Product Subcategory and Product Category.

```
[Category]
=IF(ISBLANK([ProductSubcategoryKey]),"Misc",
    RELATED(Category[EnglishProductCategoryName]))

[Subcategory]
=IF(ISBLANK([ProductSubcategoryKey]),"Misc",
```

RELATED(Subcategory[EnglishProductSubcategoryName]))Hide the Category and Subcategory tables from any client tools. If the ProductSubcategoryKey is blank, fill in the Category and Subcategory columns with "Misc". Finally, create a hierarchy with the Product Category and Product Subcategory columns named **Prd Cat**.

Create Measures

Add the following measures to the ResellerSales table:

```
Month Sales:=TOTALMTD(SUM([Sales Amount]),'Date'[Full Date])

Prev Month Sales:=CALCULATE(Sum([Sales Amount]),PREVIOUSMONTH('Date'[Full Date]))

Monthly Sales Growth:=[Month Sales] - [Prev Month Sales]

Monthly Sales Growth %:=DIVIDE([Monthly Sales Growth],[Prev Month Sales],0)
```

Test your measures by creating a pivot table as shown in Figure 14-2.

Row Labels ▼	Month Sales	Prev Month Sales	Monthly Sales Growth	Monthly Sales Growth %
⊟ 2011				
July	$489,328.58		$489,328.58	0.00 %
August	$1,538,408.31	$489,328.58	$1,049,079.73	214.39 %
September	$1,165,897.08	$1,538,408.31	($372,511.23)	-24.21 %
October	$844,721.00	$1,165,897.08	($321,176.08)	-27.55 %
November	$2,324,135.80	$844,721.00	$1,479,414.80	175.14 %
December	$1,702,944.54	$2,324,135.80	($621,191.25)	-26.73 %
2011 Total	$1,702,944.54		$1,702,944.54	0.00 %
⊟ 2012				
January	$713,116.69	$1,702,944.54	($989,827.85)	-58.12 %
February	$1,900,788.93	$713,116.69	$1,187,672.24	166.55 %
March	$1,455,280.41	$1,900,788.93	($445,508.52)	-23.44 %
April	$882,899.94	$1,455,280.41	($572,380.47)	-39.33 %
May	$2,269,116.71	$882,899.94	$1,386,216.77	157.01 %
June	$1,001,803.77	$2,269,116.71	($1,267,312.94)	-55.85 %
July	$2,393,689.53	$1,001,803.77	$1,391,885.76	138.94 %
August	$3,601,190.71	$2,393,689.53	$1,207,501.19	50.45 %
September	$2,885,359.20	$3,601,190.71	($715,831.51)	-19.88 %
October	$1,802,154.21	$2,885,359.20	($1,083,204.99)	-37.54 %
November	$3,053,816.33	$1,802,154.21	$1,251,662.11	69.45 %
December	$2,185,213.21	$3,053,816.33	($868,603.11)	-28.44 %
2012 Total	$2,185,213.21	$1,702,944.54	$482,268.67	28.32 %

Figure 14-2. *Viewing the measures in a pivot table*

Now you need to create a measure to determine if a store was open for at least a year for the month you are calculating the sales for. In the Reseller table, add the following measures:

```
Years Open:=Year(FIRSTDATE('Date'[Full Date])) - Min([Year Opened])
```

```
Was Open Prev Year:=If([Years Open]>0,1,0)
```

Create a pivot table to test your measures, as shown in Figure 14-3. Remember that the measures only make sense if you filter by year.

Row Labels	Years Open	Was Open Prev Year
A Bicycle Association	19	1
A Bike Store	24	1
A Cycle Shop	-6	0
A Great Bicycle Company	23	1
A Typical Bike Shop	12	1
Acceptable Sales & Service	6	1
Accessories Network	10	1
Acclaimed Bicycle Company	15	1
Ace Bicycle Supply	2	1
Action Bicycle Specialists	2	1
Active Cycling	-4	0
Active Life Toys	-3	0
Active Systems	6	1
Active Transport Inc.	4	1

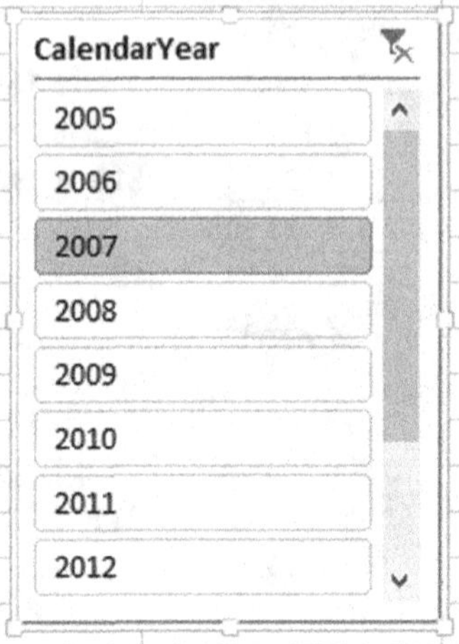

CalendarYear:
2005
2006
2007
2008
2009
2010
2011
2012

Figure 14-3. *Testing the measures*

Now you can combine these measures so that you are only including resellers who have been in business for at least a year at the time of the sales. Create the following measures:

```
Month Sales Filtered:=Calculate([Month Sales],FILTER(Reseller,[Was Open Prev Year]=1))

Prev Month Sales Filtered:=CALCULATE([Prev Month Sales],
    Filter(Reseller,[Was Open Prev Year]=1))

Monthly Sales Growth Filtered:=[Month Sales Filtered]-[Prev Month Sales Filtered]

Monthly Sales Growth Filtered %:=DIVIDE([Monthly Sales Growth Filtered],
    [Prev Month Sales Filtered],0)
```

Test your new measures by creating a Power Pivot table as shown in Figure 14-4. You should see a difference between the filtered and the nonfiltered measures.

Row Labels	Month Sales	Month Sales Filtered	Monthly Sales Growth %	Monthly Sales Growth Filtered %
⊟2011				
July	$489,328.58	$459,838.43	0.00 %	0.00 %
August	$1,538,408.31	$1,192,341.84	214.39 %	159.30 %
September	$1,165,897.08	$1,007,879.27	-24.21 %	-15.47 %
October	$844,721.00	$783,711.37	-27.55 %	-22.24 %
November	$2,324,135.80	$1,837,106.56	175.14 %	134.41 %
December	$1,702,944.54	$1,473,461.12	-26.73 %	-19.79 %
2011 Total	$1,702,944.54	$1,473,461.12	0.00 %	0.00 %
⊟2012				
January	$713,116.69	$638,323.90	-58.12 %	-57.94 %
February	$1,900,788.93	$1,709,074.23	166.55 %	167.74 %
March	$1,455,280.41	$1,247,528.68	-23.44 %	-27.01 %
April	$882,899.94	$743,640.83	-39.33 %	-40.39 %
May	$2,269,116.71	$1,937,427.35	157.01 %	160.53 %
June	$1,001,803.77	$859,550.38	-55.85 %	-55.63 %
July	$2,393,689.53	$2,057,492.23	138.94 %	139.37 %

Figure 14-4. *Testing the filtered measures*

Create the Dashboard

Before creating a dashboard in Power View, you need to update some table settings to optimize the model for Power View. Table 14-3 lists the tables and settings you need to make.

Table 14-3. *Settings to Optimize for Power View*

Table Name	Row Identifier	Default Label	Default Photo	Default Field Set
Reseller	ResellerKey	Reseller Name	—	Reseller Name, Reseller Type, Year Opened
Product	ProductKey	Product	Product Photo	Product, Standard Cost, List Price, Dealer Price
Location	GeographyKey	—	—	City, State Province, Country, Postal Code

In addition, mark the columns listed in Table 14-4 as the appropriate data category.

Table 14-4. *Setting the Data Category*

Table	Column	Data Category
Location	City	City
	State Province	State or Province
	Country	Country
	Postal Code	Postal Code
Product	Product Photo	Image

In the Date table, set the fields so they do not summarize.

To create the dashboard, insert a Power View report. Name the report **Reseller Sales** and add a column chart that shows sales by month and reseller type using the filtered monthly sales. Add a slicer to the report that controls the calendar year displayed by the chart. Since there are no sales before 2011, filter the view to only show years 2011 to 2014. Your report should look similar to Figure 14-5.

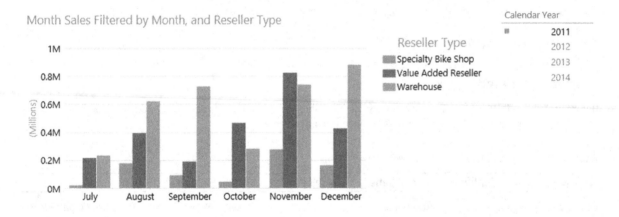

Figure 14-5. *The reseller sales report*

You now want to make another reseller analysis to find the best monthly sales for the month, quarter, and year. In order to do this, you need to add a new measure to the model. This measure uses the VALUES and the MAXX functions to find the maximum reseller monthly sales.

```
Max Reseller Sales:=MAXX(VALUES(Reseller[ResellerKey]),[Month Sales])
```

Once you have the new measure in the model, add another column chart to the Power View report that shows the maximum reseller sales for each month. Notice the charts are interactive; if you click on a column in one chart, it will filter the other chart accordingly (see Figure 14-6).

Reseller Sales

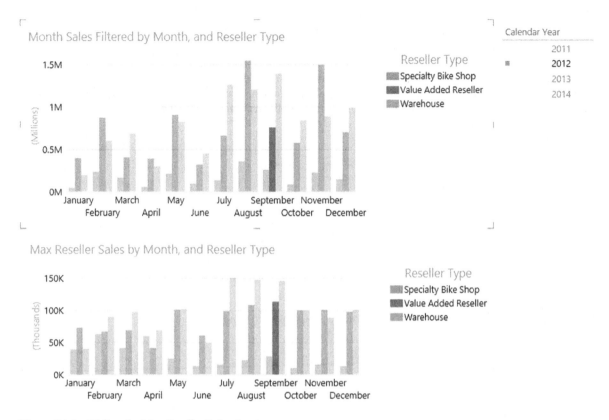

Figure 14-6. *Adding the Max Reseller Sales chart*

To take this one step further, let's say you want the name of the reseller who has the maximum monthly sales for the period. To accomplish this, you need to combine a series of expressions to retrieve the name of the reseller with the maximum monthly sales. First, you need to determine which reseller has monthly sales equal to the maximum monthly sales. If they do, they are flagged with a value of 1; otherwise they get a value of BLANK.

```
IF([Month Sales]=CALCULATE([Max Reseller Sales],
    Values(Reseller[Reseller Name])),1,BLANK())
```

The next step is to use the FIRSTNONBLANK function to find the reseller that has a value of 1.

```
FIRSTNONBLANK(Reseller[Reseller Name],
    IF([Month Sales]=CALCULATE([Max Reseller Sales],
    Values(Reseller[Reseller Name])),1,BLANK()))
```

Finally you need to make sure there were actually monthly sales during the period you are examining. Combining these formulas into the Top Monthly Reseller measure as follows:

```
Top Monthly Reseller:=If(ISBLANK([Month Sales]),
    BLANK(),FIRSTNONBLANK(Reseller[Reseller Name],IF([Month Sales]=
    CALCULATE([Max Reseller Sales],Values(Reseller[Reseller Name])),1,BLANK())))
```

This time, build the dashboard in an Excel worksheet. Add a chart that shows the percent sales growth for the months of the year you are interested in and a pivot table that shows the maximum reseller sales and reseller name for each month. Also include a slicer for the year, one for the reseller type, and one for the country. Your dashboard should look similar to Figure 14-7.

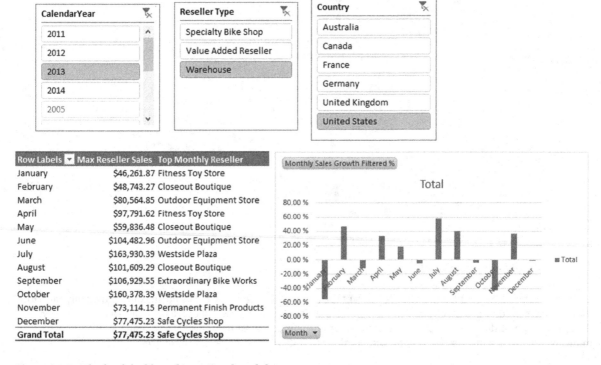

Figure 14-7. *The final dashboard in an Excel worksheet*

After completing and experimenting with the dashboard, save and close Excel.

Use Case 2: Sales Quota Analysis

For this scenario, you will use the sales data for the sales team of the same bike company from Use Case 1. This time, using Power View, you need to create a dashboard that allows the sales manager to track the performance of the sales team. You will compare actual sales to the sales quotas for the sales team. Although the measures you need for this comparison are not that complex, the grain of the data for sales and quotas is at different levels, which presents a challenge.

Load the Data

Create a new Excel Workbook named SalesRepAnalysis.xlsx. In the Chapter14Labs folder is a folder named UseCase2; this folder contains a SalesRepAnalysis.accdb Access database. Using this as a data source, import the data tables and columns listed in Table 14-5.

Table 14-5. *Tables and Columns to Import*

Source Table	Friendly Name	Columns	Filter
dbo_DimDate	Date	DateKey, FullDateAlternateKey, EnglishMonthName, MonthNumberOfYear, CalendarQuarter, CalendarYear	
dbo_DimEmployee	Sales Rep	EmployeeKey, ParentEmployeeKey, FirstName, LastName, MiddleName, Title, HireDate, EmployeePhoto	SalesPersonFlag = TRUE
dbo_DimSalesTerritory	Sales Territory	SalesTerritoryKey, SalesTerritoryRegion, SalesTerritoryCountry, SalesTerritoryGroup, SalesTerritorryImage	
dbo_FactResellerSales	Sales	OrderDateKey, EmployeeKey, SalesTerritoryKey, SalesOrderNumber, SalesOrderLineNumber, OrderQuantity, UnitPrice, SalesAmount	
dbo_DimSalesQuota	Quota	SalesQuotaKey, EmployeeKey, CalendarYear, CalendarQuarter, SalesAmountQuota	

Create the Model

After importing the tables, rename the table columns and show or hide the columns from client tools according to the information listed in Table 14-6.

Table 14-6. *Table and Column Property Settings*

Table	Column	New Name	Hide From Client
Date	DateKey	—	X
	FullDateAlternateKey	Full Date	
	EnglishMonthName	Month	
	MonthNumberOfYear	Month Number	X
	CalendarQuarter	Calendar Quarter	
	CalendarYear	Calendar Year	

(continued)

Table 14-6. (*continued*)

Table	Column	New Name	Hide From Client
Sales Rep	EmployeeKey	—	X
	ParentEmployeeKey	—	X
	FirstName	First Name	
	LastName	Last Name	
	MiddleName	Middle Name	
	HireDate	Hire Date	
	EmployeePhoto	Employee Photo	
Sales Territory	SalesTerritoryKey	—	X
	SalesTerritoryRegion	Region	
	SalesTerritoryCountry	Country	
	SalesTerritoryGroup	Group	
	SalesTerritoryImage	Territory Image	
Quota	SalesQuotaKey	—	X
	EmployeeKey	—	X
	CalendarYear	—	X
	CalendarQuarter	—	X
	SalesAmountQuota	Sales Quota	X
Sales	OrderDateKey	—	X
	EmployeeKey	—	X
	SalesTerritoryKey	—	X
	SalesOrderNumber	Order Number	
	SalesOrderLineNumber	Order Line Number	
	OrderQuantity	Quantity	
	UnitPrice	Unit Price	
	SalesAmount	Sales Amount	X

In order to create the appropriate relationships between the tables, you need to create a Sales Period table that contains the calendar year and quarter. To get this table, use the existing connection to the SalesRepAnalysis.accdb Access database. This time, use the following query to get the data (make sure the friendly query name is Sales Period):

```
Select distinct CalendarYear & CalendarQuarter as PeriodKey,
CalendarYear as [Period Year], CalendarQuarter  as [Period Quarter] from dbo_DimDate
```

Using the DAX CONCATENATE function, create a PeriodKey column in the Quota table.

```
[PeriodKey]
=CONCATENATE([CalendarYear],[CalendarQuarter])
```

The Sales table is a little trickier. First create a relationship between the Sales table and the Date table. Next, use the RELATED function to create a Period Year and Period Quarter in the Sales table. Then use the CONCATENATE function to create the PeriodKey column in the Sales table.

```
[Period Year]
=Related('Date'[Calendar Year])
[Period Quarter]
=RELATED('Date'[Calendar Quarter])
```

Hide the PeriodKey in the tables from client tools. Also hide the Period Year and Period Quarter columns in the Quota and Sales tables.

Now you can finish creating the table relationships in the model. Figure 14-8 shows what the final model should look like.

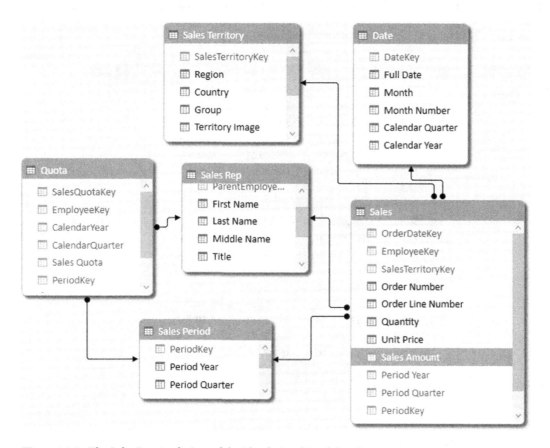

Figure 14-8. *The Sales Rep Analysis model with relationships defined*

Next create a Territory hierarchy in the Sales Territory table using the Group, Country, and Region fields. Create another hierarchy in the Sales Period table called **Period** using the Period Year and Period Quarter fields. Add a calculated column called **Sales Rep Name** to the Sales Rep table by concatenating the Last Name and First Name columns separated by a comma.

Create Measures

Add the following measure to the Sales table:

```
Total Sales:=SUM([Sales Amount])
```

Add the following measures to the Quota table:

```
Total Quota:=Sum([Sales Quota])
```

```
Variance:=[Total Sales]-[Total Quota]
```

Variance %:=[Variance]/[Total Sales] Create a Key Performance Indicator (KPI) for the sales reps where sales 5% above their quota is good and sales below 5% is bad. Base the KPI on the Total Sales measure and compare it to the total Quota measure.

Test your measures by creating a pivot table, as shown in Figure 14-9.

Row Labels	Total Sales	Total Quota	Varience	Varience %	Total Sales Status
Abbas, Syed	$172,524.45	$164,000.00	$8,524.45	4.94 %	
⊟ 2013	$145,944.10	$137,600.00	$8,344.10	5.72 %	
3	$111,924.93	$105,600.00	$6,324.93	5.65 %	
4	$34,019.17	$32,000.00	$2,019.17	5.94 %	
⊟ 2014	$26,580.35	$26,400.00	$180.35	0.68 %	
1	$5,313.01	$5,600.00	($286.99)	-5.40 %	
2	$21,267.34	$20,800.00	$467.34	2.20 %	
Alberts, Amy	$732,078.44	$700,800.00	$31,278.44	4.27 %	
⊞ 2012	$86,380.60	$86,400.00	($19.40)	-0.02 %	
⊟ 2013	$547,374.88	$520,800.00	$26,574.88	4.85 %	
1	$30,957.99	$26,400.00	$4,557.99	14.72 %	
2	$95,514.66	$88,000.00	$7,514.66	7.87 %	
3	$145,220.25	$147,200.00	($1,979.75)	-1.36 %	
4	$275,681.98	$259,200.00	$16,481.98	5.98 %	
⊟ 2014	$98,322.96	$93,600.00	$4,722.96	4.80 %	
1	$97,650.67	$92,800.00	$4,850.67	4.97 %	
2	$672.29	$800.00	($127.71)	-19.00 %	

Figure 14-9. *Testing the sales KPI in a pivot table*

Create the Dashboard

Before creating the dashboard in Power View, update some table settings to optimize the model for Power View. Table 14-7 lists the tables and settings you need to make.

Table 14-7. *Settings to Optimize for Power View*

Table Name	Row Identifier	Default Label	Default Image	Default Field Set
Sales Rep	EmployeeKey	Sales Person	Employee Photo	Sales Person, Title
Sales Territory	SalesTerritoryKey	Region Territory Image	Group, Country, Region	

In addition, mark the columns listed in Table 14-8 as the appropriate data category.

Table 14-8. *Setting the Data Category*

Table	Column	Data Category
Sales Rep	Hire Date	Date
	Employee Photo	Image
Sales Territory	Region	Country/Region
	Country	Country/Region
	Territory Image	Image

In the Period and Date tables, set the fields so they do not summarize.

Insert a Power View report and name the report **Sales Rep Performance**. Using Tiles, show the different sales reasons in the title area, and in the details area, show the sales rep information in cards (see Figure 14-10).

Figure 14-10. *Using tiles and cards to display sales rep information*

Add a matrix inside the tile detail area showing the total sales KPI by period and sales rep. Turn off the totals for the matrix. Outside the tile area, add a period year slicer and a table showing the total sales for each sales region. You can also add view filters to filter out years without sales and the NA region. Your final dashboard should look similar to Figure 14-11.

Figure 14-11. *The final sales rep performance dashboard*

After completing and experimenting with the dashboard, save and close Excel.

Use Case 3: Sensor Analysis

For this scenario, you work for a power company that monitors equipment using sensors. The sensors monitor various power readings including power interruptions and voltage spikes. When the sensor senses a problem, it triggers an alarm signal that is recorded. You need to create a map that allows analysts to view and compare power interruptions and voltage spikes over time.

Load the Data

The data you will need is in several text files. You will have to clean and process the data before you can load it into the Power Pivot model. Because of this, Power Query is the tool you will use to load the data.

Find the folder called UseCase3 in the Chapter14Labs folder. This folder has four files that contain the sensor data and the related data you need to complete the analysis. Create a new Excel workbook named PowerAnalysis.xlsx. Using Power Query, connect to the Alarms.csv file in the UseCase3 folder. You should have the following columns: PREMISE_NUMBER, METER_NUMBER, OP_CENTER, Type, and DateKey. Rename the query to **Alarms**, uncheck the Load Settings, and save the query. Add a second query, **AlarmTypes**, which gets the alarm type data from the AlarmType.txt file. You can now delete the SHORT_CODE column and save the query.

Reopen the Alarms query and merge it with the AlarmTypes query using the appropriate keys (see Figure 14-12).

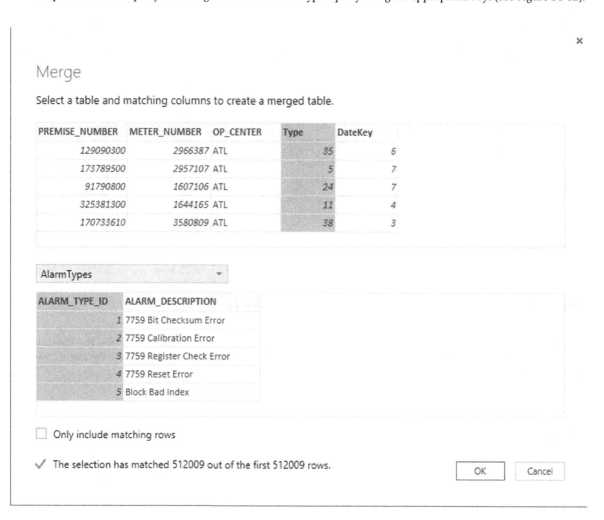

Figure 14-12. Merging the AlarmType query with the Alarms query

You can remove the Alarm Type keys and rename ALARM_DESCRIPTION to Alarm Type.

Repeat the previous procedures to replace the DateKey column with the dates in the Date.csv file. Use the Locations.txt file to add the longitude and latitude values to the Alarms query based on the OP_CENTER. You can rename the columns so that they use the same naming convention. Your alarm query should look similar to Figure 14-13.

▦	Premise	Meter	Op Center	Alarm Type	Date	Latitude	Longitude
1	129090300	2966387	ATL	ROM Fail	7/25/2014	33.8979	-85.09886
2	11490200	2964378	ATL	7759 Bit Checksum Error	7/25/2014	33.8979	-85.09886
3	164889600	3043592	ATL	ROM Fail	7/22/2014	33.8979	-85.09886
4	173789500	2957107	ATL	Block Bad Index	7/26/2014	33.8979	-85.09886
5	275189600	4450418	ATL	7759 Calibration Error	7/26/2014	33.8979	-85.09886
6	91790800	1607106	ATL	Meter Read Fail	7/26/2014	33.8979	-85.09886
7	325381300	1644165	ATL	Configuration Error	7/23/2014	33.8979	-85.09886
8	314790200	1666554	ATL	Meter Read Fail	7/24/2014	33.8979	-85.09886
9	14574700	2111210	ATL	7759 Reset Error	7/22/2014	33.8979	-85.09886
10	28989500	2915841	ATL	7759 Reset Error	7/25/2014	33.8979	-85.09886
11	170733610	3580809	ATL	Soft EEPROM Error	7/22/2014	33.8979	-85.09886
12	141668300	3113114	ATL	Power Failure	7/26/2014	33.8979	-85.09886
13	518990500	1621877	ATL	Power Failure	7/23/2014	33.8979	-85.09886
14	88326020	1983770	ATL	Block Buffer Size Error	7/26/2014	33.8979	-85.09886
15	79715900	1241441	ATL	Block Buffer Size Error	7/24/2014	33.8979	-85.09886
16	18764710	2907292	ATL	Low Battery Error	7/23/2014	33.8979	-85.09886
17	808890300	2981854	ATL	Low Battery Error	7/26/2014	33.8979	-85.09886
18	253990200	2893007	ATL	Block Can't Mark Bad	7/22/2014	33.8979	-85.09886

Figure 14-13. *The Alarm query with Latitude and Longitude data added*

Next filter the data to limit it to alarm types of power failure and high AC volts. Once you do this, you may notice some error values in the Meter column; go ahead and remove these errors. Now you can aggregate the alarm counts grouping by the Date, Op Center, Alarm Type, Longitude, and Latitude (see Figure 14-14).

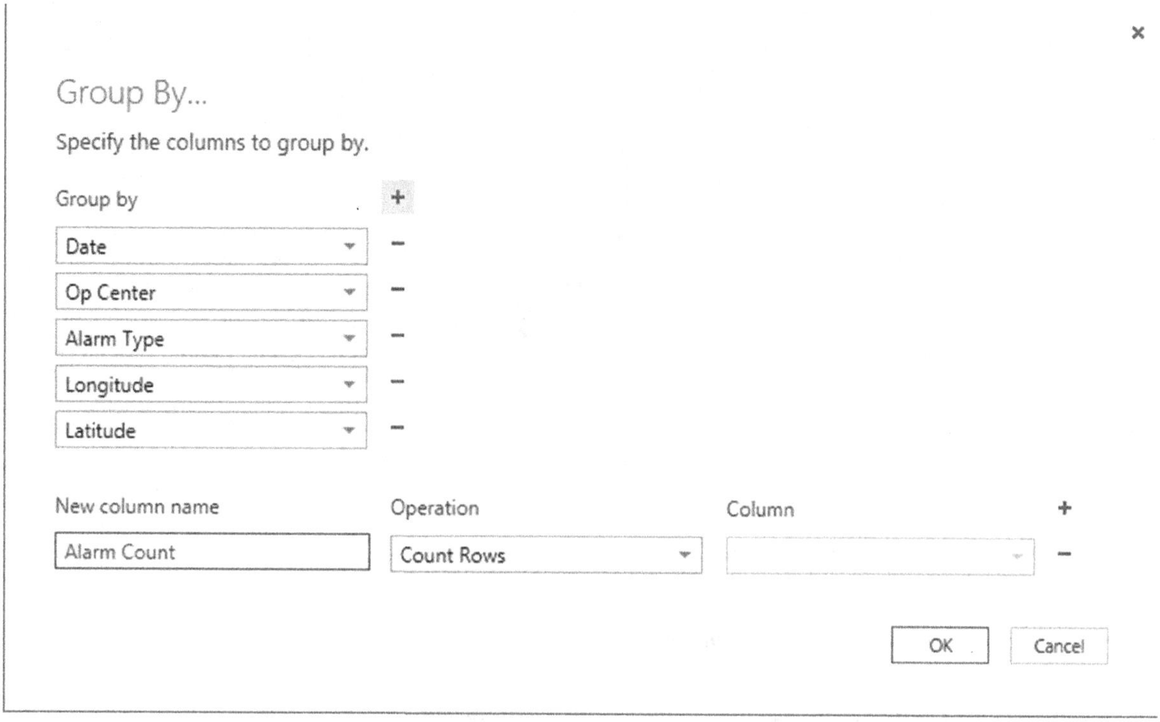

Figure 14-14. *Aggregating and grouping the alarm data*

After aggregating the data, check Load To Data Model under Load Settings and apply and close the query.

Now that you have the data ready for mapping, launch the Power Map designer and create a column chart showing the average counts over time, as shown in Figure 14-15.

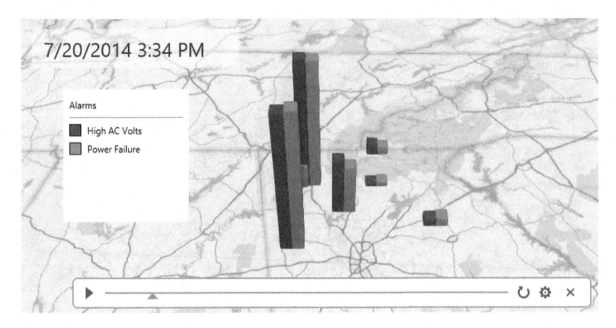

Figure 14-15. *Power Map showing alarm counts over time*

After creating and exploring the alarm data in Power Map, save and close Excel.

Summary

This chapter provided you with some use cases to help you gauge your mastery of the topics in the rest of the book. The goal of this book was to expose you to the various tools in Microsoft's self-service BI stack. Although this book used the desktop version of Excel and the BI add-ins, you can also use the Office 365 versions of these tools. I hope you have gained enough confidence and experience with these tools to start using them to analyze and gain insight into your own data.

Now that you have a firm understanding of how to use these tools you should be comfortable tackling more complex topics. There are many good resources available that cover various techniques and patterns that can be used to analyze your data. Microsoft's Power BI site (www.microsoft.com/en-us/powerbi/default.aspx), Bill Jelen's site (www.mrexcel.com), and Rob Collie's Power Pivot Pro site (www.powerpivotpro.com) are excellent resources. For more advanced topics, check out Chris Webb's BI Blog at http://cwebbbi.wordpress.com and Marco Russo's and Alberto Ferrari's SQLBI site at www.sqlbi.com/.

Index

Get the eBook for only $10!

Now you can take the weightless companion with you anywhere, anytime. Your purchase of this book entitles you to 3 electronic versions for only $10.

This Apress title will prove so indispensible that you'll want to carry it with you everywhere, which is why we are offering the eBook in 3 formats for only $10 if you have already purchased the print book.

Convenient and fully searchable, the PDF version enables you to easily find and copy code—or perform examples by quickly toggling between instructions and applications. The MOBI format is ideal for your Kindle, while the ePUB can be utilized on a variety of mobile devices.

Go to www.apress.com/promo/tendollars to purchase your companion eBook.